Pilot Error

Dedicated, with respect, to Captain James Thain

Calamity comes like the whirlwind
PROVERBS 1.27

Edited by **Ronald Hurst** and **Leslie R. Hurst**

Pilot Error
The Human Factors
Second Edition

GRANADA
London Toronto Sydney New York

Granada Publishing Limited — Technical Books Division
Frogmore, St Albans, Herts AL2 2NF
and
36 Golden Square, London W1R 4AH
866 United Nations Plaza, New York, NY 10017, USA
117 York Street, Sydney, NSW 2000, Australia
100 Skyway Avenue, Rexdale, Ontario, Canada M9W 3A6
61 Beach Road, Auckland, New Zealand

ISBN 0 246 11499 1

First published in Great Britain 1976 by Crosby Lockwood Staples
Reprinted 1977, 1978
(Original ISBN 0 258 97072 3)
Second edition 1982 by Granada Publishing

Typeset by
CAMBRIAN TYPESETTERS
Farnborough, Hants
Printed in Great Britain by Mackays of Chatham

Granada ®
Granada Publishing ®

Contents

Foreword

Accident cause attributed to pilot error is all to often an oversimplification. Many accidents are due to a sequence of events rather than to a single event. This brings about a situation where the human pilot is simply unable to cope with a level of task that exceeds any reasonable capability. In other circumstances where a pilot has obviously made a mistake, we need to ask ourselves the reasons; is it due to incorrect or inadequately presented information? Are we spending enough money to ease the pilot's task under the most adverse circumstances?

Clearly a great deal of progress has been made in the last few years and the aircraft now coming into service are greatly improved on some of their earlier forbears. Nevertheless, it is still probably not enough.

I commend this book to all who will read it and I support the theme of vigorous research and development in the area of human factors studies as a means of eliminating pilot error.

Brian Trubshaw, CBE, MVO, FRAeS
Director, Flight Test and Concorde,
British Aerospace Aircraft Group,
U.K.

Preface to the Second Edition

The first edition of *Pilot Error* examined the nature of that verdict as an explanation for so many aircraft accidents, revealed the frequent injustice of its application and surveyed some of the contributory factors masked by a ready acceptance of that term. That edition closed by marking the painful advance of aviation towards a better understanding of its human problems and expressed the hope that air transport would benefit increasingly from the efforts of those who '. . .seek not for scapegoats, but for answers. . .'

It may be seen from the content of this, the second edition, that that goal is being pursued with integrity and determination and that much has been achieved since this book first appeared.

Yet it may be seen, too, that it is the waywardness of human behaviour which remains as the fundamental challenge and that although we have come to abhor so bitterly the victimisation which characterised such accidents as Ciampino (1952), Munich (1958) and Nantes (1973) we have latterly met their counterparts —in terms of unfounded allegation and actual victimisation—following the disasters of Zagreb (1976), Mt Erebus (1979) and Tenerife (1980). Indeed in the first case—the mid-air collision over the Zagreb beacon—a Yugoslav air traffic controller was sentenced to seven years imprisonment· and in the second—the crash of an Air New Zealand DC10 on Mt Erebus, Ross Island, Antarctica (which killed 257 people), the original finding of 'pilot error' by the New Zealand Ministry of Transport was later overturned by a Royal Commission.

For the sake of improvement we can bring about changes in aviation technology. It is a longer haul to do the same for its human servants in order to ensure our greater safety, and for that reason there can be no definitive version of this book.

Yet the steps towards the understanding we seek have been honourably pioneered and have culminated in modern research programmes equally formidable in terms of invested effort and ultimate value to the aviation community.

The contributors to the second edition of *Pilot Error* are among the foremost participants in these endeavours and we are grateful for the collective support which now enables this study to depart from the overview of the problem presented in the first edition, in order to focus on the areas of challenge in which they have earned an international recognition.

Only one of the original chapters of this work has been retained. For the rest, the material is either entirely new or has not previously seen wide circulation. It is hoped, therefore, that like its predecessor, this edition will stimulate discussion

and, where it is thought to be invited, controversy; for all of these things sustain
that vigilance which is the only real safeguard for civil aviation.

This book has received generous support, now sincerely acknowledged, from
Dr Stanley Ross Mohler, MD, MA, currently Professor, Wright State University
School of Medicine and formerly Chief, Aeromedical Applications Division,
Federal Aviation Administration, USA, and Brian E. Trubshaw, Director, Flight
Test and Concorde, British Aerospace Aircraft Group. Our only remaining
contributor from the First Edition is Dr Martin Allnutt, formerly of the
Aviation Medicine Division, Royal Aircraft Establishment and now engaged
on Accident and Simulation research at HQ Director Army Air Corps (UK), has
again provided a solid foundation, by offering an essential insight into the major
theme.

Thanks are due to Mervin K. Strickler, Jr, Vice-President of the World Aerospace Education Organisation and former Director of the FAA Education
Programs Division; and, with a smile at the recollection of a very congenial
meeting, to Richard S. Jensen, Assistant Professor, Department of Aviation, The
Ohio State University.

We are equally grateful for the opportunity of reinforcing this book with the
joint study by Dr Earl L. Wiener, Professor of Management Science, University of
Miami and Renwick E. Curry, Ames Research Center, National Aeronautics and
Space Administration. Their essay on 'Flight-Deck Automation: Promises and
Problems' was published in the journal *Ergonomics* and as NASA Technical
Memorandum 81206. Similarly, the two chapters by Dr Wiener dealing with
'Controlled Flight into Terrain' and 'Mid-Air Collisions' have appeared in the
journal of the Human Factors Society of the United States. Permission to reprint
this material is acknowledged and sincerely appreciated.

The editors are particularly happy to welcome to this fellowship Richard
C.W. Weston of Aviation Consultants International Inc. and to express a special
indebtedness to Dr Stanley N. Roscoe, Head of the Behavioral Engineering
Laboratory, New Mexico State University, both for his own important chapters
and, in addition, for invaluable help in gathering this distinguished group of
contributors.

Not for the first time in our long association, John Cutler AFRAeS
shouldered the burden of the illustrations: in an area which is so often dismissed
with the barest acknowledgement it is pleasant to record sincere appreciation of
time and ability placed so cheerfully at our disposal.

And finally, to David Fulton, Managing Director of Granada Technical Books
Ltd, for unfailing good humour and, above all, patience. . .

This book is the sum of those efforts.

Ronald Hurst, Leslie R. Hurst,
Dean Gate, Gallows Tree Common,
Oxfordshire, England.

Introduction

Safety in flight is the product of pilot behaviour as modified by aircraft characteristics, flight environment factors and ground personnel influences.

The editors have assembled a group of authors who have each concentrated on a major area related to pilot error aircraft accidents. These authors have placed before us the major areas needing attention if we are to significantly reduce the continuing threats to the present air safety record. Three of the various fatal accidents that have occurred since the first edition of this book illustrate the ever-present nature of the human factors problems remaining with us. The accidents are as follows:

(a)   On 27 March 1977, a KLM Boeing 747 initiated take-off at Tenerife while a Pan Am Boeing 747 was still on the take-off runway ahead. The KLM 747 became airborne but collided with the Pan Am aircraft and the worst accident in aviation history occurred. The official report lists 583 fatalities. The accident investigators found that the captain of the KLM aircraft took off without a clearance. They also concluded that the strictness of certain rules on limitation of duty time influenced the Captain's flexibility in this respect, and may have contributed to a compulsion to leave within a very limited time frame. Certain language misinterpretations with regard to air traffic control communications are also cited.

(b)   A United McDonnell-Douglas DC8 passenger flight ran completely out of fuel at night, 28 December 1978, Portland, Oregon. Ten persons received fatal injuries in the ensuing dead-stick landing. The investigators determined that the pilot did not properly monitor the fuel state while his attention was diverted to a landing gear malfunction. It was also felt that the First Officer and the Flight Engineer did not fully comprehend the development of a critically low state of fuel. The investigators concluded that these two crew members could have been more alert to the state of fuel and could have more adequately communicated the developing problem to the captain.

(c)   A Transamerica Lockheed L188 experienced failure of the attitude indicators at night near Salt Lake City, 18 November 1978. The turn needle and directional heading indicator were functioning but the Captain became spatially disoriented attempting to integrate unreliable attitude information with that of these instruments. This large turbo-prop aircraft described a typical 'graveyard spiral' and broke up in flight, killing the three crew members. This accident illustrates that insidious failures of critical flight instruments still remain a major hazard in flight activities.

Key human factor safety issues for the 1980s and 1990s derive from flight operational experiences and carry-over concepts from earlier eras. The investigative reports of incidents and accidents provide major directions for aviation research, training and operational programmes.

Among the key issues for the next decade are:

(a)   crew workload levels as quantified at specific flight phases (including sensory, cognitive and motor elements);
(b)   crew fatigue, including aspects related to multiple night flights, trans-meridian desynchronosis, 24-hour lay-overs following night arrivals, and multiple take-offs and landings;
(c)   flight display characteristics, emphasising the increasing replacement of mechanical instruments by electronic instruments;
(d)   crew fitness and behaviour, medical standards, exceptions to these standards and pilot ageing;
(e)   alcohol and drug effects, acute and protracted, on crew performance;
(f)   in-flight environmental factors, including G forces, hypoxia, and spatial disorientation;
(g)   an increasingly automated air traffic control system that will further remove the human controller from the loop.

The new generation of aircraft contain increasing levels of automation. Many new civil aircraft are also pushing closer to the limits of aerodynamic envelopes. The human factors area must today, more than ever, ensure that adequate attention is given to the failure mode in the human equation. This book will alert persons in aviation to the various possibilities as shown through actual events. Awareness is the first step in the process of prevention.

Stanley R. Mohler, MD
Professor and Vice-Chairman
Director of Aerospace Medicine
Department of Community Medicine
Wright State University School of Medicine
Dayton, Ohio
(16 October 1981)

Chapter 1

Human Factors: Basic Principles
M. Allnutt

*Martin Allnutt surveys some of the basic premises of research into human
behaviour and provides an essential background for the studies which appear in
later pages.*

*This chapter was considered to be of sufficient significance to be utilised in the
submission by the American Airline Pilots' Association during its own
investigation into the runway collision at Tenerife Airport in 1977, in which 583
people died.*

The search for an understanding of this topic is the province of psychologists
and specialist workers, and the range of their endeavours is highlighted by other
contributors to this book. Less apparent, however, are the disciplines which have
been evolved to support these studies. Certain of these approaches concern
themselves with the identification of 'specific features', i.e. with one type of
accident or with one type of human failure. Study groups such as those set up
by the British Airline Pilots' Association to investigate problems of pilot fatigue,
or by other bodies with equally clearly defined terms of reference, are typical
examples in this category—as are such contributions as the work by Kraft[6] on
visual clues during night landings.

For other researchers, the 'statistical approach' offers a possible key to pilot
behaviour. The proportion and type of pilot-error accidents by day and night are
tabulated. Critical decisions and critical elements of the occurrence are analysed,
and a 'cluster analysis' used to reveal the factors common to a number of
accidents.

This approach may probe even more deeply in order to show the frequency
with which any breakdown in the pilot function may have contributed to an
accident. Thus, a statistical evaluation of eighty-three pilot-error accidents[16]
produced the following table of causes:

Improper flight technique	15
Over-confidence	16
Insufficient care	18
Other causes	34

Such categorisations have long been established as research groundlines. Pilot
error has been defined, for example, in terms of failures of coordination and
technique; or, as a consequence of shortcomings in the exercise of alertness and
observation, or intelligence or judgement; or again, as a phenomenon influenced
by personality and temperament.[8]

Similarly, other analyses list among accident causes those which may have been induced by design factors or operational procedures, by ignorance, by deliberate acts of omission or commission, by environmental factors, or by psychological or physiological causes.

Approaches such as these are most necessary, since their findings serve to indicate the areas in which research should be concentrated and remedial action sought; but primarily these methods are concerned with reconstructing a sequence of events. The focus, in fact, is on what happened, rather than on *why* it happened.

The normal pilot

It is the need to answer the latter question which motivates the third avenue of research—the 'normal pilot' approach—adopted in the author's own field of aviation psychology and considered in some detail here. Essentially the basis of this method is summed in the self-evident truth that all pilots are human.

This acknowledgement charges the psychologist with the task of unravelling the cognitive and psychomotor processes which determine not only the level of the pilot's professional performance, but also his response to demanding or critical situations; and it is this task which is aided, in great measure, by the fruits of particularly hard-won experience.

It is recognised, for instance, that the undoubted individuality to be found among this professional group is fortunately not reflected in the diversity of pilot errors on record; in fact, a significantly repetitive strain is manifest among those occurrences. This characteristic permits the classification of the major types of error under headings which are appropriate to behavioural areas, e.g. information processing, illusion, false hypothesis, habit, motivation, and stress and fatigue. The typical examination of these sectors in the following pages is therefore fundamental to that 'closer look' at the pilot which is the researcher's avowed aim.

1. How does the pilot process information?

A simple model of the human information-processing system is shown in Fig. 1.1. The model is, of course, greatly simplified, with no attempt to reproduce the actual profusion of associated filters and feedback loops. It will nevertheless suffice for the purpose of tracing an item of information through the system and for some illustration of the variety of stages at which errors may occur. For example, an aircraft captain might tell his co-pilot to 'stop number one', meaning that he wants the number one engine closed down. But before the co-pilot complies with this order a few seconds later, the information must pass at least five hurdles.

(a) *Sensation*. In order to be 'heard' or 'seen' the incoming signal to the human body must register on the appropriate sense organ. However, these sense organs

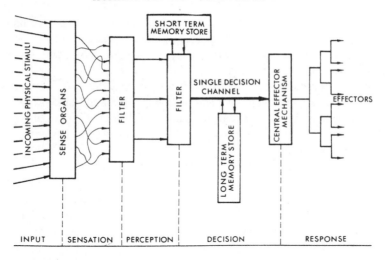

Fig. 1.1 \Human information processing sequence

are both limited and, in some cases, missing. Thus, man can hear sounds only within a fairly narrow frequency band and when they are of sufficient loudness. Similarly, he has no sense of velocity, but only one of acceleration. In the above example, the message 'stop number one' was of the correct loudness and frequency for it to register at the ear, and so the first hurdle is passed.

(b) *Perception*. The fact that the auditory nerve passes a particular message to the brain is no guarantee that the brain will always deduce the same meaning from that message. What is perceived will depend on the stimulus, i.e. the action, word, or phrase used in the context in which the message is passed, and on the hearer's previous experience.

The word 'chopper', for instance, may have an entirely different meaning for, and may evoke a different behaviour pattern in, the woodcutter who knows that the word describes a handaxe, and the helicopter pilot, to whom the word is a colloquialism for his aircraft. The stimulus, it must be noted, is exactly the same in each case. In the example, the co-pilot might perceive 'stop number one' very differently if the message were passed in a bar, or if it were the key to a joke which he and the captain had shared the previous evening. In this case, however, the co-pilot perceives the message correctly and the second hurdle is passed.

(c) *Attention*. It is a sad fact of life that incoming messages do not reach us at convenient intervals, but rather arrive irregularly, and often just at the wrong time. This fact is of special importance, since research has shown that man possesses only a *single decision channel*, and *all* information must be passed sequentially through this channel, i.e. if two items of information arrive at the brain at the same time, one of these items must wait until the other is processed.

The concept of the single decision channel is well established, of course;

nevertheless, many people's first reaction to this idea is to protest that they *can* in fact do two things at the same time. Close inspection of any such demonstration shows that the person concerned is simply scanning from one source of information to another very rapidly. An obvious parallel is provided in the case of a passenger in a car being driven by a friend: at first the driver appears to be doing two things at the same time, namely driving the car and talking. But when he pulls out to overtake and finds an approaching vehicle in his path, it is noticeable how quiet he becomes. He has given up scanning and is concentrating on only one source of information.

Anecdotal evidence, too, is confirmed in the laboratory, where different messages are put into the right and left ears. It is found that when the listener attends to the input to one ear he can tell his questioner virtually nothing about the message arriving at the other ear. Nor does it matter whether the other message comes to the ear, the eye, or to the seat of the pants, that area popularly renowned as the location of a mysteriously 'instinctive' knowledge. Man, in fact, can *only attend to one thing at a time*; and it is his central decision channel which limits the speed at which he can process the information.

The function of a device such as the klaxon horn—the 'attention-getter' in the aircraft cockpit— is to ensure that a warning signal takes precedence over all other inputs and goes immediately down the decision channel. Yet there are numerous examples of warning signals being ignored, either because the pilot was dealing with more important information, or because he could not shift his attention from one input to another.

A number of accident findings typify this situation, for it is with distressing frequency that 'preoccupation' is attributed as a factor in those events:

'. . .Preoccupation with a malfunction of the nose landing gear. . .distracted the crew's attention. . .';

'. . .Preoccupied with the task of flying the aircraft. . .he mentally transposed the first and last figures. . .';

'. . .Insufficient attention. . .to altimeter indications by the crew. . .because of their preoccupation with other matters. . .';

'Too busy. . .timing the let-down procedure. . .the entire crew forgot to change the basic altimeter setting. . .'.

It is worth dwelling on the point that, while one item of information is going through the decision channel, other items which have arrived at the same time must await their turn in, effectively, a short-term memory store. It has been shown, however, that items waiting in such a store are quite likely to be forgotten very quickly. Particularly is this true in the case of the older pilot, for laboratory experience indicates that if such a pilot is given simultaneously, say, both a new clearance and a relatively more important piece of information—perhaps the proximity of another aircraft—he may have forgotten the first piece of information by the time he has processed (i.e. considered and acted upon) the 'priority' message.

The limited capacity of man's single decision channel means that situations arise in which, even though all the component parts of the system are working well, there is still so much information that the channel becomes overloaded. The pace and stress of modern living, indeed, has made people all too familiar with situations in which they are required to attend to too many inputs. Familiar, too, are the number of well-recognised techniques which human beings adopt in dealing with this overload situation. Depending upon temperament and capacity, individuals may deal with each piece of information quickly and badly, or may concentrate entirely on one source of information to the exclusion of all others. They may confuse information obtained from two or more sources, or may even seek to escape from the situation by ignoring all the inputs, possibly by indulging in a totally irrelevant activity.

The co-pilot in our present example has many inputs which require his attention; but he decides to concentrate on the message 'stop number one' and so surmounts the third hurdle.

(d) *Decision*. Once the co-pilot hears and understands what his captain wishes him to do, the decision to comply should be, and in the vast majority of cases is, a simple one to make. He merely closes the throttle and passes on to the next decision. However, there may be occasions when the decision is not an easy one. Perhaps the co-pilot looks at his instruments and sees that it is, in fact, not the number one unit, but another engine which is malfunctioning. His decision now becomes far more complex. At a subconscious level such a situation may trigger what is in effect an internal 'pay-off' matrix, whereby the mind assesses the decision in terms of the probable outcome and its consequences. A pilot, for instance, might wish to be 'reasonably' confident that a minor instrument was functioning correctly before trusting it, but would need a far higher level of confidence in the correct functioning of a major instrument, where a malfunction might prove fatal.

Fortunately there are no complications when the message 'stop number one' is passed; therefore the co-pilot's brain sends a message to his hand to close the throttle of the number one engine.

(e) *Action*. This phase is the final part of the sequence and yet another source of error. The co-pilot might intend to move the throttle for the number one engine, but in fact moves that for the number two engine—a type of error too often compounded by poor ergonomic design. For if the controls are designed on a cosmetic rather than a functional basis, Murphy's law—which states that anything that can go wrong, will go wrong—must be fulfilled.

In this case, however, the co-pilot closes the correct throttle and so complies with the order of his captain. This action sequence is concluded when the co-pilot's brain receives feedback information from his hand, and perhaps visual confirmation from the appropriate r.p.m. gauge, that the throttle has been closed. The complete sequence from command to action has probably taken less than a second, and yet it has contained at least five 'error-possible' points. The realisation that thousands of such sequences are completed on every trip brings one fact into a truly startling focus—namely, that gross errors are so few, and disastrous errors extremely rare.

2. Visual illusions*

Most of the information which the pilot receives comes to him through his eyes. Some of this information comes from instrument displays in the cockpit, but a large amount is obtained from outside the cockpit, often under conditions which may be far from ideal. Indeed, certain conditions may prevent the necessary information even from reaching the eye—for example a pilot may fly into an obstruction obscured by cloud.

More often a signal reaches the eye, but the brain misinterprets it and the pilot 'sees' something else; in other words, he experiences a visual illusion. Such illusions are extremely common, and we all probably 'see' several of them each day—simply because the visual signal reacts with previous personal experience to produce the picture which is actually 'seen'. Thus experience teaches us that objects usually maintain their size, so that when they appear to be getting larger, i.e. when they form a larger image on the retina, they must in fact be getting closer; and behaviour is adjusted accordingly. A pilot makes thousands of such simple interpretations on every trip, but there are other more subtle illusions which require all his experience and concentration if he is not to be led astray by them.

The relationship between visual illusions and aircraft accidents has been excellently covered, among others, by Pitts[11] who lists the causes of visual illusions commonly encountered in aviation. Some of these are described below.

(a) *Refraction*. The curvature of the windscreen, or perhaps water on it, may cause refraction so that the pilot thinks that he is higher than he really is, and consequently lowers his approach.

(b) *Fog*. In fog, objects may appear to be larger and farther away than usual, so tempting the pilot to fly below the glide path.

(c) *Texture*. The texture of the ground gives cues as to the observer's distance from it, while objects of unusual size, e.g. stunted trees or a particularly large building, may cause distance to be misjudged. Similarly, terrain which is nearly devoid of textural cues—such as still water—can make the judgement of distance extremely difficult. This is also true when there is little contrast between the runway and the surrounding terrain; 'degraded visual cues' because of snow was cited as one of the factors which caused the accident to a Viscount aircraft at Castle Donington in 1969 (see CAP 337, HMSO, London).

*See treatment of this subject in chapter 8.

(d) *Autokinetics*. A stationary light in a dark environment can sometimes appear to move. This can be demonstrated by staring fixedly at a faint point source of light in a dark room; after a while the light will appear to be moving around of its own volition. Similarly, when flying over uninhabited terrain on a dark night, a faint stationary light on the ground might be 'seen' to move and thus be misidentified as another aircraft.

One of the purposes of giving a captain familiarisation trips to an airport, before allowing him to approach it on his own, is to let him learn the vital cues which he will need for a visual approach. He will learn what sort of visual picture to expect at various stages in the approach and let-down, and what snares or illusions are waiting for him: e.g. that the forest on the top of the hill is composed of dwarf trees and so appears to be farther away than it really is; or that the dip in the ground before the start of the runway is far deeper than it looks from 2 miles out.

It is said that a pilot becomes 'tuned' to the visual picture provided by a three-degree glide slope, and provided that the visual cues on the approach to a particular airport are fairly typical, or are sufficiently plentiful to overcome any illusions, this tuning is both necessary and safe. When neither of these provisos is met, an accident situation may develop—as witness the circumstances highlighted by Kraft.[6]

Kraft found that 16 per cent of all the major aircraft accidents to US carriers between 1959 and 1967 occurred during night approaches over unlighted terrain or water, towards well-lighted cities. He studied these accidents, setting up laboratory simulations of night approaches to certain airports, and found that a major cause of height misjudgement under these conditions was a descent path which nulled out visual information. The change in visual information from the airport lights during the approach was not sufficient to be perceived, nor were there other visual cues. Thus, the pilot had no visual indication from outside his cockpit that he was dropping below the glide path. On the basis that motion must exceed about one minute of visual angle per second to be perceived, Kraft calculated that at a speed of 240 miles an hour and at a height of 3000 ft—a typical approach configuration—such perception would occur at a distance of about 9 miles from touch-down; the distance at which several accidents have in fact occurred.

Such visual illusions are exacerbated by:

(a)   Complete darkness both beneath and to the side of the approach.
(b)   A long straight-in approach to an airport located on the near side of a city.
(c)   A runway of unusual length or width.
(d)   A sloping runway, i.e. the pilot assumes that the runway is horizontal and approaches it at an angle of 3°. If the runway slopes *up* at an angle of 3°, his approach may be disastrously low.
(e)   A sprawling city with irregular lights on hills behind the runway; this provides the pilot with false cues as to height, distance, and the horizontal.

3. The false hypothesis

The false hypothesis is such an important contributor to human error that it deserves special attention.

For a simple demonstration of the characteristic thought processes involved, the reader should ask a friend to say the word 'toast' five times, as quickly as possible, and then to repeat the process with the name of the object he puts into the toaster. If he says 'toast' rather than 'bread'—as well he might, since his mind has become 'conditioned' to a phonic pattern—he has made a false hypothesis.

Such a vast amount of information impinges on the brain that it cannot possibly process it all in detail. The human reaction therefore is to take in only a small part of the information, and make an assumption about the rest. Typically, a pilot may see lights below him, assume that they are the lights of Airport A, and start to set up his landing pattern on this assumption. Usually they are indeed the lights of Airport A and his action is appropriate; but occasionally they are the lights of Airport B and he has made a false hypothesis which may lead to disaster.

On 14 January 1969 a BAC 1-11 crashed near Milan due to a loss of power, although both engines were subsequently found to be virtually fully serviceable.* Shortly after take-off a compressor bang surge occurred in the number two engine. For reasons which may well have been rooted in fatigue, a training captain who was sitting in the jump-seat thereupon made the false hypothesis that it was the number one engine which had failed, and ordered that engine to be closed down. Unfortunately the thrust from the number one engine had already been partially reduced due to 'an inadvertent displacement of the relevant throttle lever', and the aircraft crashed.

An early account of the 'false hypothesis' situation is provided by Davis[4] who cites examples from the railways in which a driver looked at a red signal, read it as green, and caused an accident. Many pilots will doubtless recognise parallels in their own experience, and Davis describes four specific types of situation in which a false hypothesis is particularly likely to occur.

(a) *When expectancy is very high.* Long experience of an event which has always happened in a particular manner generates a strong probability that it will be 'seen', 'heard' or 'felt' to happen in that manner in the future, regardless of the precise nature of the stimulus. An example, in Britain, is the official blue and white sign which reads: 'Police Notice, No Parking'. A sign of similar design which contains the words 'Polite Notice, No Parking' is often used by harassed residents to encourage motorists to move on and park elsewhere. The stimulus received at the eye is the letter 't'; but because people are used to seeing a 'c' in this context, it is read as such.

Man has a great need to structure situations, that is to give them order and meaning. A pilot who hears a message over a distorted radio/telephone channel

---

* CAP 347: *Report of the Italian Commission of Inquiry on the accident to BAC 1-11 G-ASJJ at S. Donato Milanese, Italy, 14 January 1969.* HMSO, London.

may make a number of hypotheses before asking for the message to be repeated. He knows that the airport tower would not pass a meaningless message to him, so he tries to fill in the gaps and believes that he heard what he thinks he *should* have heard. If he is expecting a particular message to be passed at that time, or if he is under great pressure—such as shortage of time or the intimidating influence of a domineering captain—this tendency to accept a dubious hypothesis is given even greater impetus.

(b) *When the hypothesis serves as a defence*. Human beings are prone to interpret incoming information in such a way as to minimise anxiety. It is, in fact, commonly witnessed that a person who is suffering from an incurable illness may readily believe an implausible hypothesis if it offers hope. And it is equally common for the student who receives a card informing him that he has failed an examination to assume that it has been sent to him in error. Both these people might be objective where the events pertain to others unknown to them; but they become irrational when they themselves, or people dear to them are concerned. The objective evidence is there, but people so affected have no wish to see it. Such disregard for reality is frequently evident when two people become involved in a violent argument. Both persist in advocating hypotheses which grow progressively less tenable because of the anxiety with which each disputant views the prospect of backing down.

However senior his rank, and however great his experience, a pilot is still subject to anxiety and, because of this, to the pitfalls of false hypothesis. Happily, his experience may have taught him appropriate lessons, and he may realise and guard against the circumstances which can lead to this type of error. Occasionally, however, his very seniority and status may be an even greater bar to admitting his mistakes—and he will only publicly reject his false hypothesis when it is too late, and when disaster is imminent.

(c) *When attention is elsewhere*. If a pilot has a number of immediate tasks, and if one of these requires special attention, he is likely to be less critical in accepting hypotheses about other components of the work load. Thus, if a great deal of the pilot's effort is devoted to spotting runway lights in bad weather, he is more likely to misread—that is, develop false hypotheses about—other instruments. Again, if the pilot *already* holds a false hypothesis about some item of information upon which he is concentrating very closely, he may ignore other vital information which conflicts with this hypothesis.

Davis[4] cites as an example an accident in which the aircraft's starboard engine began to surge and lose power. The pilot reported to the tower that the propeller constant-speed unit had failed, and attempted to clear the surging by operating the throttle and pitch levers throughout their full range, but without effect. Shortly afterwards, the aircraft crashed.

The subsequent investigation showed that the cause of the accident was the single and simple fact that the fuel tanks were empty. But having made up his mind that the propeller constant-speed unit was defective, the pilot failed to carry out checks elsewhere in the cockpit.

(d) *After a period of high concentration*. Every pilot knows about 'end-of-tripitis' —that time at the end of a brilliantly flown sortie when the concentration drops. The most difficult part of the flying procedure has been successfully completed, but it is all too often at this juncture that an accident occurs.

Among the examples offered by Davis is that of a railway driver who drove through fog from Crewe to London—a distance of 160 miles. A few miles away from the terminus the fog cleared and the sun came out. The driver relaxed, drove through a red signal and crashed into another train. Clearly, the greater part of the trip—in poor visibility—had made great demands on his concentration. The remainder of the journey must have seemed so easy, in contrast, that the unfortunate driver had obviously considered himself 'as good as home'.

A false hypothesis need not be spontaneous but may be an idea with which a person has lived for many years. On a light aircraft such as the Chipmunk, the stalling speed of the clean aircraft is about 35 knots; this fact, too often, becomes a broad concept of the aeroplane's stalling characteristics. When the aircraft is in a turn with the flaps down, however, as may well be the case in an attempted forced landing into a field, the stalling speed is nearly doubled. In about one in two of all light aircraft accidents in the UK the penultimate act in the drama is a stall in the turn at low altitude. Virtually all light aircraft pilots know the stalling speed of their clean aircraft in straight and level flight, but how many know the other, and more vital figure? One who may not have done so was the pilot of a Nipper T66 who stalled in the turn at 200 ft. The figure for a power-on stall in this aircraft is 32 knots, but becomes 65 knots at a 75° angle of bank.*

4. Man, the creature of habit

A basic tenet of human behaviour which is of vital importance to aviation is that the more times an action has been performed in a particular way in the past, the more likely it is to be performed in that way in the future. Indeed, much of the pilot's training is devoted to establishing a repertoire of habitual actions so that when he is flying he can concentrate on coordinating whole groups of actions, instead of devoting inordinate attention to one comparatively simple task. His basic role is therefore that of monitor of a number of low-level activities.

The majority of aircraft, too, are standardised, so that actions appropriate to one aircraft are also appropriate to another, i.e. controls are usually in the same place and operate—and are operated—in the same way. For the most part, such previously learned habits are beneficial, and may often be essential, to the present situation; but occasionally they are inappropriate and a potential accident looms large.

A much-quoted episode from the records of aviation medicine is provided by the case of the Auster aircraft which, shortly after take-off, was seen to porpoise and dive into the ground.[1] The pilot had applied excessive elevator trim, probably because he had been flying a different aeroplane—a Tripacer—for much of the

* Civil Aviation Authority Accident Report No. 8, 1973.

preceding year. Both the Auster and the Tripacer are fitted with a similar trim control in the same place, but whereas the Tripacer requires several turns of the control wheel to effect a small change in trim, the Auster needs only a single turn to cover the full range. The pilot probably carried out the right action for a Tripacer; unfortunately, he was in an Auster at the time.

This accident, and others like it, illuminate one great disadvantage of the human system when it is compared with a machine: namely, that man has no erase button on his memory. *He cannot make himself forget.* Rather, old and no longer appropriate habits must be slowly and laboriously eliminated, whenever man must adapt to new conditions and demands. This situation can be exacerbated in certain circumstances when people are more likely to revert to earlier and well-learned patterns of behaviour.

It is known that two situations of this type encourage such reversion—firstly, when little attention is being paid to the task in hand. An example is the familiar experience of the driver who changes from a floor-mounted gear lever in a car, to one which is mounted on the steering column. While the driver concentrates on changing gear, his actions are appropriate, but as soon as he attempts to change gear with his attention elsewhere he finds his hand waving about at knee level.

A second cause of reversion to earlier behaviour patterns is stress. It can be shown in the laboratory that a person under stress is much more likely to repeat an earlier, and possibly inappropriate action.

The possibility of such an occurrence is suggested in the Report of the Italian Commission of Enquiry which investigated the crash of the BAC 1-11 aircraft referred to earlier. The report states

Psychologists consulted think that there may have been a return to a former behaviour pattern acquired during operation of aircraft types which required immediate action by the pilot in the case of an engine failure on take-off.

During the nine years preceding his service in the BAC 1-11 (the pilot) did in fact fly piston-engined and propeller turbine multi-engined aircraft and during that period he experienced an engine failure on take-off.

Investigators concerned with specific cases of pilot error must therefore consider not only the pilot's present habits, but also those of his past. It is not always possible to assess the relevance of these patterns, or even to pronounce with any accuracy that an old and inappropriate habit has ceased to be a danger. This depends both on the strength of the original habit and on the subject's subsequent behaviour patterns. Suffice it to say that all habits go very deep, and lack of attention, or the prevalence of stress, may awaken a habit which has lain dormant for months, *or even years.*

As a pilot's experience increases, so does his repertoire of responses and so, alas, does his age. Questions on the relationship between accident rates and age and experience are often posed, and are rarely answered satisfactorily, but it requires little effort to appreciate how complex this relationship is. Age and experience and their corollaries are usually correlated, i.e. the older pilot is frequently more experienced than his younger colleague, but may be in a slightly worse physical condition, although he may counter the latter effect by pacing himself more efficiently. He may be more worried about status, but will have learned to live with many of life's other problems. The list of such compensatory adjustments is endless. Yet in a simplistic review of age and experience it is true to say that in the context of physical fitness the human body reaches a peak in the years of the 'teens and early twenties, and from then on the progress is downhill; whereas relevant (and irrelevant) experience increases throughout life.

The ideal, and probably the safest, age for any job depends upon the nature of that job. A female swimmer usually reaches her peak in her late 'teens, whereas a High Court judge is usually in his late fifties or may be even older. Similarly the fighter pilot who has a hard physical task which needs good reactions may be at his best in his late twenties, while the captain of a large aircraft who has a large management element in his job may reach his peak somewhat later. Graphs purporting to show the relationship between accident rates and age and experience should always be considered with these provisos in mind.

Recent experience, i.e. current familiarity with the aircraft type, is an important factor in flight safety, for statistics show that the pilot who flies less than 100 hours per year is the more likely to have an accident.[15] Current acquaintance with specific manoeuvres is of equally crucial importance—a fact confirmed by such events as the crash of a twin-engined Apache which came to grief after one of the engines failed. The investigators could find no record that the pilot had practised asymmetric flying at any time during the previous twelve years.*

A large proportion of the professional pilot's training, however, is devoted to preparing him for situations which it is hoped he will never meet, that is, for real emergencies. The object of this training is two-fold. Firstly, it is to ensure that the pilot's responses to the emergency are made as automatic as possible in order to 'free' his mind to a great extent for concentration on the crisis; in other words, the pilot 'over-learns' the emergency-response sequence. This process of over-learning is essential, since the shock of an emergency may well diminish the pilot's ability to a considerable degree. Secondly, over-learned responses and realistic simulations give the pilot the confidence to remain calm. In actual emergencies, however, responses are likely to be elicited by less intense and less specific stimuli, and tend to be more forceful, more extensive, and more rapid; at the same time they are somewhat less well organised, less regular, and in all probability, uncoordinated.

However realistic the simulator, the emotional shock of a genuine emergency is missing, and so the margin of over-learning of the safety procedure must be large. The ability to climb slowly into a rubber dinghy in a warm swimming pool is of little use; what counts is to be able to do it quickly in darkness, and in freezing water, while nursing a bruised head and rehearsing an exoneratory story for the board of enquiry. In the event, no responsible pilot neglects his emergency training and all pilots would endorse the quotation from the UK's National Safety Council: 'No one gets ready for an emergency in a moment.

* CAP 342. Report on Accident to Piper PA-23 (Apache) G-ARHJ at Hilfield Reservoir, near Elstree Aerodrome, Herts, 27 January 1968. HMSO, London.

What a person does in an emergency is determined by what he has been doing regularly for a long time.'

5. Motivation

One glib definition of the difference between a man and a machine is that a man cares about getting home safely, whereas a machine does not. Apart from the occasional aviation suicide, this is true and so motivation must be seen as a major factor in any consideration of pilot error. The investigator must therefore consider not only whether the pilot had the ability to carry out a particular task, but also whether he was sufficiently motivated to do so.

This is not, of course, the task of getting home safely, but rather the thousands of component tasks which are carried out on every trip. Any failure to carry out even one of these tasks successfully may lead to an accident.

Exploration of the many elements of motivation represents a profound field of research. It may, however, be convenient here to consider motivation as one of the major components of arousal. There is, unfortunately, no single agreed definition or measure of arousal, but basically it is the general state of human alertness as shown by certain physiological and psychological indicators. At any one time, man's level of arousal varies on a continuum from deep sleep, up through the various states of wakefulness, to a state of blind panic. His level of arousal is determined by many internal and external forces, and of these perhaps one of the most compelling internal forces is his motivation. Two major aspects of motivation are level and direction.

(a) *Level of motivation*. It is a simple, but quite useful, dictum that performance is best at moderate levels of arousal. If arousal is too low, energy is insufficient and nothing is achieved; if arousal is too high, there may be plenty of action but it is ill-directed and useless. This 'day-dream-to-panic' continuum is described by Lager[7] as a situation in which the brain is 'switched out' at low and high levels of arousal. At a low level the effect is analogous to low-level programs (in the computer sense) becoming muddled up, while at the high end a man may display random, i.e. purposeless, activity. Alternatively, at the high-arousal end, the brain's channel-selector may become jammed, causing the person to fixate on one thing to the exclusion of all others. As a typical consequence of this condition the passenger trapped in the blazing wreckage of an aircraft may continue to struggle with an unyielding emergency door and ignore the gaping hole in the fuselage. Given the emergency situation without the fire, and consequently a much lower level of arousal, he would easily spot the alternative exit.

Although it is the panic end of the arousal continuum which is the more spectacular, it is often the other end which is the more dangerous, for at the low end of the continuum lies complacency. Aircraft have crashed into each other in clear skies; experienced pilots have landed wheels-up; and many pilots have begun what proved to be a final flight secure in the knowledge that 'it can't happen to me'.

Complacency is ubiquitous and not easy to prevent. Artificial signals to raise the pilot's arousal to an optimum level are of limited use because he soon becomes adapted to the signal. It has been found, for example, that it is not possible to prevent wheels-up landings by burdening the pilots with the onus of an additional call to say that the undercarriage is down, for this call soon becomes part of the routine, and thus non-arousing. The only real answer lies in education and propaganda so that every pilot is always aware that every safe landing he makes is, on the complacency index, making matters worse.

There have been numerous accidents which can be described as having been due either to too high or too low a level of arousal, but for many years to come researchers will have to remain content with descriptions rather than proof. At the moment it is only possible to hypothesise, and to use evidence from witnesses or voice-recordings to estimate a pilot's level of arousal at the time of an accident. Lager has tried to close the gap between description and proof by measuring pilot performance in a flight simulator. He reports that he can distinguish groups of pilots who possess either a very low or a very high level of arousal, as measured by certain physiological indicants. Both groups perform significantly worse than the pilot population as a whole, and also have a poorer, i.e. more frequent, accident record. The low-arousal group show very little emotion after an accident or a poor trip in the simulator; while the high-level group are very active, but subject to performance breakdown if energy alone cannot solve their problem.

The levels of motivation which people appear to experience vary greatly. There are numerous stories of people who have exerted a superhuman effort in moments of great stress: unaided they have lifted a huge weight from a trapped friend, or suffered dreadful hardships at the behest of that supreme motivator, survival. But be it noted that virtually all these actions are fairly simple physical acts; what is more rare is the demonstration of a balanced and rational approach to a problem when the motivation to succeed is very high—a situation exemplified by the trauma of examination nerves.

(b) *Direction of motivation*. To say that a pilot is motivated merely to fly from place *A* to place *B* is to over-simplify the associated problems. The pilot's decision is not whether to fly safely or to have an accident, but often whether to take very slight risks, or just slight risks. In this context there are inevitably conflicting pressures on a pilot who is about to make a landing in marginal weather conditions. The decision is his and he knows he *could*, and perhaps *should*, divert to an airport some distance away. On the other hand, his mind is processing the counter-arguments: 'The company would be glad if I managed to land there; the passengers are waiting; I'd like to get home tonight; and I don't want to miss my golf/theatre/dinner appointment. . .'

One factor in particular may play a major part in such a dialogue, yet in any discussion the issue of manhood versus safety is usually swept under the carpet with alacrity.

Our culture and training teach us that men are brave; that it is natural, desirable and indeed heroic to struggle through adversities such as pain, bullies, strong teams of opposing sportsmen, and enemy troops. Man's lowly instincts therefore often generate a contempt for bad weather, or a risky flight, as just another hazard which will yield to bravery. This distortion of logic is compounded by social attitudes offering a combination of censure and sneaking admiration for the man who breaks the rules and wins; while of course, the wrath of righteous indignation is called down upon the man who breaks the rules and loses. But most, if not all, men have the occasional desire to kick over the traces and to take risks they would not ordinarily take, as the accident statistics on young drivers confirm. For them, as for many other people, the safe course often carries with it a slight, but nevertheless perceptible loss of face, and 'face'—as the antithesis of weakness—must be preserved.

Pilots are trained to control the urge to express 'manhood' by flying dangerously, and the urge *is* controlled, but not entirely destroyed. Mason[9] quotes the case of a Convair Metropolitan aircraft which came in to land at a small, fogshrouded coastal town. The weather was below limits but the pilot succeeded in landing at his third attempt. A second Convair approached and was told by the airport tower that the first aircraft was already on the ground—information which clearly represented sufficient challenge to the incoming pilot to sustain him through two abortive approaches before his aircraft crashed into a group of houses, killing forty-one people.

6. Stress and stressful environments

Man is equipped with a number of defence mechanisms which counter the effects of any stressful environment in which he may find himself. If he is too hot therefore, he sweats; if he is tired, he may try harder; and if he is feeling the effects of age, he may adopt a more philosophical approach to life. But for all such stresses there may come a time when the defence mechanism can no longer cope adequately with the stress, and performance suffers. The degree to which pilots can be so affected, and in what manner, is a matter calling for some clarification of the stresses to which they are exposed.

For convenience, three categories of stress may be identified: firstly, the physical stresses such as temperature, vibration, turbulence, and lack of humidity; secondly, the physiological stresses such as sleep-loss or disturbance, irregularity in eating patterns and the effects of drugs such as alcohol, nicotine, etc.; and thirdly, the psychological stresses such as fear, frustration and social and commercial pressures. By and large, research workers know more about the effects of physical stresses than they do about those which are physiological; and more about those which are physiological than about those rooted in psychology.

In the aftermath of an accident it may be possible to establish the presence and approximate magnitude of the physical and physiological stresses; but it is far harder to do the same for the psychological element. In a crash investigation, for example, the acceleration to which the cockpit was subjected might have been recorded and enquiries can reveal the pilot's sleep patterns for the previous few days. But establishing the importance of the real relationship between the crew members as a factor in the accident, or the degree to which the captain was worrying about his child's health or his own possible impotency, may well be virtually impossible.

The situation is the same in the laboratory, for stresses such as are imposed by large variations in temperature or by an excess of alcohol are measurable and reasonably well documented. It is possible to say that if, for instance, the body temperature exceeds 38.0°C, then human performance may change in the direction of increased speed and tendency to error, together with diminished accuracy and greater irregularity. Equally, more than 80 milligrams of alcohol in a blood sample convinces the police that a car driver's erratic performance was influenced by drink. Unfortunately certain stresses are not so well documented as others, and for many of those which are of the greatest interest to commercial aviation —such as disturbances in eating and sleeping patterns, low humidity, conflict and frustration—the data on performance effects are very limited. Yet, even when the better-documented stresses are relevant, there is still a wide gulf between the laboratory experiment and the responsibility of providing a definitive answer to the question posed at an accident enquiry: 'Did the presence of this stress contribute to the accident?' The question in turn poses others for the competent investigator, who would want to know a good deal more about the nature of the stress, the work which the pilot had to do—and about the pilot himself.

Besides the severity of the stress, the investigator would want to know its duration; the suddenness of its onset (a factor of considerable importance); and the presence of other stresses. Thus, one night of poor sleep may have effects very different from a week of such nights; and gradual adaptation to a hot climate is less deleterious than a sudden change of environment. Many (not quite all) of the data on the effects of stress have been obtained using single stresses whereas real-life situations almost invariably contain a number of stresses. To predict the effects of a multi-stress environment from the known effects of its component stresses is a most unreliable procedure, however, for the stresses may combine in an additive, more-than-additive, independent or even antagonistic manner. The effects of some of the vast number of stresses which plague modern man have been reviewed by many authors, among the more recent being Poulton[12] and Appley and Trumbull.[2]

Both the nature and difficulty of the task are important variables, as the pilot may well be able to cope with the associated stress when the flight is routine, but cannot manage when events begin to pile up on him. A 'chapter of accidents' is a common description of events in which a number of minor difficulties has occurred—either simultaneously and/or progressively—and their combined effect has made the pilot's task impossible. A further complication is posed by the fact that man is often a very bad judge of how well or badly he is performing a task— as witness the drunken driver who drives badly, while believing that he is driving well. Similarly, a senior pilot who is angry because his flying is suffering from the effect of stress may not be over-receptive to remarks to this effect from his juniors.

Lastly, the effects of stress depend on the pilot himself, his physical fitness, his competence and his personality; and here again the relationship between these factors challenges positive affirmation. Every reader knows people who have coped with stresses in far better fashion than would ever have been predicted of them. Men such as Byrd, Bombard, Lovell and hundreds of nameless pilots have responded magnificently to great stresses; others have failed at the first hurdle. The scientific selection of stress-resistant people is still in its infancy, although it has proved successful in the astronaut selection programme and is now in use with an increasing number of organisations. But, in general, it is true to say that the study of the physical and physiological stresses which affect a pilot is still in a state of virtual adolescence, and the picture of what happens when man is subjected to these pressures is being completed only slowly.

In recent years, psychological or 'life' stresses have been receiving a great deal more attention, as their ubiquity and great importance are being recognised. A pilot may say that he does not allow his work and his domestic life to mix; but this statement can only be partly true. Human beings are 24-hour-a-day people, possessing only one brain with which to control all their activities; and this brain has to cover both work and play. In sum, events which happen in one segment of daily life may therefore influence what happens in other segments.

The pilot who has just quarrelled violently is in a dangerous state,* for although he may have moved away from the person with whom he has quarrelled, and climbed aboard his aircraft, the physiological and psychological effects of the quarrel may last well into the flight, and the crushing retort which he wishes he had thought of at the time of the argument may crowd his single decision channel to the exclusion of more important information.

Few discussions of pilot error proceed very far before mention is made of 'accident-proneness'—the idea that some pilots are inherently more likely to have accidents than are others. This concept comes in and out of fashion as the years pass and as new studies are published, but at best the thesis is of very limited use in an aviation context for the following reasons:

(a)   The number of aviation accidents is small and so data are scarce.
(b)   If accidents are normally distributed amongst the pilot population there are, quite naturally, pilots who have had more than one accident.
(c)   Commercial and military pilots are very highly selected and what may apply, say, to the motoring public at large, probably does not apply to such a small select group.
(d)   Even were the concept of accident-proneness to be proven, there is little practical action which can be taken. By the time that it had been shown that the chances of a particular pilot having an accident had increased from one per million units to five per million units a great deal of money will have been spent on his training. Singling him out for special treatment —restriction to good weather flying or to daylight flying only—would, of course, be disastrous for his own and his colleagues' morale.

A much more useful and perhaps more realistic concept than accident-proneness is that of a short-term accident liability—the proposition that a pilot becomes more likely to experience an accident because of the personal pressures on him at the time. More specifically, in this attempt to rationalise cause and effect, the man whose child is ill, or who has quarrelled with his wife, or who is worried about his job, may be more likely to have an accident until he emerges from the trauma which is disturbing him. It follows, of course, that given an appreciation of this situation, the responsible pilot or manager should appreciate these stresses and make the necessary adjustments.

7. Fatigue

Fatigue might have been considered with the other stresses to which a pilot is subjected; but it is a topic which is discussed so often in the pilot-error context that it deserves special attention.

Captain Bressey was correct in his claim that '. . .there is still no definition of fatigue acceptable to all interested parties; nor has medical science been able to define, in specific terms, what produces fatigue. . .'*

Nevertheless, definitions have been attempted and many of them may be subsumed under that of Bergin.[3]

Fatigue is a progressive decline in man's ability to carry out his appointed task which may become apparent through deterioration in the quality of work, lack of enthusiasm, inaccuracy, ennui, disinterestedness, a falling back in achievement or some other more indefinable symptoms.

A distinction is sometimes made between single-trip fatigue, where a good night's sleep will effect recovery, cumulative fatigue, in which a state of rest between trips is not adequate and which may necessitate several days' rest for complete recovery, and chronic fatigue, which usually calls for medical help. The behavioural symptoms of all three types of fatigue are similar, however, and usually include increased irritability and irrational behaviour, as well as complaints about physical discomfort, the whole accompanied by a deterioration in flying skill. Thus, at the end of a tiring day's flying a pilot may perform less accurately and attentively, may require a higher than normal level of stimulus to evoke the appropriate responses, and may show increased fixation of both perception and behaviour.

A plethora of facts hasten the onset of fatigue. Organisational factors, for instance, may include badly planned or delayed trips, unnecessary delays, unproductive time or inadequate stop-over facilities. Any or all of these factors may be compounded by poor ergonomics in the cockpit, high work-load, temperature, noise, vibration, low humidity and bad weather. These pressures may be intensified by the physiological factors, by any decline in the pilot's fitness, or by the effects of mild hypoxia (oxygen deficiency), lack of food or

---

* In *Pilot Error*, First edition (1976): Chapter 1, p. 27.

disturbed diurnal rhythms. They may be even further intensified by psychological factors such as responsibility, morale, crew cooperation, and worry.

All of these, and many other factors relevant to aviation fatigue, are described in an excellent work by Hartman.[5]

Most people connected with flying recognise the symptoms of fatigue both in themselves and in others. It remains, nevertheless, difficult to provide a quantitative measure of the condition and nearly impossible to prove that it may have caused an accident. Post-flight psychological and hormonal measures of fatigue have met with only limited success, since fatigue is usually only one of a number of influences on these measures. Others, such as the attitude of a tired pilot in having to carry out a 'damn-fool' psychological task at the end of a long day, may be equally important.

Post-Accident Information

A variety of sources may provide post-accident clues to human behaviour. Tape recordings of communications between the pilots, or between the pilots and the ground, may tell the investigators just what was said, and the manner in which it was said—the latter facet perhaps indicating the presence of stress. Unfortunately the tapes may give no information about the pilot's plans or fears, nor may they give any indication as to whether or not he had actually seen a particular warning light. Experts, too, may not agree that the pitch of a pilot's voice is necessarily a useful index of stress.

A second major source of information is provided by the evidence of the pilot, and of other parties involved in the accident; and here there are many possible sources of distortion. Occasionally one or more people may lie, either in an attempt to save themselves, to avoid embarrassment, to protect their jobs, or out of misplaced loyalty to a colleague. The word 'misplaced' is used with some reluctance, but it is clear that the vital necessity for total honesty and objectivity in accident investigation may well conflict with some very deep emotions.

A far more important source of distortion lies in the poorness of the human memory. Man absorbs a truly vast amount of information during every moment of his life. Much of this remains in the memory for a very short time; a very little dwells for longer periods. But every moment, memories are decaying and are being contaminated with the arrival of fresh information. A pilot may, therefore, remember the pressure setting he used on the trip from which he had just landed, but probably does not remember what value he set last Tuesday week; and the thousands of such settings which he has made over the years form a general blur.

Closely controlled laboratory experiments confirm the everyday experience that memories are distorted in the direction of simplicity and coherence. If a story is repeated many times from one witness to another, it is progressively simplified until only the bare bones remain. Similarly, the human desire for order out of chaos means that nonsequiturs in a story are gradually eliminated until a clear and logical account of events emerges. However, this final account usually bears very little resemblance to the original message.

The pilot who repeats his story a number of times, and who discusses the accident with many people, may, with total integrity, give a false account of what actually happened. He 'remembers' that the reading on a dial was such and such because that reading would make sense in the context of his story.

Distortion can be minimised, although not eliminated, when statements are taken from the parties concerned as soon as possible after the accident. However, pilots have yet to be trained to crash alongside the investigator's office, and prevention of any discussion of the accident pending the arrival of the investigator is not without its difficulties.

It is an unfortunate fact, too, that the investigator himself may be a source of distortion, for the answers to his questions depend, at least in part, on the questions he asks and the way in which he asks them. Every investigator has his personal bias, and a pilot, a lawyer and a psychologist in search of a common truth may ask very different questions and receive very different answers.

The non-directed interview, in which the witness talks and the interviewer merely records his statement, goes some way towards solving this problem. Eventually, when the enquiry is completed, the pilot-error cause is coded and entries appear against certain categories in a record card. This information is handed down to posterity, but again, may be a distorted version of what actually occurred.

Finally, eye-witness accounts may provide a little cheer in the tragic circumstances of an accident, since such witnesses are often victims of many of the pressures mentioned above. They may have talked to a number of people about the accident; they have almost certainly read graphic accounts of it in the newspapers; and they are usually motivated by a strong desire to appear both knowledgeable and helpful. 'The port engine backfired and the aircraft yawed sharply to port in a marked nose-up attitude—I make model aircraft so I know about these things.' This may appear to be a helpful statement but the investigator has to satisfy himself that the witness really did understand the meaning of each term, and, what is more important, that he understood them at the time of the accident. The tendency for distortion in the direction of what *must* have happened rather than what *did* happen must not be forgotten. If a piston-engined aircraft passed overhead, appearing to be both 'low and slow' before it subsequently crashed, an obvious corollary for the lay observer is that an engine must have been running roughly.*

---

* This syndrome was plainly in evidence following the Moorgate tube train crash in London on 28 February 1975, in which forty-one passengers were killed.

Following conjecture in the press that the driver had suffered a heart attack (refuted by subsequent medical evidence) one British newspaper reported as follows:

Eye-witness reports—taken by British Transport police—of [the driver's] last moments at the controls of the train indicate that he was a sick man. One said: 'The driver looked as if he were mesmerised. He was staring in front of him and just looking ahead.'
Another said that the driver had a blank expression.
    A statement from a passenger waiting to board the train said. . .'the driver had a glazed look in his eyes and looked as though he was frozen'.

(*Daily Telegraph*, 5 March 1975)

It is salutary to conclude this chapter by reiterating that mistakes are a normal feature of human behaviour and that aviation is a human activity. It is nevertheless equally human that the logic of this proposition should be challenged by the continuing pursuit of twin goals—firstly, the reduction of the possibilities for pilot error; and secondly, the lessening of the consequences of such mistakes.

The achievement of these goals, however, depends on much more than an acceleration of the present trend towards a better understanding of pilot behaviour. It requires, in addition, a far more rational attitude toward their mistakes. That 'better understanding' is essential for all those concerned with aviation safety: for pilots, managers, the designers of aircraft and procedures, those responsible for the selection and training of pilots, research workers, accident investigators and many others. For all of these, the data-producers must present their evidence in a usable format wherein research findings and experience are collated and state-of-the-art reviews are readily accessible. The decision-makers must seek these data and use them. But, above all, the attitude to pilot error must be unemotional and constructive; for until the pilot's errors are viewed as dispassionately as are those of the aircraft in which he is flying, there will be more than a ring of truth in the cynical phrase: 'If the accident doesn't kill the pilot, the enquiry will.'

References

1. Allnutt, M. F. (1971) 'Human factors: their significance in an investigation'. Paper presented to the DTI seminar on Aircraft Accidents, London.
2. Appley, M. H. and Trumbull, R. (1967) *Psychological Stress*, Appleton-Century-Crofts, New York.
3. Bergin, K. G. (1948) *Textbook of Aviation Medicine*, J. Wright, London.
4. Davis, R. D. (1958) 'Human engineering in transportation accidents', *Ergonomics*, 2, 24–33.
5. Hartman, B. O. (1969) 'Psychological factors in flying fatigue', *International Psychiatric Clinics*, Winter (4)1, 185–96.
6. Kraft, C. L. (1969) 'Measurement of height and distance information provided to the pilot by the extra-cockpit visual', *MIT Conf. Proc.*, 257–64, 16–19 April.
7. Lager, C. G. (1973) 'Human Factors.' Paper presented to a seminar on Aviation Accident Prevention at the Royal Institute of Technology, Stockholm.
8. McFarland, R. A. (1953) *Human Factors in Air Transportation*, McGraw-Hill, New York.
9. Mason, C. D. (1972) 'Manhood versus safety'. Paper presented to the Third Oriental Airlines Association Flight Safety Seminar, Singapore.
10. Masters, R. L. (1972) 'Analysis of pilot error-related aircraft accidents'. Paper submitted to the National Transportation Safety Board.
11. Pitts, D. G. (1967) *Visual Illusions and Aircraft Accidents*. Technical Report No. 28, School of Aviation Medicine, Brooks Air Force Base, Texas.
12. Poulton, E. C. (1971) *Environment and Human Efficiency*, Charles C. Thomas, Illinois.

13.   Rolfe, J. M. (1972) 'Ergonomics and air safety', *Applied Ergonomics* **3** (2), 75–81.
14.   Shaw, L. and Sichel, H. (1971) *Accident Proneness*, Pergamon, Oxford.
15.   Smith, E. M. B. (1966) 'Pilot error and aircraft accidents', *ZBL Verkehon-Med.* **12**, 1–13.
16.   Wansbeek, G. C. (1969) 'Human factors in airline incidents'. Paper presented to the 22nd Annual International Air Safety Seminar at Montreux.

Chapter 2

Accident Prevention: The role of Education and Training *M. K. Strickler, Jr.*

We have learned something of aviation's human material. What we need to know with increasing confidence is what can be taught and what is the best way to teach it effectively.
Here Mervin Strickler looks at training and educational programmes designed to reduce aviation accidents and suggests approaches which he believes could bring about significant improvements.

Concurrent with Wilbur and Orville Wright's historic experiments with flight, the Russian psychologist Ivan Petrovich Pavlov postulated and proved a psychological law that is basic to safety training and accident prevention:

The human organism can be so programmed that reflexes become automatic.

Introduction

Man's early trial and error methods since the dawn of aviation have been more recently modified by what we have learned about learning and what we have created via new technology: both of these achievements teach that we should be wary of panaceas, and none deserves more caution than the approach to training. Clearly, training *per se* is not an automatic assurance of safety. Factually, since the earliest days of aviation to the present, training has been and still can be hazardous and indeed, the wrong type of training can prove fatal. However, a combination of aviation education and training based on fundamental psychological principles can assist in reducing those accidents that most authorities agree are preventable.

Since the first flight, the role of training in accident prevention has been foremost in the mind of anyone concerned with the successful and safe accomplishment of the operation. Early flights and accidents led to trial and error procedures, and word-of-mouth or hangar-flying types of communication.

It is remarkable that there were not more accidents in the pioneering phases of aviation. By the standards of today, of course, there were far too many that objectively fall in the category of preventable. In fact, today there are still areas for improvement if we will simply use the knowledge and technology that is available.

Most authorities agree that civil aviation operations in most parts of the world today present two faces at once.

(a)   Civil aviation operations are as safe—accident free—as they have ever been considering the diversity of aviation instruction, aircraft, the variety of operational conditions and personnel maintaining and operating them. Further considerations include the range of technological advances, aids to navigation, complexity and capacity of air space, regulatory standards, surveillance and enforcement and the total system of which the man/machine is but a part.[1] (See Fig. 2.1.)

(b)   In spite of all the scientific, technological and related areas of clear and measurable progress, there are still far too many examples of preventable accidents.

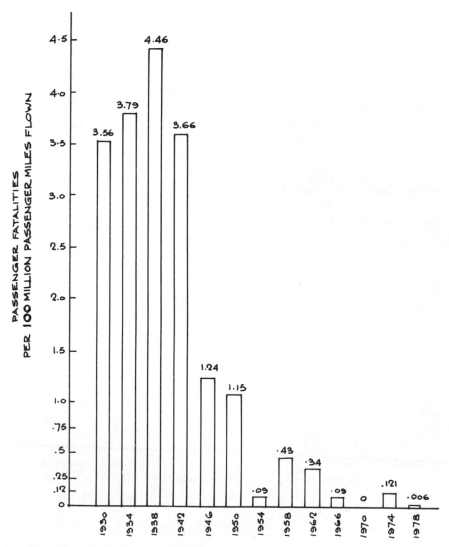

Fig. 2.1   Air carrier fatality rate 1930—78

Resources allocated for the education and training of aviation personnel have steadily increased. In the decade of the 1980s, worldwide resources devoted to civil aviation education and training are in the category of multi-billions of dollars. Concerns for aviation safety are no longer local or national, or simply of interest to an extremely limited group of nations. The global transportation network of civil aviation now touches lives in every region of the planet and there is, therefore, a wide interest in any progress in using new techniques, resources, and technology to reduce accidents.

In analysing past accidents and proposing methods to prevent similar occurrences, it is clear that one cannot take a portion of the system and deal with it in isolation—rather a total system approach must be used. For example, is it appropriate to use the term 'training' alone? Should one consider 'education' and 'training'? If so, what is the distinction between the two?

For the purposes of this chapter, training is defined as follows:

. . .the teaching, drill and discipline by which powers of mind or body are developed. . .instruction in an art, profession, or occupation.[2]

Education is defined as:

. . .the art or process of providing with knowledge, skill, competence. . .[3]

To put the terms training and education in a context directly related to aviation the author suggests the following:

With what we know of behavioural psychology, conditional response, reward and punishment or reinforcement, combined with currently available navigation, computer, sensing, automated feedback systems, it is possible to 'train' a crew that includes a chicken, a pigeon and a chimpanzee to react to programmed stimuli and—in effect—'fly' a modern jet transport coast-to-coast or an intercontinental flight from start-up, through taxi, take-off, climb, cruise, descent, landing, taxi and stop. All of this can be done via training. However, such a crew cannot be 'educated' to handle a missed approach.

In short, for the purposes of this chapter, training is a vital, crucial element in safe, successful profitable aviation operations. Training, however, relates to manipulative skills coupled with the appropriate analytical functions related to decision-making. Education is a broader concept. It includes elements of training and it includes the element of judgement which Richard Jensen considers in some detail in chapter 3.

While it may, at first reading, appear oversimplified, training can be regarded as being an assurance of performance of proper tasks to attain a pre-determined goal. Education, however, is really synonymous with behaviour change. For a flight crew member, the hope is to provide training to plan and operate a flight safely at all times. Education is meant to take flight crews from a point of behaviour manifest before their exposure to aviation and modify that behaviour —reaction to various stimuli, information, etc.—so they will behave in an acceptable, safe and efficient manner. In this instance, training for certain functions would be a part of the aviation education that a flight crew member would receive.

Aviation education is not limited to flight personnel. Using the total system approach, it is essential that certain kinds of values, standards and behavioural norms are demonstrated by those who plan all elements of the aviation system: aircraft, airports, aids to navigation, the total system; and those who regulate and enforce elements of the system.

In critically examining the past, and hopefully looking to the future, it is clear that innovations have been made in education and training historically. There are opportunities today to continue to make progress.

There are new understandings in the field of psychology in general, and some psychiatric principles that have relevant applications to training in aviation in particular. Further, opportunities to share information on an international basis abound via various professional organisations, as well as international bodies such as the International Civil Aviation Organisation (ICAO), International Air Transport Association (IATA) and the various industrial, educational, professional and regulatory bodies of various nations. While the opportunities are available for communication, there are still examples of failure to share widely data that might help prevent future similar accidents or incidents. Thus more communication sharing must be encouraged.

Decision-making for Safety Education

It is instructive to note how decisions are made for resource allocations aimed at improving safety, training and related activities in aviation. An innovative analysis of decision-making, developed by Dr H. Gene Little in his doctoral dissertation of May 1979, is called STEP—meaning the relationships of Safety—Technology—Economics—Politics. In his analysis, Little developed a flow chart to be used as an evaluation tool. He devised what he termed 'the STEP test' to show the relationships of various events (accidents, fuel shortage) and factors (political decisions) to the central theme of his study. For example, he cites the following historic accidents and relationships:

(a)   In 1931 the Fokker F-10 crash carrying Knute Rockne '. . .caused a political uproar which resulted in economic pressures on the builder, General Motors Corporation, the designer, Fokker, and technical evaluation of wood-wing structure integrity, which ultimately forced the F-10 from the skies in the US'.[4]

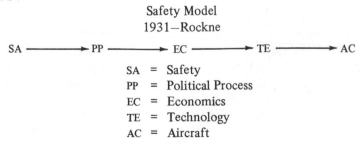

Safety Model
1931—Rockne

SA ⟶ PP ⟶ EC ⟶ TE ⟶ AC

SA = Safety
PP = Political Process
EC = Economics
TE = Technology
AC = Aircraft

(b)   The 1935 crash of the TWA DC-2 in which Senator Cutting of New Mexico was killed '. . .resulted in the initiation of a new air traffic control system for aviation. Although very minimal, the basis of an airways system began after overwhelming political forces had run their course. This accident resulted in a change in the in-flight environment of the 1935–1938 period.'[5]

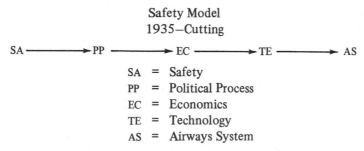

Safety Model
1935–Cutting

SA ────────► PP ────────► EC ────────► TE ────────► AS

SA = Safety
PP = Political Process
EC = Economics
TE = Technology
AS = Airways System

(c)   The 1956 mid-air collision of a United Air Lines DC-6 and a TWA Constellation over the Grand Canyon '. . .resulted in the positive control of all flights above 24 000 feet flying instrument flight rules (IFR). With Congress alerted to the inadequacy of the air traffic system, funding for an airway plan gained approval.'[8]

Safety Model
1956–Grand Canyon

SA ────────► PP ────────► EC ────────► TE ────────► AS

As in the 1935 accident, Congress up-graded the airways system (AS).

(d)   In March of 1974, the Turkish Airlines DC-10 was the first crash of a widebody aircraft. Departing from Orly Airport near Paris the DC-10 '. . .crashed after the rear cargo door opened during the climb to cruising altitude. This occurred even though a program had been designed to obviate such a recurrence.'[7]

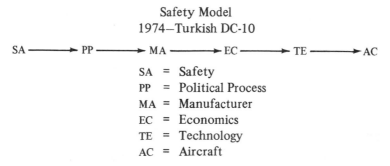

Safety Model
1974–Turkish DC-10

SA ────────► PP ────────► MA ────────► EC ────────► TE ────────► AC

SA = Safety
PP = Political Process
MA = Manufacturer
EC = Economics
TE = Technology
AC = Aircraft

In the example the manufacturer (MA) is introduced as a factor.

(e)   In September of 1978 the mid-air collision over San Diego, California between a Pacific South-west Airlines Boeing 727 and a single-engine Cessna Skylane '. . .occurred even though both pilots were in contact with the San Diego Lindbergh tower and apprised of the other aircraft's proximity.'[8]

Safety Model
1978–San Diego

SA ————————▶ PP ————————▶ EC ————————▶ TE ————————▶ AS

Little points out:

This accident precipitated major political pressures. The Federal Aviation Administrator, Langhorne Bond, issued a press release less than 60 days later announcing a satellite airport system to separate traffic, providing radar control, instrument landing systems for satellite airports, more new terminal control areas (TCAs) and terminal radar service areas (TRSAs). The technology was available before the San Diego crash; however, the monies were not.[9] *

Clearly, the examples cited by Little demonstrate that, historically, forward steps are made largely as a result of a crisis. Little uses a similar technique in showing the influence of a Technological Model, Economic Model and Political Model. He then shows the relationships of technology, economics and political decisions on aviation in general, and maintenance and pilot personnel in particular.

For a detailed chronology of technological characteristics for the period 1928–70 see Table 2.1.[10]

For the economic impact of selected civil transport Aircraft Unit Prices 1935–1975, see Fig. 2.2.[11]

In the final analysis, Little states:

Political policy can create the environment for technology, which results in aircraft that influence career qualifications. In fact, it is most likely that the political influence is the most obvious force in play.

Through the five decades examined for relationships which caused change in the career qualifications for aviation maintenance and flight personnel, political events and factors have provided the economic power to cause significant technological advances. The vast majority of these advances are now an integral part of the modern civil air transport fleet. This same statement could have been made at any stage through the evolution of the airplane.[12]

Furthermore he writes:

Regardless of specific factors which influence the ultimate characteristics of the aircraft and the resultant operational environment, these characteristics and environment dictate the specific career qualifications for the skills and knowledge necessary to successfully maintain and operate civil air transport aircraft. The safety record of civil air transportation reflects the success of the applied educational and training technology and philosophy of the US civil air carrier system.[13]

* For a more detailed discussion of this accident, see chapter 6.

Table 2.1

TECHNOLOGICAL CHARACTERISTICS
1928–70
Aircraft

	Structure	Systems	Powerplants
1928 Fokker F-10 Tri-motor 10 passengers 125 m.p.h.	Steel tube Fabric Wood wing	Hydraulic brakes Magnetic compass Basic instruments	Air-cooled radial
1935 DC-3 21 passengers 180 m.p.h.	24-ST All metal aluminium alloy Cantilever wing Wing flaps NACA cowling	Retractable landing gear-hydraulic-1000 p.s i Hydraulic flap system Gyro instruments Two-way radio De-icing Auto-pilot	100 octane fuel Constant speed propellers
1942 DC-4 (C-54) 45 passengers 220 m.p.h.	Flush riveting	Tricycle landing gear	Three-blade propellers

Table 2.1 cont.

	Structure	Systems	Powerplants
1950			
	DC-6 85 passengers 300 m.p.h	7075-T6 Aluminium alloy Pressurised	Skydrol fluids (fire resistant) High pressure hydraulics 3K-p.s.i. Cabin supercharger Pressurisation	Compound radial
1959			
	707 165 passengers 550 m.p.h	Titanium Swept wings Honeycomb Compound materials Fail-safe philosophy	System redundancy Servoflight controls Alternating current Powered/on-board Alternators Doppler navigation Integrated instrument systems Weather radar	Gas turbines Thrust reversers
1970			
	DC-10 280–300 passengers 600 m.p.h.	Wide body Compound structures	High redundancy Inertial navigation system On-board computers Micro electronics Auto-landing	High-bypass Turbine engines (fan jet)

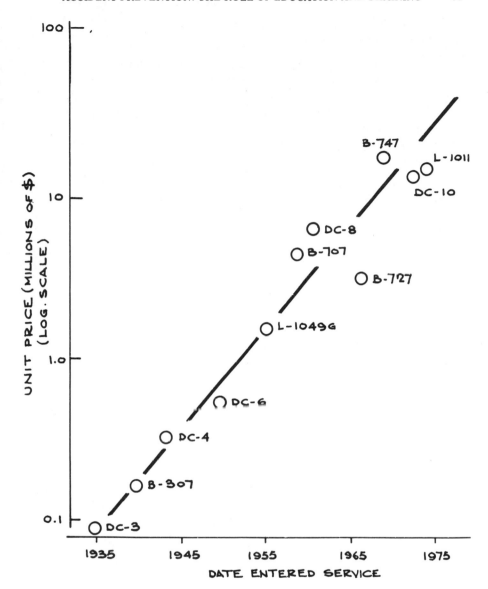

Fig. 2.2   Civil transport aircraft unit price 1935–75

Educational and Training Requirements for Air Crews

A report published in 1977[14] compares data on airline training and personnel practices of countries including Great Britain, Switzerland, France, West Germany, Sweden, Denmark, Norway, the Netherlands, the Soviet Union, and two typical airline companies in the United States.

The major differences shown in this study as far as European and US practices are concerned are as follows:

(a)   Almost all European airlines have some *ab initio* training for commercial pilots which is subsidised by the government.
(b)   Many of the European pilots do not have a college or university degree.
(c)   US airline pilots come from the military, college and university programmes and the general aviation flight schools.
(d)   European airline pilots tend to be employed at an earlier age thus providing more years of productive return to the employer.

A large proportion of US airline pilots in recent years have completed a college education or its equivalent.*

Government subsidy of US pilot trainees is mostly in the form of that for military pilots, veterans who receive partial subsidy, and government guaranteed college student loans.

US airlines new-hire pilots tend to be older than their European counterparts and have fewer years of productive service available to their employers.

In terms of airline transport pilot Federal Qualification Standards 1928—78 Little traces the evolution of the requirements.[16]

The question to be considered is: What new standards may result from the needs, technology and safety record of this decade?

One clue to what the future holds may be noted from suggestions made by Jack R. Hunt, the President of Embry Riddle Aeronautical University of Daytona Beach, Florida and Prescott, Arizona. His suggestions came during an international scientific and technical exchange meeting between representatives of civil aviation in the United States and officials of the USSR Ministry of Civil Aviation.†

President Hunt stated during his discussion of future trends for airline pilot training: 'The best kept secret in aviation is this—airline pilots do not fly airplanes. They manage and monitor systems.'[17]

Proposal for an airline pilot education programme

Hunt first broached this subject in April 1977 during a discussion with Soviet officials at Daytona Beach. At that time, the joint US—USSR concerns had to do with what might be done to help ensure more accurate predictions of success for

* The Air Line Pilots Association (ALPA), Federal Aviation Administration personnel, and representatives of several colleges and universities offering aviation education and training programmes have formed a volunteer Aviation Education Review Organization (AERO) to produce a guide to assist colleges and universities in evaluating aeronautical educational experiences. Many colleges and universities use this AERO college credit standards guide for awarding credit for various aviation ratings, licences and certification. The most recent guide was published in 1977.[15]

† The governments of the United States and the Soviet Union have conducted a civil aviation education and training scientific and technical exchange under a programme known as The US—USSR Joint Cooperation in Transportation. The cooperative exchange took place between 1974 and 1979. This report is based upon discussions during the Seventh Session of this Exchange which took place in the United States, 12—18 August 1979.

pilot applicants and trainees, and reduce the failure rate of pilot trainees. At that time too, Hunt suggested that study should be made of planning pilot training as an '. . .integrated system designed to produce pilots for specific missions'.[18]

In the August 1979 discussion in Prescott, Arizona, Hunt stated:

We must replace our romantic approach to 'flight' training with objective airline pilot training in order to properly prepare pilot trainees to effectively manage and monitor sophisticated, integrated flight director systems.

He recognised that this will not be easy:

We can anticipate considerable resistance to necessary changes in our training programs. We must differentiate between the two basic types of pilot training programs that will be necessary to prepare pilots for various careers in aviation flight. The first step is to classify airline pilots in one category and all other pilots in another category. For the time being, all other pilots will continue to be trained in accordance with present pilot training programs.

In fact, Hunt pointed out:

In developing the airline pilot training program, we must adopt a systems approach that will articulate academic subjects with practical on-line training using computers, procedure trainers and simulators. There is no reason to conduct any portion of the airline pilots' training in a basic training airplane. In fact the use of such an airplane can be counter productive to the skills required by an airline pilot.[19]

In making this point Hunt used the analogy of conversations he had with captains of large surface ships with regard to their training. They indicated that there is simply no correlation between training in a small boat and the large ship. Indeed, as Hunt said, 'Any training in a small boat would be useless and similarly counter productive.' The training for large ship commanders '. . .was conducted on board a large ship and by the use of simulators.'[20]

Hunt then proceeded to describe in some detail both a rationale and specific recommendation for an Airline Pilot Educational programme at the college level:

Society, in the USA and most other countries, considers a college degree to be the mark of a professional person. Yet, approximately one-half of the airline pilots in the United States do not have a college degree. This situation is changing rapidly. Virtually every airline requires a pilot applicant to have a college degree. We at Embry-Riddle Aeronautical University have concluded that the professional pilot of the future will be required to have a college degree. Therefore, we no longer offer a flight training program that is not part of a degree program. Appropriate college credit is given for all flight training courses.

In an attempt to develop a dialogue about airline pilot education and to provide a basis to explore the content of a college degree program that will produce airline pilots, this suggested program outline is submitted for further consideration and discussion:

AIRLINE PILOT (BS Degree)
Length: 8 Academic Semesters

Required Courses

Nomenclature of Aviation
Flight Rules and Regulations
Basic Navigation
*Inertial Navigation
Basic Aerodynamics
Aircraft Turbine Engines
Governments in Aviation (ICAO)
Aviation Law
Typing (computers)
Computer Language
*Introduction to Cockpit
*Cockpit Systems
*Emergency Procedures
Oral Communications
Technical Report Writing
Basic Aviation Math
Basic Accounting
Basic Physics
Basic Psychology
Cross-Cultural Communication

History of Aviation
Meteorology
*Electronic Navigation
Radio Voice Communications
Basic Aircraft Systems
Hydraulic Systems
*Aircraft Performance
Flight Safety
Introduction to Computers
Computer Programming
*Cockpit Procedures Training
*Cockpit Teamwork
*Flight Engineer Training
Written Communications
Introduction to Logic
Advanced Aviation Math
Management Concepts
Applied Physics
Applied Psychology
(123 credit hours)

*Controlled Environment Training

Elective Courses
Approximately six courses in a field to be chosen by the student in such areas as Language, Geography, Cross-Cultural Communications, International Relations, History of Economic Thought, International Aviation Law, etc. (15 credit hours).

The complete BS Degree Airline Pilot program would take four academic years to complete and entail a total of 138 credit hours.

Rationale
Flight Training conducted under FAR 141 or ICAO Regulations requires specific minimum hours of flight time as well as specified maneuvers which must be mastered before being issued a license but which cannot be performed in an airliner. Consequently, a student who has completed his flight training and earned his Flight Certificate and Ratings has spent at least 22 months in training, has not earned a college degree and is barely qualified to become an airline pilot *apprentice*. He must serve as a Flight Engineer or as a Co-pilot for several years in order to learn about operating an airliner.

The suggested Airline Pilot Education Program provides a systems approach which equates simulator training with an academic education, producing a graduate who is qualified to assume Flight Engineer duties immediately. This means that the average age of entry into airline service would be 22 years of age with a productive expectancy of 38 years service to the airline. This is in contrast to the average airline entry age of 28 years old with a productive expectancy of 32 years service.

Summary
Safety of operations, cost effectiveness, professional competence and high morale in the cockpit will result from an Airline Pilot Educational Program.[21]

In considering Hunt's suggestions the key points to keep in mind are:

(a)   state-of-the-art of simulators;
(b)   attitudes of management, trainees; and
(c)   regulatory bodies.

Flight Simulation: its Status

Remarkable progress has been made throughout the world in the design and use of procedural trainers, part-task training devices and flight simulators. In fact, the proposal by Hunt for total training of airline pilots in simulators draws ever closer to reality.

Dr Robert C. Houston of American Airlines in his paper entitled 'Developments in Training Technology' given in September 1979 at the Hague Symposium on Human Factors in Civil Aviation stated:

There are many challenges remaining for the future. . .For the near future there is the full substitution of the simulator for the training airplane; a step that not only requires well designed equipment, but a complete training system that uses all the human inputs to best advantage as an integral part of the system.[22]

Captain J. A. Brown, Director, Flying Training, of American Airlines in November of 1975 presented a paper at the twentieth technical conference of the International Air Transport Association entitled 'Safety in Flight Operations'. Brown traced the evolution of his airline's approach to safe operations. A major element of the programme he described is the progress made in the increased use of flight simulators for captain transition programmes. The average flying training hours are graphically shown in Fig. 3.3 (from his paper) describing 707, 727, 747 and DC-10 transition hours of actual aircraft and simulator time.[23]

The benefits of fuel savings, air space use, and reduced accidents in training are obvious and substantial.

It should be noted that this progress in simulator fidelity and use results largely from the initiative of manufacturers, aviation users and regulatory bodies working cooperatively.

Aircraft flight hours saved—recurrent training

In 1977 D. C. Killian of American Airlines surveyed and reported on the increasingly widespread use of simulator time being substituted entirely for flight time for recurrent checks.[24] He noted that:

The eighteen reporting airlines account for over 28,000 flight crewmen who receive approximately 40,600 annual proficiency training/checks (twice yearly

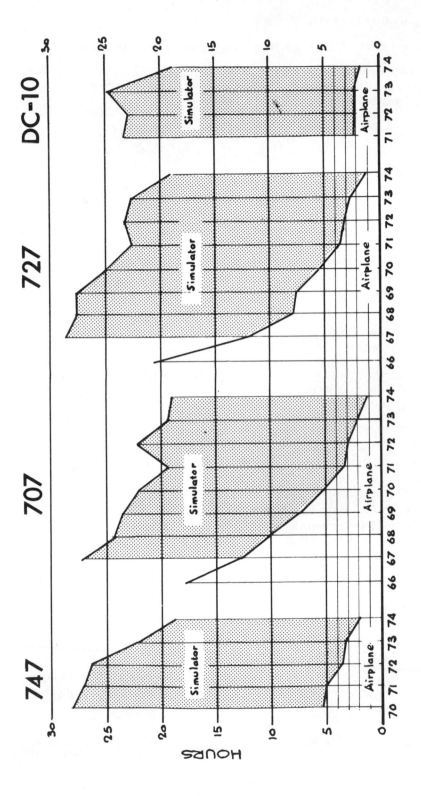

Fig. 2.3   Flying training average hours captain transition programmes

for captains, and annually for other crewmen). American Airlines, with 4,183 flight crewmen, conducted 5,934 recurrent training/check sessions in 1976. If these checks had been conducted without the availability of any flight simulator time, each captain and first officer check would have required an average of 1.5 hours of aircraft time. The total aircraft hours would have been more than 6,830 flight hours resulting in an additional fuel burn for American Airlines of more than 11.5 million gallons of jet fuel. Extrapolating American Airlines' fuel savings to all airline flight simulator users, it can be estimated that, for recurrent training/checks alone, these 18 airlines saved upward to 97 million gallons of fuel in 1976.[25]

As Killian points out, the airlines '. . .have a stated goal of total training through simulation.' Recent events verify that this goal is well on the way to attainment and may well be reached in this decade. However, says Killian, four major areas remain key to meeting the goal of total training via flight simulators.

(a) Simulators '. . .must be programmed to simulate all regimes of operational flight.'
(b) Training programme development must be improved.
(c) Training must be tied to line operations. 'Only when a continuity is established between training and line operations, can we make certain that the real world problems are brought back into the flight simulator environment where they can be effectively researched, improved and made a part of both training and operations.' '. . .only through such continuity in the instruction and checking process, can we be certain that proven procedures are routinely made a part of line operations.'
(d) 'The fourth key to a successful flight simulator training lies in a step-by-step program of proving and selling each new concept to the pilots who are involved, the management who must support these programs, the approval and authorizing agencies and the instructor group who can make or break any program. Many studies have been conducted by the industry to explain and validate the changes that have led the airlines to their present position of near total training through simulation. Extensive instructor training, many briefings and a lot of selling have all taken place, and much more will be required.'[26]

In summary Killian adds:

It takes a careful amalgamation of all four of these key elements, and maximum involvement by the many participating groups, such as the airframe manufacturer, the simulator manufacturer, airline user, engineers/computer programmers, instructors, pilots and the regulatory agencies to move successfully toward total simulation. However, the rewards are great. They include much more effective training, fuel savings that can make a real contribution to national resources, reduced noise and air pollution in many population centers and reduced training costs which can contribute to better transportation at less cost. Most importantly for everyone, flight simulation has contributed to a marked improvement in the safety record of scheduled operations and has provided the ultimate in safety for training.[27]

What does the future hold?

Captain R. E. Norman, Jr, Chairman, Pilot Training Committee of ALPA in a presentation entitled 'Training—Economic and Safety Considerations' in June 1979, reported the results of a 1974, and later updated, survey of ALPA's most experienced safety and training representatives. According to Captain Norman these professionals '. . .indicated overwhelming agreement on the necessity to revise required recurrent proficiency training and checking'.
He goes on further to indicate:

We propose the following briefly stated outline as an improved method of conducting recurrent training for flight deck air crews:

(1)   Recurrent pilot training should be conducted on an annual basis in an approved flight simulator.
(2)   Flight simulator training should include a review of instrument approaches and selected abnormal and emergency procedures.
(3)   The training will be designed to realistic line operational concepts with emphasis on crew coordination.
(4)   Training may include selected weather, wind shear, turbulence and unusual approach conditions or other circumstances that are likely to cause accidents.
(5)   Annual training for flight deck crew members should include appropriate review of aircraft systems, aircraft performance and emergency procedures, including ditching if over water.
(6)   Annual training for flight deck crew should include a review of recent or recurring problems for the aircraft type and additions or revisions to the navigation and instrument equipment or traffic control procedures.

We estimate that the above procedure would require approximately six hours of ground training and four hours of flight simulator training.
    Several simulator sequences are recommended and would be revised and approved on an annual basis.
    The preceding briefly stated outline provides more training for air crews than is now required by the regulations. The training would be more useful than the present stereotyped check requirements. Training equipment would be better utilized and scheduling of flight crews for training would be simplified and more efficient.[28]

Quite clearly, the attitudes of these professionals suggest they are ready and willing to accept simulator and related line-oriented and crew-coordinated training that exceeds current regulatory standards. As previously indicated, willing acceptance by the personnel to be trained is an essential ingredient for success.

Flight simulator approval status

The goal of total qualification with, or even increased use of, simulators and related devices requires both the availability of the technology and the approval of the regulatory authorities.

Regulatory bodies are increasingly positive in their study, analysis, evaluation and approval of validated devices and techniques. In August 1980 the United States Department of Transportation, Federal Aviation Administration issued Advisory Circular 121-14C entitled 'Aircraft Simulator and Visual System Evaluation and Approval'. The Federal Aviation Administration's attitude is clearly reflected in the background statement of this Advisory Circular which stated in part:

Simulators can provide more in-depth training than can be accomplished in the aircraft. There is also a very high percentage of transfer of learning from the simulator to the aircraft.

The FAA policy and regulatory position is fully supportive of the pioneering work done by airline management and training personnel, as well as the designers and manufacturers of modern simulation and visual system technology. FAA goes on in AC 121-14C to declare that:

During the last 10 years, as simulator technology has improved, changes to the FAR were made to permit the increased use of simulators in air carrier training programs. In the late 1960s, visual attachments appeared on the market. Since that time, a breakthrough in computerization has permitted the development of computer-generated image visual systems. In December 1973, FAR Amendments 61−12 and 121−108 permitted additional use of visual simulators. Amendments to § 121.439 of the FAR permitted a simulator approved for the landing maneuver to be substituted for the aircraft in a pilot recency-of-experience qualification. These changes to the FAR constituted a significant step toward the development of Amendments 61−69 and 121−161 issued June 24, 1980, which contain FAA Advanced Simulation Plan.[29]

With the subsequent progress made as spelled out in FARs 61 and 121 and their relevant appendix material, it is now possible from a regulatory point of view to have five levels of aircraft simulators approved−non-visual, visual and Phase I, II and III, the latter being the most advanced. At the end of 1981, there were still no Phase III simulators approved; however, one US airline had approval for Phase II simulator-use and twenty additional airlines were working on programmes at, or leading to, approval. This means that for certain recurrent and up-grading qualifications all training may be done in approved simulators and programmes. No actual aircraft time is required and this is truly remarkable progress.

For a full understanding of the available scope of the new approval authority, one may note the summary of the FAR part 121, Appendix H, Advanced Simulation Plan, that is summarised in a presentation given by Northwest Orient Airlines Captain Kenneth J. Warras. Captain Warras serves as a member of the Air Line Pilots Association (ALPA) Pilot Training Committee and works extensively in the ground training section of the Northwest Airlines Training Department. In November of 1981 he presented a paper to the RTCA entitled 'Total Simulation For Air Line Applications'. Captain Warras describes the FAA three-phase Advanced Simulator Plan as follows:

Phase I
A.   Training and checking permitted:
    1.   Recent experience requirements (three take-offs and landings each ninety days)
    2.   Night take-offs and landings
B.   Simulator requirements:
    1.   Aerodynamic programming
       a.   Ground effect, i.e. roundout, flare and touchdown
       b.   Ground reaction—reaction of the aircraft on ground contact to include strut deflection, side forces, etc.
       c.   Ground handling characteristics to include crosswind, braking, thrust reversing, turning radius, etc.
    2.   Minimum of three-axis freedom of motion system
C.   Visual requirements:
    1.   Visual compatibility with aerodynamic programming
    2.   Minimum visual system lag in response to pilot inputs
    3.   Visual cues to assess sink rate and depth perception during landing

Phase II
A.   Training and checking permitted:
    1.   Transition training between airplanes in the same group
    2.   Upgrade training to pilot in command (under certain conditions)
B.   Simulator requirements:
    1.   Representative crosswind and three-dimensional wind shear dynamics
    2.   Representative stopping and directional control on various runway surfaces (dry, wet, icy, etc.)
    3.   Representative brake and tyre failure dynamics (including anti-skid and decreased brake efficiency due to high brake temperatures)
    4.   A motion system which provides motion cues equal to or better than those provided by a six-axis freedom of motion system
    5.   Operational NAV systems, including INS, OMEGA, etc., if applicable. This requirement is to enhance LOFT*
    6.   Sound of precipitation and significant aircraft noises such as gear extension, thrust, reversal, etc.
    7.   Duplication of aircraft feel comparable to those encountered in flight
C.   Visual requirements:
    1.   Dusk and night visual with at least three specific airport representations
    2.   Radio navigation aids properly oriented to the airport runway layout
    3.   Various weather representations below 2000 feet and within a ten mile radius of the airport, including the following:
       a.   Variable cloud density
       b.   Partial obscurity
       c.   Gradual breakout
       d.   Patchy fog
    4.   Continuous minimum field of view of $75°$ horizontal and $30°$ vertical
    5.   Capability to present other visual ground and air hazards

Phase III
A.   Training and checking permitted—all except:
    1.   Annual line check requirements
    2.   Operating experience requirements
    3.   Static airplane requirements

* Line-Oriented-Flight Training, see pp. 41–43.

B.   Simulator requirements:
    1.   Characteristic buffets (Mmo, Vmo, turbulence, flap extension, etc.)
    2.   Realistic amplitude and frequency of cockpit noises and sounds
C.   Visual requirements:
    1.   Daylight, dusk and night visual scenes
    2.   Visual scenes portraying certain landing illusions such as short runway, rising terrain, landing over water, etc.
    3.   Special weather representations which include the sound, visual and motion effects of entering various types of precipitation
    4.   Wet and snow covered runways, as appropriate for the operator

In order for an air carrier to take advantage of the benefits of this three-phase program, that carrier must submit a simulator upgrade plan to the FAA. Many of the major US carriers are now operating under Phase 1 of this program. At the present time only one US carrier has met the requirements for Phase II operations. Phase II of the Advanced Simulator Program incorporates a requirement for the air carriers engaged in the program to implement a LOFT program.[30] This important system of line operations simulation merits further examination.

Line-Oriented Flight Training (LOFT)

In the evolution of flight training one notes the early emphasis on the rudimentary skills of manipulation of controls and the use mainly of psychomotor skills. As the air route systems, aids to navigation, air traffic control, and more diverse high speed and complex aircraft entered the system, the tasks for pilots grew in complexity. Today, the major emphasis in airline operations is on crew training rather than individual skill attainment. Obviously, satisfactory crew performance assumes a sufficient level of individual skills on the part of each member. Relatively new, however, is the interest in, need for and recognition of crew, rather than individual, training. The use of simulation technology and devices to accommodate crew training oriented to line operations is a remarkable challenge, and one to which the airlines, manufacturers and regulatory bodies are rising with success.

In a recent National Aeronautics and Space Administration (NASA) Conference publication, Line-Oriented Flight Training (LOFT) was described thus:

Line-Oriented Flight Training (LOFT) is a developing training technology which synthesizes high-fidelity aircraft simulation and high-fidelity line-operations simulation to provide realistic, dynamic pilot training in a simulated line environment. LOFT is an augmentation of existing pilot training which concentrates upon command, leadership, and resource management skills.[31]

The operational origins of LOFT may be found in simulation conducted by the United States Air Force Strategic Air Command, and when, in 1974, Northwest Orient Airlines established a task force to work on a programme, they referred to it as Coordinated Crew Training or CCT.

Recognizing that CCT met certain training objectives that were not being effectively achieved by recurrent training programs conducted under FAR 121

Appendix F, Northwest petitioned the FAA for an exemption to permit a one-year test and evaluation of this training concept. The exemption was granted in February 1976. On the basis of the positive results observed at Northwest, the FAA issued an additional exemption in October 1977, which allowed other air carriers to utilize LOFT on a voluntary basis. Finally, in May 1978, Advisory Circular AC 120-35 was published, and FAR 121 was amended to permit LOFT to be utilized in any airline recurrent training program.[32]

Essential features of LOFT

During the NASA workshop, Captain H. T. Nunn, Director, Flight Training of Northwest Orient Airlines characterised this approach as follows:

LOFT is a line environment flight-training program with total crew participation in real-world incident experiences, with a major thrust toward resource management.[33]

Captain A. A. Frink, Vice-President, Flight Training of Pan American World Airways said:

. . .line-oriented flight training, in principle, has filled a long existing need in airline-crew training, that of command and resource management in the total crew resolution of realistic line-type problems.[34]

As brought out during the NASA Workshop, the features which characterise LOFT are as follows:

(1)   LOFT is the application of line-operations simulation to pilot-training programmes. LOFT is a combination of high-fidelity aircraft simulation and high-fidelity line-operations simulation.
(2)   LOFT involves a complete crew, each member of which operates as an individual and as a member of a team just as he does during line operations.
(3)   LOFT involves simulated real-world incidents unfolding in real time. Similarly, the consequences of crew decisions and actions during a LOFT scenario will accrue and impact the remainder of the trip in a realistic manner.
(4)   LOFT is casebook training. Some problems have no single, acceptable solution; handling them is a matter of judgement. LOFT is training in judgement and decision-making.
(5)   LOFT requires effective interaction with, and utilisation of, all available resources; hardware, software, and 'liveware', or the human resources. A LOFT scenario requires the exercise of resource management skills.
(6)   LOFT is a training and learning experience in which errors will probably be made, not a checking programme in which errors are not acceptable. The purpose of LOFT is not to induce errors, but cockpit resource management is, in part, the management of human error. Effective resource management recognises that under some circumstances, such as high-workload situations, human error is likely; steps must be taken to reduce the probability of

error. However, it is also necessary to maximise the probability that error, when it does occur, will be detected and corrected, thereby minimising the probability of adverse impact upon the overall safety of the operation. Just as it is necessary to practise landing skills in order to gain and maintain aircraft-handling proficiency, it is necessary to practise human-error— management skills; the former requires a simulator or airplane, and the latter, the presence of errors or error-inducing situations.[35]

With all the obvious benefits of LOFT there are limitations.

(a)   LOFT will not solve all training problems
(b)   LOFT is resource management training but it is not skill training. Manual skills are an essential prerequisite.
(c)   LOFT will succeed only as a part of a total training and crew education programme that ensures that basic knowledge and skill norms are met.

The real success of LOFT programmes will depend upon the scenarios that are designed for the use of the crews. An airline contemplating using the technique would do well to consult the excellent NASA Conference Publication for guidelines in developing a programme that can be of positive benefit to the education and training of crews. The techniques now being used in both Line-Oriented Flight Training (LOFT) and Line-Operations Simulation (LOS) are moving closer to the day when total simulation will be reached and time in the actual aircraft will be used only for revenue producing operations.

The Role of Aviation Education

The role of formal education in the preparation of aircrews is typified by educational bodies such as the Guggenheim Fund, the Flight Safety Foundation and the Embry-Riddle Aeronautical University, etc.

There is a clear trend on an international basis to make more use of formal education in general and college and university or technical institutes in particular, to develop well-trained and educated aviation personnel.

In the Soviet Union for example, the Ministry of Civil Aviation operates twenty-six higher education institutions that prepare personnel for Aeroflot, the Soviet airline. These institutions prepare pilots, maintenance technicians and engineers, electronics specialists, air traffic controllers, managers, administrators and ground service personnel. In short, the total civil aviation personnel staff for Aeroflot is now being prepared in higher education institutions which operate under the policy guidelines of the Ministry of Secondary and Higher Education, but under the budget, staffing and technical guidance of the Ministry of Civil Aviation personnel. The resources for training aids, simulators, teaching devices, laboratory equipment, faculty and staff assistants have steadily increased. The quality of research being done by the students and faculty members is first rate. Specialised degrees are granted to the graduates of many of these programmes. In short, the Soviet Union is making huge resources available to provide the best possible education and training to their civil aviation personnel. The author has visited many of the Soviet education and training establishments and recognises in them significant progress and innovation.*

In the United States more and more colleges and universities are offering programmes ranging from pilot training to programmes for aviation technical, engineering and management personnel. In 1981, there were nearly 200 colleges and universities offering courses, majors and/or degrees with emphasis on aviation.[36]

In looking to the future, it appears that more and more use will be made of higher education resources for the aviation education and training of aviation personnel.

The role of general aviation

In the United States, general aviation continues to play a major role in total aviation and in supplying qualified personnel for the airlines. Furthermore, from a safety viewpoint, general aviation contributes significantly to the total numbers of aircraft in the system as well as to the accidents. If one notes the most recent year for which total transportation accident data in the United States are available, a perspective of where civil aviation fits may be readily seen. (See Fig. 2.4 depicting transportation fatalities for 1980.)

A better understanding of the total US aviation system may be had by noting the following numbers of aircraft by category:†

Air Carriers	3 805	(including commuter and air taxi aircraft)
Military	19 402	
General Aviation	255 735	(including 40 000 inactive aircraft)

When one notes the combinations of aircraft in the system and the variety of qualifications of personnel, the education and training challenges are readily seen.

In general aviation there are many successful pilot seminars and refresher courses sponsored by the Federal Aviation Administration (FAA); the Aircraft Owners and Pilots Association (AOPA) Air Safety Foundation; and the Civil Air Patrol (CAP).

Since the inception of the FAA's accident prevention programme, nearly a million general aviation pilots have participated in refresher courses. The General Aviation Manufacturers Association reports that during the past several years 18 000 pilots have participated in the GAMA–FAA sponsored safe pilot programme that requires attendance at special ground school sessions and three hours of flight and/or simulator time stressing basic manoeuvres, en route capability, and landing and take-off experience. None of the 18 000 participants in this programme has had a fatal accident.

---

* International civil aviation needs to share these benefits. Access to the lessons contained in Soviet civil aircraft accident reports would be an important beginning (Editors).
† As of late 1981.

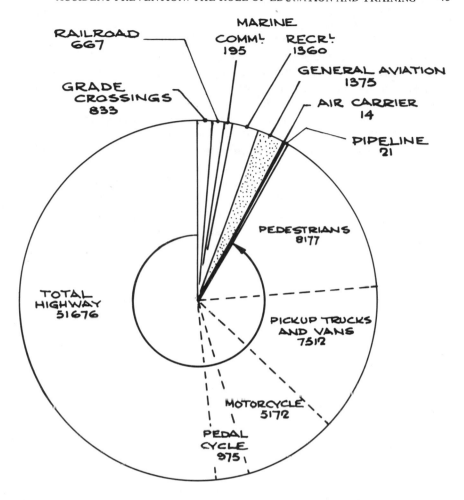

Fig. 3.4   U.S. transportation fatalities in 1980
(preliminary figures). Source: National Transportation Safety Board (Washington D.C.).

The AOPA Air Safety Foundation has conducted special refresher courses for hundreds of thousands of pilots and flight instructors. These courses are well attended and participants often return for other courses because they prove of benefit to them. All of the above programmes are examples of voluntary programmes that are well attended and appear to contribute to air safety.

The role of the flight and ground instructor

Future flight safety progress may well be linked directly to the quality of ground and flight instruction. This is one of the reasons flight simulation is so important.

In the author's view, one of the neglected areas of research and investigation is the role of the instructor in accident prevention and as a contributory cause to accidents. The reason for this point of view is based on the well-established but too infrequently considered psychological principle which in effect says: in an emergency situation, one's response will be as close as possible to earlier similar responses. But if the early acquired experience is incorrect for a given emergency response at a later date, the results are often disastrous. Many pilots used to single-engined aircraft have experienced difficulty when moving unexpectedly from VFR to IFR conditions, and fail to control the aircraft by reference to instruments instead of visual cues outside the cockpit. Accident investigators believe many stall-spin weather-related accidents stem from this cause.

In the United States, within professional and safety organisations and the FAA, there is increasing discussion of the need for more emphasis on the part of both ground and flight instructors on principles of learning and teaching. This trend also appears to be of interest in other countries.

The idea of developing better attitudes on the part of instructors and, in turn, finding ways to 'transfer' these attitudes to students, appears to be crucial for further success in accident prevention. Yet there are some hitherto untapped principles and techniques that can help to facilitate better, and safer, pilot performance by improving instructor communication skills. The principal key to this potential is inherent in a relatively new field of psychiatric practice known as transactional analysis, or TA.

The potential role of transactional analysis in accident prevention

Everyone who has learned to fly has experienced at least one instructor who could be characterised as having a 'bad' attitude. Similarly, any discussion by aviation instructors will elicit comments about the 'poor', 'improper' or 'bad' attitudes of students. This apparent dilemma can be solved.

The author believes that the field of transactional analysis (TA) holds great potential for improving the quality of communications in aviation and thereby helping to promote aviation safety and more efficient instruction.

The late Eric Berne, MD, psychiatrist, first described his technique in 1961 in a book entitled *Transactional Analysis in Psychotherapy*,[37] and in 1964, described in detail his theory and technique in a book entitled *Games People Play—The Psychology of Human Relationships*.[38]

Berne describes three major ego states that all adults manifest:

(a)   Those resembling parent figures.
(b)   Those which relate to 'objective appraisal of reality'.
(c)   Those which are really 'archaic relics. . .' which were established '. . .in early childhood'.[39]

He labels these three states Parent (P), Adult (A), Child (C) (respectively). As Berne says:

. . .at any given moment each individual in a social aggregation will exhibit a Parental, Adult or Child ego state, and that individuals can shift with varying degrees of readiness from one ego state to another.[40]

Describing transactional analysis Berne writes:

The unit of social intercourse is called a transaction. If two or more people encounter each other in a social aggregation, sooner or later one of them will speak, or give some clear indication of acknowledging the presence of the others. This is called the *transactional stimulus*. Another person will then say or do something which is in some way related to this stimulus, and that is called the *transactional response*. Simple transactional analysis is concerned with diagnosing which ego state implemented the transactional stimulus, and which one executed the transactional response. The simplest transactions are those in which both stimulus and response arise from the Adults of the parties concerned. The surgeon, estimating from the data before him that a scalpel is now the instrument of choice, holds out his hand. The respondent appraises this gesture correctly, estimates the forces and distances involved, and places the handle of the scalpel exactly where the surgeon expects it. Next in simplicity are Child-Parent transactions. The fevered child asks for a glass of water, and the nurturing mother brings it.[41]

The types of transactions described above are complementary and what one would expect of normal, healthy human relationships. Thus, Berne points out that 'the first rule of communication is that communication will proceed smoothly as long as transactions are complementary. . .'[42] Communication, of course, is shut off if transactions are perceived to be destructive or condescending.

One needs to be cautioned here to understand that transactional analysis is a form of psychiatric therapy and analysis and that the concepts do not transfer directly to aviation. But it is the author's personal belief that flight instructors are often role models for students and If the instructor does not demonstrate behaviour of a positive kind, the results for the student—even a long time afterwards—can be detrimental. In short, it is felt that controlled experiments and demonstrations need to be planned in an aviation learning environment to test the hypothesis that communication processes may well be an underlying cause of accidents which have hitherto gone unidentified.

The field of transactional analysis holds great promise for exploration and experimentation in an aviation training environment. It may well be that research in this field will enable us to combine emerging computer-based instruction with high fidelity simulators and so reinforce the effort to achieve a zero-defect record in accident prevention.

References

1. Little, H. G. (1979) 'An Analysis of the Major Factors Effecting the Maturation of Career Qualifications For Aviation Maintenance Technicians and Professional Pilots'. Unpublished doctoral dissertation, Nova University.
2. (1966) *Webster's Third New International Dictionary*, G. & C. Merriam Company, Springfield, Massachusetts, USA.
3. *Ibid*.
4. *Ibid*., 73

5. *Ibid.*, 73
6. *Ibid.*, 74
7. *Ibid.*, 75
8. *Ibid.*, 76
9. *Ibid.*, 76
10. *Ibid.*, 82
11. *Ibid.*, 87
12. *Ibid.*, 91
13. *Ibid.*, 91, 92
14. Bernberg, R. E. and Pierson, W. R. (1977), *Educational Requirements for Civil Aircrew*, Flight Safety Foundation Inc., Arlington, Virginia, USA. Note this study was sponsored by and made for N. V. Philips Gloeilampenfabrieken, Eindhoven, The Netherlands.
15. Aviation Education Review Organization (AERO), College Credit Standards Guide 1977, Air Line Pilots Association, Washington, DC.
16. Little (1979), 38–9
17. Hunt, J. R. (1979), 'Highlights of the Seventh Session, US–USSR Exchange 12–18 August 1979, on the topic Civil Aviation Education and Training as a part of the US–USSR Joint Cooperation in Transportation'. Report prepared by Embry Riddle Aeronautical University for Aviation Education Programs Division, Office of Aviation Policy, Federal Aviation Administration, Department of Transportation.
18. *Ibid.*, 1
19. *Ibid.*, 3, 4
20. *Ibid.*, 4
21. *Ibid.*, 5, 6, 7, 8
22. Houston, R. C. (1979), *Developments in Training Technology*, American Airlines Symposium on Human Factors in Civil Aviation, The Hague, September 1979, 6.
23. Brown, J. A. (1975), 'Safety in Flight Operations'. Paper presented for American Airlines at Twentieth Technical Conference, International Air Transport Association, Istanbul, Turkey, 10–15 November 1975.
24. Killian, D. C. (1977), *The Impact of Flight Simulators on US Airlines*, American Airlines, Table II, 888.
25. *Ibid.*, 889
26. *Ibid.*, 892
27. *Ibid.*, 892
28. Norman, R.E. (1979), *Training–Economic and Safety Considerations*, Pilot Training Committee, Air Line Pilots Association, June 1979, Attachment I
29. Advisory Circular, AC 121–14C dated 29 August 1980, Aircraft Simulator and Visual System Evaluation and Approval, Department of Transportation, Federal Aviation Administration, Washington, DC, 1.
30. Warras, K. J. (1981), *Total Simulation for Airline Applications*, for Northwest Orient Airlines, presented to Radio Technical Committee for Aeronautics (RTCA), November 1981, 1–3.

31. Lauber, J. K. and Foushee, H. C. (1981), 'Guidelines for Line-Oriented Flight Training,' Volume 1. NASA Conference Publication 2184, proceedings of a NASA/Industry Workshop held at NASA Ames Research Center, Moffett Field, California, January 13–15 1981, Preface.
32. *Ibid.*, 3
33. *Ibid.*, 5
34. *Ibid.*, 5
35. *Ibid.*, 5, 6
36. *Directory of Aviation Majors and Curricula Offered by Colleges and Universities*, Aviation Education, GA-300-130, Department of Transportation, Federal Aviation Administration Office of Aviation Policy, Washington, DC, 1979.
37. Berne, E. (1961), *Transactional Analysis in Psychotherapy*, Grove Press Inc., New York.
38. Berne, E. (1964), *Games People Play—the Psychology of Human Relationships*, Grove Press Inc., New York.
39. *Ibid.*, 23, 24
40. *Ibid.*, 24
41. *Ibid.*, 29
42. *Ibid.*, 30

Chapter 3

Pilot Judgement: Training and Evaluation
R. S. Jensen

An analysis of accident statistics reveals that over 50 per cent of the pilot-caused civil aviation accident fatalities are the result of faulty pilot judgement. Although the US Federal Aviation Administration, for example, requires examiners to evaluate it, no definition or critique is provided against which an evaluation of a pilot judgement can be made. In spite of the statistics implicating pilot judgement in many aviation fatalities, attempts to teach it are almost non-existent. It is but a slight overstatement to say that good pilot judgement is learned by the lucky and the cautious over many years of varied flying experiences.

This chapter examines some of the decision research literature in an attempt to provide an operational definition of pilot judgement and to suggest ways that pilot judgement may be taught and evaluated in civil aviation.

Introduction

Pilots have always been expected to exercise a considerable amount of judgement in the overall task of flying an aircraft. However, in recent years, increasing demands in our society for safety, dependability, economy, effectiveness, and reduced energy consumption have increased the complexity of civil and military flying operations, magnifying the pressures on good pilot judgement. Furthermore, technological advances that have eased much of the pilot's burden for precise aircraft control have not greatly eased the pilot's decision-making workload. In many cases these advances have only created demands for higher levels of skill, knowledge, and judgement for which few pilots have been trained, and the training costs to prepare them to operate effectively in the changing system are becoming prohibitive.

If it were merely a matter of teaching flying skills, the training of pilots to operate safely in our complex aviation system would be a much smaller task than it is. Unfortunately, because actual conditions are never quite the same as those used to develop aviation regulations, procedures, and performance limitations, the safety of a given flight also depends upon a significant amount of evaluation and interpretation of existing conditions by the pilot.

For example, the conditions used to develop flight performance values for a particular type of aircraft may be ideal—including clean airplane surfaces, a new engine, a new propellor, an unrestricted air filter, and a company test pilot. In actual conditions the pilot must compare the book values obtained in ideal conditions with those in which he finds himself. These actual conditions may include a dirty aircraft, a slightly used engine, a few marks on the propeller, a slightly dirty air filter, and a less than perfect pilot. He must then evaluate many other conditions such as gross weight, centre of gravity, wind, temperature, humidity, altitude, etc., for comparison with those used in the book to determine his expected flight performance. Finally, he must check the present and forecast weather, the terrain, and expected traffic density and compare them with an estimate of his own capability before determining whether or not his planned flight will be safe. Examples such as these, requiring decisions with less than perfect information, can be found in all areas of flight activity.

Furthermore, every decision that the pilot makes is coloured by physiological, psychological, and social pressures that are virtually impossible to weigh properly on the spot. For example, just as persons watching a sporting event may 'see' an infraction or foul differently depending upon their vantage points and which team they support, a pilot may be influenced to view the weather outlook or his own abilities differently depending upon the importance or value he assigns to a given flight. Some pilots may be susceptible to social pressures which result in less than rational pilot judgement. Irrational pilot judgement has been exhibited by such unsafe practices as flying under bridges, landing on busy highways, attempting to land in football stadiums, and flying 'formation' on other unsuspecting pilots. Potential sources of social pressure that may lead to these types of activities include peer reaction, fear of failure, censure from superiors or family members, and many others.[12]

The problem

An analysis of accident statistics by categories of pilot behaviour activities reveals the serious nature of the problem in civil aviation. Most analyses of aviation accident statistics have found that 80–85 per cent can be assigned broadly to 'pilot error' and the remainder to mechanical malfunctions. To determine why pilots are making accident-causing errors, it is useful to provide a more molecular examination of pilot behaviour activities. One such classification (Roscoe, 1980) divides these activities into three categories as follows:

(a) Procedural activities–the management of the powerplant, fuel, vehicle configuration, autopilot, displays, navigation, and communication.
(b) Perceptual–motor activities–including vehicle control, judgement of distance, speed, altitude, and clearance, hazard detection, and geographic orientation.
(c) Decisional activities–including the self-assessment of skill, knowledge, physical and psychological capabilities, the assessment of aircraft and ground system capabilities, hazard assessment, navigation planning, and flight priority adjustment.

To determine the relative importance of each of these activities in civil aviation accidents, statistics from the National Transportation Safety Board (NTSB) Automated Aircraft Accident and Incident Information System, from 1970 to

1974, were classified into the three behavioural categories given above.[13] Then the total numbers of both fatal and non-fatal accidents during the five-year period were determined for each of these behavioural categories. The results of these analyses are shown in Table 3.1.

Examination of these data provides valuable indications of possible weaknesses in current civil aviation programmes. For example, a majority of the non-fatal pilot-caused accidents (56.3 per cent) were the result of faulty perceptual–motor behaviour. The most significant factors here ('failure to maintain flying speed' and 'misjudgement of distance, speed, altitude, or clearance') represent one type of pilot judgement. On the other hand, a majority of the fatal pilot-caused accidents (51.6 per cent) were the result of faulty decisional behaviour, another type of pilot judgement. The most significant factors in this area were the familiar 'continued VFR into known adverse weather' and 'inadequate pre-flight planning or preparation'.

Table 3.1 Number and percentage of the total general aviation accidents in which the pilot is listed as a cause or factor, between 1970 and 1974

	Fatal		Non-fatal	
	no.	%	no.	%
Procedural	264	4.6	2 230	8.6
Perceptual–Motor	2 496	43.8	14 561	56.3
Decisional	2 940	51.6	9 087	35.1

It is apparent from these accident statistics that both aspects of the deciding function are important to safe flight and possibly suffer from neglect in the present training and testing process. However, because it suffers from greater misunderstanding in aviation circles, pilot judgement as represented by the general decisional activities is the topic of concern here. Although a significant amount of research has been done on this aspect of judgement in recent years,[12] no one has specifically examined this judgement problem as faced by the pilot, the flight instructor, and the pilot examiner.

There appear to be three major problems requiring solution before major improvements to pilot training and evaluation can be realised in this area. The first is the establishment of a common definition of 'judgement' as it applies to flying. At present, even though the term is used repeatedly in aviation circles, and FAA examiners are required to evaluate candidates on the basis of judgement, no such definition exists.

The second major problem is to determine whether or not pilot judgement can be taught, and if so, how one can best teach it. Because some aspects of pilot judgement are closely linked to personality characteristics, they may be difficult to modify. It may be necessary to use testing and selection procedures to improve aviation safety and effectiveness from these standpoints. Other aspects of pilot judgement are more easily modified through systematic training procedures.

The third major problem is to determine whether or not pilot judgement can be evaluated reliably, meaningfully, and objectively. Because judgement is primarily a mental process, it may be difficult to evaluate in any reliable way. On the other hand, behavioural events frequently have been used to indicate mental activity. Although personality tests have proved to be somewhat unreliable, research results using these instruments may be useful in the development of instruments for evaluating and predicting judgemental behaviour.[5]

Judgement definition

As indicated above, the word 'judgement' has been used to describe two somewhat different mental processes in aviation. Perhaps its most common usage has been to describe the mental activity that takes place at the perceptual–motor level. The second describes the mental activity involved in choosing a course of action from among several alternatives. Obviously, this second usage of the term is similar to the first in that both involve making choices. However, there is a basic difference.

The first refers to highly learned perceptual responses that must be made in a very short time, in some cases continuously. The second refers to cognitive decisions for which set procedures have not been established or may have been forgotten. Flight instructors have used various terms in referring to this type of judgement including 'headwork', 'thinking ahead', and 'staying ahead of the aircraft'. In a more general sense, pilots have referred to it as professionalism or commandability. Usually, more time is available to evaluate the situation, a larger number of possible courses of action must be considered, and there is a greater degree of uncertainty concerning the existing situation and possible outcomes than is the case in perceptual judgements. For these reasons, cognitive judgements have been the source of greater misunderstanding in pilot training and evaluation.

These two aspects of judgement may be considered as two ends of a continuum based on cognitive complexity and decision time. One such representation is shown in Fig. 3.1. At one end of the continuum are the common perceptual judgements of distance, altitude, speed, and clearance. These perceptual judgements are less complex in that they involve fewer pieces (frequently one) of fairly accurate information, from which responses are determined with highly learned motor behaviour. They may require simple responses but frequently call for immediate control movement.

At the other end of the scale are what might be called cognitive judgements and, as noted, these judgements are complex in that they usually involve a large number of relevant pieces of highly probabilistic information, they usually require the specification of and choice from among several alternatives, and they are frequently affected by emotions, values, and social pressures. In addition, cognitive judgements usually permit some deliberation before a control response is required.

Fig. 3.1   Pilot judgement continuum based on cognitive complexity and time

Candidate judgement definition. Considering these factors a candidate definition of cognitive judgement in flying aircraft is:

(a)   The ability to search for and establish the relevance of all available information regarding a situation, to specify alternative courses of action, and to determine expected outcomes from each alternative.

(b)   The motivation to choose and authoritatively execute a suitable course of action within the time frame permitted by the situation, where: (i) 'suitable' is an alternative consistent with societal norms; and (ii) 'action' includes no action, some action, or action to seek more information.

The first part of the definition refers to intellectual or discriminating abilities. It depends upon human capabilities to sense, store, retrieve, and integrate information. This function is what Van Dam calls the 'discriminating ability' in professional pilots.[13] It is analogous to detectability (d') in signal detection theory.* It is purely rational and could be stated mathematically. If it were possible to separate this part of human judgement from the second part (which it is not), we would solve problems in much the same way as a computer. This is not to say that our decisions would be error-free. Probabilistic information is used and the performance is dependent upon the amount, type, and accuracy of information stored as well as inherent and learned capabilities to process information.

The second part of the definition refers to motivational tendencies. The emphasis in this case is on the directional aspects of motivation rather than intensity. It says that a part of human judgement is based upon bias factors (costs and pay-offs) or tendencies to use less than rational information (defined by society) in choosing courses of action. Society would probably consider the use of any information other than that required to define the safety risk (e.g. convenience, monetary gain, gain in self-esteem, adventure seeking, etc.) as less than rational. This part of human judgement is analogous to the response bias (B) in signal detection theory. It is what Van Dam has called the 'response pattern' of the professional pilot. If properly developed, this part of human judgement would tend to halt the use of information not directly related to the

* See p. 55 post.

safety of the flight and to direct the pilot's decision toward the use of rational processes.

Judgement training

One of the most important questions to be addressed following the establishment of the definition is whether or not pilot judgement, as defined, can be modified through training. The paucity of judgement training guidelines in pilot training and training research literature leads one to doubt that judgement can be taught. Literature such as the FAA Instructor's handbook[4] and syllabi commonly used in flight instructor courses contain large sections on how to teach the motor skills of flying but very little on how to teach pilot judgement. The typical private pilot course offers a scattering of judgemental instruction in the areas of weather avoidance and power-plant emergencies but no systematic judgemental training.

However, there is evidence in aviation showing that at least one form of judgemental training, assigning procedures for every conceivable situation that might arise, may be effective. In the military these are referred to as 'Boldface' training procedures.[20] Similar training procedures used by the airlines have even been more successful than those used by the military.[8,21]

Looking outside the field of aviation one finds other evidence indicating that judgement may be taught. For example, although the theory of signal detection (TSD) was not designed specifically to handle cognitive judgements, many of its methods can be used to explain and perhaps even modify pilot judgement behaviour. TSD divides an individual's decision behaviour into two components representing his sensitivity (d') and his response criterion or bias (B), roughly corresponding to the two aspects of our judgement definition.

The sensitivity is affected both by the physical value of the stimuli in the situation (signal v. background noise) and the quality of the sensory apparatus of the observer. In cognitive judgement this is the intellective component. It refers both to the strength of the evidence for one alternative over another, and to the knowledge and intellectual ability of the pilot to use effective strategies in gathering and processing the evidence.

On the other hand, the response criterion represents the point in the signal-to-noise distribution at which the observer is willing to say 'signal'. It is the amount of relevant information in the presence of non-relevant information or noise, needed to tip the decision one way or the other. It is influenced by motivation, knowledge of the signal's probability of occurrence, and the costs and pay-offs attendant with a given response. In cognitive judgement the response criterion is the motivative component.

The response criterion can be manipulated through a wide range of values by adjusting probabilities, costs, and pay-offs.[3] We can infer from the vast amount of psychophysical decision data that cognitive judgements can be modified in a similar way. Decision biases, attitudes, risk tendencies, consideration for passenger safety, and pilot motivation can and are being taught by the flight instructor by example, if not by design, at all levels of pilot training. These tendencies are taught, perhaps unconsciously, by the assignment of probabilities, costs, and pay-offs to actions of the student by the instructor.

Although TSD says that the sensitivity component is quite stable for a given individual, there is a growing field of research indicating that, if considered as the intellective component of cognitive judgement, sensitivity can be modified as well. For example, attempts have been made to discover the mental processes that are used by expert judges such as stockbrokers, livestock judges, and medical diagnosticians in making their decisions.[2,11,15,18] The hypothesis is that if models of the mental processes used by these experts in decision-making were available, they could be used in training others to use similar processes. In each of the areas studied, judgemental training traditionally occurs over a fairly long apprenticeship programme in which the trainee observes the expert make decisions and learns by this observation. However, in aviation, because of the complexity of the information used to make decisions, observation or even trial and error are inefficient training methods.

The research on the motivative aspect of cognitive judgement also indicates that training can have a beneficial effect. The major research efforts in this area are reported by Janis and Mann.[12] These authors, speaking from a clinical perspective, begin with the assumption that psychological stress is a frequent cause of errors in decision-making. They say that stress arises from at least two sources. First the decision-maker is concerned about the material and social losses he may suffer from whichever course of action he chooses, including the costs of failing to live up to prior commitments. Second, he recognises that his reputation and self-esteem as a competent decision-maker are at stake. The more severe the anticipated losses, the greater the stress.*

Janis and Mann have constructed a 'conflict-theory' model of decision-making postulating that the way we resolve a difficult choice is determined by the presence or absence of three conditions: 'awareness of risks involved', 'hope of finding a better solution', and 'time available in which to make the decision'. They have developed several clinical procedures to improve decision-making under the titles, 'awareness-of-rationalisations', 'emotional role playing', 'balance sheet', and 'outcome psychodrama'. They report that these procedures have demonstrated effectiveness in changing decision-making tendencies and in attitude modification.

Some learning principles

Because of the common misapplication of some well established learning principles in many training programmes, a discussion of these principles as applied to pilot judgemental training is needed. Perhaps the most popular of these is the assumption that the best way to learn an activity is to practise that activity. This assumption is rooted in much of the educational literature and is often identified by the catch-phrase 'learning by doing'. Gagne[7] points out that it may also be a

*Compare with Martin Allnutt's description of landing decisions in marginal weather conditions, chapter 1 pp. 15.

generalisation of the research on the conditioned response in which learning, particularly in animals, appears to have occurred only after a response (practice) has been made.

However, Gagne argues that practice is not an effective training method by itself, even for the acquisition of such motor skills as field gunnery. He says that 'instruction about the correct sighting picture for ranging is more effective in bringing about improved performance than is practice on the task'. The point is that training should emphasise the principles and procedures (thought processes) involved, and practice should be directed to take advantage of these principles or take a minor role. If this is the proper emphasis for teaching motor skills, it is even more important in the teaching of judgemental skills which are more deeply rooted in thought processes.

A second learning principle that is frequently misapplied in training situations is variously called reinforcement, feedback, or knowledge of results during practice. This principle has been found to be most effective in choice behaviour. However, Gagne points out that some manipulations that artificially improve feedback during practice failed to show reliably better transfer to the operational environment, and others showed negative transfer perhaps because of a learned dependence on the artificial cues. Apparently the form of the feedback is important.

Any novice flight student will confirm that the usual feedback information such as 'you did it right' or 'you did it wrong' is almost useless. The time period between trials and feedback may be long, it is often cluttered with interfering information, and the trials themselves are often so complex that the student may learn very little from such a response by his flight instructor. The student really needs to know *why* he did it right or wrong. He needs to know what rules he should have followed and where he strayed from those rules. Although practice and right/wrong types of feedback may be useful in some training situations, they should be de-emphasised in favour of these 'thought' oriented teaching principles in all types of pilot training, but especially in judgemental training.

Judgemental training media

Because of the nature of the subject matter to be taught (i.e., attitudes, principles, and motivation), the primary load of pilot judgemental training must be borne by the flight instructor. Practice and conventional self-teaching techniques (e.g., solo flying in a practice area) are highly inefficient methods for imparting these concepts. The following is a discussion of some suggested judgemental training media and techniques that could be applicable to pilot training in civil and military aviation.

Ground school. There are a number of excellent ways that pilot judgement could be taught from the perspective of the conventional ground school. To afford it proper emphasis, it is suggested that judgement should be given a special section of ground school with the same status as meteorology, navigation, and Federal

Air Regulations. This section could include lectures and/or discussions of aviation accident scenarios in which the pilot was a cause or factor, interactive movies, video tapes, slide presentations requiring student judgemental responses at critical points in flight scenarios, and independent study of the principles involved in good pilot judgement.

In addition, this ground school might include instruction in information integration and subjective probability estimation.[9] Judgemental behaviour in expert judges is characterised by 'chunking', or the formation of clusters of stimulus attributes and response alternatives, for economy in the thought process. Ground school students could be taught to use these processes in their judgemental activity. The instructor would show how various types of probabilistic information such as weather forecasts, predicted aircraft system malfunctions, and predicted Air Traffic Control problems should be combined in making flying decisions.

The instructor would teach the student how to 'think ahead' or anticipate decisions that might have to be made later resulting from present choices of action. Such anticipation permits the gathering of relevant information under lower levels of stress, when errors are less frequent than later in the flight when time-to-decide may become an error-causing factor. This section of ground school could also include decision-making training using procedures suggested by Janis and Mann[12] such as 'balance sheet' and 'emotional role playing'.

Computer-assisted instruction. An instruction technique which holds unusual promise for pilot judgemental training and evaluation is computer-assisted instruction (CAI). The great advantage of CAI systems is that they can teach principles and then permit the student to participate in decision processes, a highly effective learning technique.[5] The disadvantage of these systems in the past has been their limited availability and high cost. However, recent advances in technology are making them more readily available at a relatively lower cost.[22]

Although CAI programmes are available in several forms, the dialogue systems permitting student–computer interaction unrestricted by preset response alternatives[1] show the greatest potential for application to judgemental instruction. These systems depend upon a set of stored algorithms which are used by the computer to construct a great variety of responses to student questions. In addition, student responses are not limited to exact duplicates of pre-stored expected responses. The programme recognises a variety of student responses and is able to proceed accordingly.

Although practice and feedback are frequently-used concepts in CAI programmes, these could be augmented by presenting principles and reasons for taking a certain course of action. In judgemental training the student could be presented with a flight situation requiring judgement. He could then be asked to respond by listing all of his alternatives and the factors affecting each. He could even be asked to estimate the probability of success for each alternative.

The computer, after examining the flight experience data on the student (entered previously) and the stored accident statistics from similar circumstances, would respond with comments on the appropriateness of the student's responses, the alternatives that may have been omitted, and the principles that should have been followed in making the decision. The program could then branch to another problem, the difficulty of which would be based on the level of judgemental capability evidenced by the student's responses to the previous problem.

Complexity, realism, and time constraints might be included in the judgemental task by the addition of a simple flight hand-controller and an airplane symbol with a map on the screen. The purpose of this controller would be to provide indications of progress toward a destination and time available for the decision, not for instruction in flight control.

CAI has many advantages not commonly associated with other instructional systems. The most important of these is individualisation of instruction. It can adapt to the specific needs of the individual and interact at his current level of ability.[10] Second, the unencumbered reinforcement capabilities of CAI are a real benefit to the student. It has no personality or ulterior motives to clash with those of the student. Students would no longer be handicapped by instructors who underscore weakness in the simulation. Third, CAI systems do not require the presence of a teacher, although it may be beneficial to have one present for occasional consultation. Fourth, they permit standardisation of instruction across a wide area. One central computer could potentially support terminals at every pilot instructional centre in the United States at a relatively low cost. Fifth, data gathered from student responses could be stored for as long as necessary or used in updating instructional programmes or evaluating individual pilot judgemental capabilities.

Flight simulation. In some ways, judgemental training in a simulator environment would be more cumbersome than in ground school or CAI, because, at least in current practice, it depends upon the instructor to create the simulated flight situation primarily through verbal communication.[6] Nevertheless, the simulated flight environment provides an additional opportunity to teach judgemental principles, if properly structured, in a somewhat more realistic environment than ground school or CAI can provide.

Probably the best way to begin judgemental training in the simulator is to use the airline approach, i.e. teaching procedures that are to be followed in each situation that departs from normal flight. This includes system failure detection as well as establishing courses of action to correct or counter system failures. Principles involved, as well as corrective procedures would be taught according to this method, and appropriate judgemental performance measures could be developed.

The simulator instruction could also include the creation, by the flight instructor, of judgement-demanding situations which do not involve the failure of systems. These situations would demand decisions such as whether or not to continue a flight into deteriorating weather, decisions about passenger demands for landing at an unfamiliar alternate airport, decisions about weight and balance considering field conditions, density altitude, etc. In all cases the instructor would ask the student to state several alternatives available to him and also to state which he would choose. These situations could be developed from NTSB accident briefs, and they could be a part of the flight instructor's simulator judgement instruction package.

The aircraft. Of all the media available, the aircraft is probably the most difficult to use for direct, systematic judgemental training. The reason is that for the sake of safety, convenience and cost, most judgemental problems must be halted before the student sees the final consequences of his decisions. He frequently must take the instructor at his word that his decision would have resulted in a safe or unsafe situation. However, the aircraft offers special opportunities for judgemental instruction because the environment is more realistic, it is more meaningful, and therefore, it is more likely to cause a more permanent behavioural change in the student than other training media.

Everything that has been said about instructor attitudes and approaches to judgemental training is even more important when actually flying. Effective judgemental instruction in the aircraft requires a consistent, disciplined flight instructor who always follows the rules that the student is expected to follow, or provides a good explanation for his deviation from them. It also requires that the instructor follow the learning principles stated earlier, i.e. that practice and feedback are beneficial only when accompanied by direction and explanation.

Judgemental instructions in the aircraft could take the form of simulated situations created by the instructor requiring the use of judgement. Such activities could be interspersed throughout the flight training programme. Such instruction is already being done to some extent through training in simulated engine failures, other system failures, and all types of stalls. This training could be expanded to include many of the hypothetical situations discussed above. Portions of such simulated situations could be a part of every instructional flight.

Through situational training techniques flight instructors may be able to modify the response tendencies of their students by teaching them that it is not socially demeaning to refuse to fly or to turn around in the face of deteriorating circumstances. Such situations could be made to occur several times during the student's instruction programme in the aircraft. There is a tendency in many pilots to believe that it is necessary to maintain a virile or courageous image for themselves and their profession.* Pilots have often said that it is most difficult to turn around the first time. Thus, students need to be taught how to avoid the tremendous social pressure that a group of important passengers can exert. They need to know how to isolate themselves from flight-naïve passengers in all important decisions.

Finally, one of the most difficult evaluations a pilot has to make is the self-evaluation of his own skill, knowledge, and judgemental capability relative to a proposed flight. Although research is needed to determine ways to effectively evaluate one's own capabilities, some guidelines can be suggested for its application. First, pilots should be taught to develop a list of personal limitations

* Compare with comments by Martin Allnutt, chapter 1.

on flight procedures based on an estimation of their own capabilities. Second, they should be taught that these limitations are applicable to all flights regardless of who the passengers are or how much they are willing to pay for a more risky choice. These personal limitations should be invoked during a rational moment, and the pilot's resolution should be strong enough to withstand social pressures to deviate from them either before or during a given flight.

Judgement Evaluation

Perhaps the most difficult part of any study of human judgement training programmes is the evaluation of student performance. The reason is that much of what must be evaluated cannot be observed directly but must be inferred from observation of other related behaviours. From discussions with flight instructors and pilot-examining personnel, it is clear that judgement is not being evaluated effectively today.[13]

Although flight test guides published by the FAA specify that civilian pilots are to be evaluated for their 'judgement' capabilities, no definition of judgement is provided. For this evaluation, examiners primarily depend upon the judgement of flight instructors who have the opportunity to examine their student's decision-making capability over a greater variety of circumstances. However, in interviews with flight instructors, the researchers Jensen and Benel found only one who admitted to having failed a student purely on the basis of poor judgement. Although many said that they could recognise poor judgement, students were failed on the basis of a borderline performance of some other more clearly defined flying manoeuvre involving skilled performance.

Some ideas for judgement evaluation are offered by Van Dam who directs a flight school in which pilot judgement receives a strong emphasis.[13] In his approach, the evaluation begins with psychological and intelligence testing prior to admitting students for flight instruction. Initial impressions from these pre-training examinations are augmented with other subjective indicators of judgement such as 'obvious effort and attention to instruction', 'relaxation', 'division of attention', 'response delays', 'confidence', 'capacity for problem-solving', and 'initiative'. In later pilot training, evidence of judgement development is seen through an 'eagerness to learn or high motivation', 'teachability', 'adaptability and flexibility', 'an intuitive quality in thinking or decision-making', 'a pattern of good choices', and 'application of margins and allowances'.

The requirements of pilot judgemental evaluation are even broader than these. Society expects pilots to make decisions based on the interests of passengers and property owners. Therefore, judgement must also be evaluated in an absolute sense against this poorly defined scale. Thus, there are three major dimensions along which judgement should be evaluated and each presents a unique problem to the evaluator.

(a)   The assessment of judgemental capabilities and tendencies prior to flight training.

(b)   The assessment of the effects of training on pilot judgement.
(c)   The assessment of the amount of training transferred to the operational
       flying environment.

Pre-training evaluation

It is important from the standpoints of both safety and economics to identify
persons, prior to flight instruction, who may have difficulty with some aspects
of flying judgement. If such individuals could be identified, they could either be
discouraged from seeking flight training or their training programmes could be
modified to offset this deficiency.

Unfortunately, on the basis of psychological testing research to date, the
predicted success of such a pre-training evaluation programme is not very good.
For example, psychologists and others have made many attempts, with little
success, to identify a general personality trait known as risk-taking and to link
this trait to accident-proneness.[17] In his research J. E. Shealy found that if one
were to limit the scope of the test to specific situations, such as downhill skiing,
its predictive validity would be greatly increased. Therefore, efforts to develop
pre-training pilot judgement prediction tests should not be discouraged by the
limited success of the general tests. Instead, efforts should be made to design an
aviation-specific test with judgement predictive validity.

Pre-training evaluations of judgement ability in pilot training candidates is a
potentially useful adjunct to the entire training and evaluation process. Results
from such tests could be used by training management to adapt their programmes
to emphasise training in areas identified as potentially weak in these tests. Flight
instructors could be alerted to possible weaknesses in individual students and
adapt their training accordingly. Tests which could identify risk-taking
tendencies,[14,19] tests which identify accident-proneness[16] and situation-specific
tests are potentially useful in this application.

Training evaluation

The second major dimension along which pilot judgement must be evaluated is
an assessment of the amount of change in the pilot's judgement performance
that is the result of training. This measure provides an indication of the value of
the training programme as well as indications of individual student progress.

The development of clearly defined judgemental evaluation criteria presents
the greatest challenge to effective evaluation of pilot judgement in all phases of
pilot training. To ensure that evaluations are made along the same dimensions as
the training conducted, the development of these criteria should be based on
pre-established behavioural objectives. Judgemental criteria should consist of
positive statements of acceptable pilot judgemental behaviour for each major
area of flight activity. Similar criteria could be developed for every major
manoeuvre taught. These could be graded by the instructor together with
evaluations of knowledge and skill each time the manoeuvres are attempted.

In pilot training, for each level of pilot experience, certain judgemental hurdles (proficiency levels) could be objectively specified. The instructor, or examiner who evaluates the judgements, would have a range of acceptable performances, also objectively specified. Evaluation of pilot judgement would be a matter of comparing performance against the established criteria in carefully structured situations.

The critical point for judgemental evaluation in a national system is the use of the same criteria by all judges as well as by the pilots themselves. One way to ensure standardisation of judgemental evaluations is to use a nationwide CAI system to administer tests at specific times during each student's training programme. Results of such tests could be used to modify the individual student's training or the training programme as a whole.

Transfer evaluation

The final dimension along which pilot judgement must be evaluated is an assessment of the amount of training that is transferred to the operational flying environment. This means that students who have received special judgemental training are compared with those who have not received such training after both groups have moved into the operational flying environment. The results of this evaluation are used to modify both student selection criteria (or pre-training examinations) and programme need assessments.

The criteria for this evaluation are basically the same as those used in training evaluations except that they are more highly influenced by societal demands. Measures of judgemental training transferred can be made in terms of the number of accidents or incidents due to faulty pilot judgement reported within the respective groups.

Operationalising judgemental evaluations

The definition of pilot judgement has two components: discrimination and response selection. Both components must be evaluated. To operationalise these components for use in any specific training or testing situation, the evaluator may ask the following questions:

(a) For discriminative judgement: Did the student consider all of the alternatives available to him? Did he consider all of the relevant information and assign proper weights to each item? Did he integrate the relevant information efficiently before making his choice?

(b) For response selection tendencies: Did the student exhibit any tendency to consider factors other than safety (such as his own self-esteem, adventure, or social pressure) in making his response selection? Did he seem to be highly prone to use semi-relevant factors, such as financial gain or convenience, in situations where safety should have been the primary consideration?

The initial step toward an operational evaluation of pilot judgement for experienced pilots was taken in a recent study at the Ohio State University sponsored by NASA (Flathers[6]). In this study conjoint measurement techniques were used to establish the worth functions for four factors affecting a diversion-decision during a 'paper and pencil' simulation of an alternator failure in instrument flight conditions. The four factors were air traffic control service (radar v. no-radar), the weather at the airport (ceiling of 1000 or 500 feet); the time to fly to the airport (15 v. 30 minutes), and the best approach facilities (ILS v. ADF) at the alternate airport.

Flathers reports that these techniques effectively discriminate between ATP (Air Transport Pilot) and instrument-rated pilots in terms of the value placed on certain of these four factors. Similar discriminations were found as a function of training backgrounds, type of flying most commonly done, and level of pilot ability to diagnose flying problems as determined from a separate test. Each of these are primarily measures of the discriminative component of judgement.

The study also measured the response selection tendencies of the pilot. In this test pilots were asked to state how many of their previously selected top airport choices would be avoided in favour of a more risky choice to take advantage of field maintenance facilities. Although, in this case, the results were not significant, they indicate that private and commercial pilots were more likely to take a greater risk than ATP pilots.

The Flathers study shows that objective tests can be developed to measure both aspects of pilot judgement. Obviously greater fidelity in the testing procedure could be found through computer or flight simulators. Although the first steps have been taken, a great deal of research still needs to be done to refine these tests and validate their results in operational environments.

The proper evaluation of pilot judgement requires more of the evaluator than just an occasional passing glance at the instrument panel. It requires the careful structuring of the situation, perhaps hypothetically, and a careful examination of actions taken by the student. It probably would require a dialogue between the student and the evaluator to establish what the student actually considered in making his choice. Each evaluation must be considered a training device as well, and as such, feedback should be given to the student concerning all aspects of the decision situation known to the evaluator. It is recognised that evaluations of this sort place high demands on the flight instructor. Nevertheless, they seem to be warranted in view of the high number of fatalities caused by faulty judgement, a factor that is hardly being evaluated at all under the present system.

Acknowledgements

The research for this chapter was sponsored by the Systems Research and Development Service of the Federal Aviation Administration. Patrick Russell was the Contracting Officer's Representative. The author wishes to thank Russ Benel, Jim Finnegan, Mike Kelley, and Rob Durst for their assistance in this programme.

References

1. Alpert, D. and Bitzer, D. L. (1970) 'Advances in computer-based education'. *Science* **167**, 1582–90.
2. Anderson, N. H. (1969) 'Comment on analysis-of-variance model for assignment of configural cue utilization in clinical judgment'. *Psychological Bulletin* **72**, 63–5.
3. Birdsall, T. G. (1955) 'The theory of signal detectability', in Quastler, H. (ed.) *Information theory in psychology: Problems and methods*, Free Press, Glencoe, 391–402.
4. Federal Aviation Administration (1977) *Aviation instructor's handbook*, US Government Printing Office, Washington, DC, No. AC 61–41.
5. Fishbein, M. and Ajzen, I. (1975) *Belief, attitude, intention, and behaviour: An introduction to theory and research*, Addison-Wesley, Reading, Mass.
6. Flathers, G. W. (1980) 'A study of decision-making behavior of aircraft pilots deviating from a planned flight'. Unpublished master's thesis, Ohio State University, Department of Industrial and Systems Engineering.
7. Gagne, R. M. (1962) 'Military training and principles of learning'. *American Psychologist* **17**, 83–91.
8. Gibson, J. H. (1969) Optimized flight crew training: A step toward safer operations. American Airlines, Flight Training Academy, Fort Worth, Texas.
9. Goldberg, L. R. (1968) 'Simple models or simple processes? Some research on clinical judgments'. *American Psychologist* **23**, 483–96.
10. Goldstein, I. L. (1974) *Training: Program development and evaluation*, Wadaworth, Belmont, Ca.
11. Hoffman, P. J., Slovic, P., and Rorer, L. G. (1968) 'An analysis of variance model for the assessment of configural cue utilization in clinical judgment'. *Psychological Bulletin* **69**, 338–49.
12. Janis, I. and Mann, L. (1977) *Decision making: A psychological analysis of conflict, choice, and commitment*, Free Press, New York.
13. Jensen, R. S. and Benel, R. A. (1977) 'Judgment evaluation and instruction in civil pilot training'. National Technical Information Service, Springfield, Va; Final Report FAA-RD-78-24.
14. Kogan, N. and Wallach, M. (1964) *Risk taking: A study in cognition and personality*. Holt, Rinehart, and Winston, New York.
15. Shanteau, J. and Phelps, R. H. (1977) 'Judgment and swine: Approaches and issues in applied judgment analysis', in Kaplan, M. F. and Schwartz, S. (eds.), *Human judgment and decision processes: Applications in problem settings*, Academic Press, New York.
16. Shaw, L. and Sichel, H. S. (1971) *Accident proneness: Research in the occurrence, causation, and prevention of road accidents*, Pergamon, New York.
17. Shealey, J. E. (1974) 'Risk-taking in skilled task performance.' *Proceedings of the Eighteenth Annual Meeting of the Human Factors Society*, Human Factors Society, Santa Monica, Ca.

18.   Slovic, P. (1969) 'Analyzing the expert judge: A descriptive study of stockbroker's decision processes'. *Journal of Applied Psychology* **53**, 255–63.

19.   Taylor, R. N. and Dunnette, M. D. (1974) 'Influence of dogmatism, risk-taking propensity, and intelligence on decision-making strategies for a sample of industrial managers.' *Journal of Applied Psychology* **59**, 420–23.

20.   Thorpe, J. A., Martin E. L., Edwards, B. J., and Eddowes, E. E. (1976) 'Situational emergency training: F-15 emergency procedures training program'. Williams Air Force Base, Arizona, Technical Report No. AFHRL-TR-76-47(1), June.

21.   Trans World Airlines (1969) 'Flight simulator evaluation.' Trans World Airlines, Flight Operations Training Department, Kansas City, Mo.

22.   Trollip, S. R. and Ortony, A. (1977) 'Real-time simulation in computer-assisted instruction.' *Instruction Science* **6**, 135–49.

Chapter 4

Flight-Deck Automation: Promises and Problems *E. L. Wiener and R. E. Curry*

But if pilot judgement remains an enigma, how far should flight-deck decisions be taken out of the pilot's hands?

Modern microprocessor technology and display systems make it entirely feasible to automate many flight-deck functions previously performed manually. There are many real benefits to be derived from automation; the question today is not whether a function can be automated, but whether it should be, due to the variety of human factors questions which are raised. It is highly questionable whether total systems safety is always enhanced by allocating functions to automatic devices rather than human operators and there is some reason to believe that flight-deck automation may have already passed its optimum. This is an evergreen question in the human factors profession and there are few guidelines available to the system designer.

This chapter examines the state-of-the-art in human factors in flight-deck automation, identifies a number of critical problem areas and offers broad design guidelines. Some automation-related aircraft accidents and incidents are discussed as examples of human factors problems in automated flight.

Introduction

Studies of this kind often begin with the almost mandatory statement that in future systems, automatic devices will provide for the real-time, moment-to-moment control of the process, and that the human operator will be relegated to the post of monitor and decision-maker, keeping watch for deviations and failures and taking over when necessary.* This prescription is based on the observation that inanimate control devices are extremely good at real-time control, but must be supported by the remarkable flexibility of the human as a supervisor and standby controller, in case of breakdown or other unforeseen events.

The second mandatory statement is that the human, for all his putative flexibility, is not so good at the monitoring task, and is highly likely to miss critical signals, as well as to make occasional commissive errors. Indeed, the verity of the second statement, backed up by endless accident and incident reports, tempts designers to 'automate human error out of the system'. The lure is especially great in aviation, where the cost of human failure can be so high.

While the authors have no quarrel with the two basic statements, the assumption that automation can eliminate human error must be questioned. This chapter

*See numerous papers in Sheridan and Johannsen.[27]

will therefore explain the automation of flight-deck functions, the presumed benefits and possible pitfalls, and will ask whether it is possible that cockpit automation may have already passed its optimum point. This examination is made more urgent by rapid developments in microprocessor technology, and by many present and near-future applications in the cockpit.[12, 23] The question is no longer whether one or another function can be automated but, rather, whether it should be.

Much of what will be said about automation on the flight deck may be applied equally well to other large-scale systems (e.g., air traffic control, nuclear power generation), and we invite the reader to do so. Likewise, much of what has been written about automation in other fields could apply to the flight deck: for example, the many excellent papers on process control appearing in Edwards and Lees,[8] and the overview by Shackel.[26]

The very word 'automation' is likely to conjure up, at least in the mind of the technologically unsophisticated, two rather opposite images, both of which can ultimately be shown to be exaggerated, if not incorrect. On the negative side, automation is seen as a collection of tyrannical, self-serving machines, degrading humans, reducing the work force, bringing wholesale unemployment, and perhaps even worse, offering an invitation to a technological dictator to seize power and build a society run by Dr Strangeloves, aided by opportunistic, cold-hearted computer geniuses. The classic Charlie Chaplin movie *Modern Times* depicted the subjugation of industrial man to machine, and more recently, the popular novels and movies by Michael Crichton (*Westworld, Terminal Man*) dwelled on the perils of a computer-based society gone awry. So far, there is no indication that such a thing has happened, or that it will.

Perhaps equally fallacious is the positive image of automation: quiet, unerring, efficient, totally dependable machines, the servant of man, eliminating all human error, and offering a safe and cost-effective alternative to human frailty and caprice. The traditional dream of traditional engineers has been to solve the problem of human error by eliminating its source. It is worth noting that the general public appears as sceptical of the infallibility of automation as they are fearful of its consequences.

Thus, the authors will shortly present what is popularly called 'the good news and the bad news' of flight-deck automation, as there are ample instances of each. We shall finally attempt to provide some tentative guidelines to the implementation of automatic devices in aircraft. Automation of human functions in air traffic control (ATC),* weather forecasting, dispatching, and maintenance, while vitally important, will not be addressed.

Why automate?

It is almost trite (though necessary) to say that automation may be a mixed blessing in the cockpit, as elsewhere. Already there is serious concern about the impact of automation on flight-deck performance, work-load, and ultimately, on

* . . .the measure of ATC needs is considered in Richard Weston's chapter. See chapter 7, p. 130.

aviation safety.[6, 7] Questions have arisen from accident reports, incident reports (such as NASA's Aviation Safety Reporting System), airline training, simulator studies, and our own interviews with crew members and airline flight managers about such matters as failure detection, manual takeover, skills degradation, and even job satisfaction and self-concept of pilots and flight engineers operating highly automated equipment. These are not new problems, but they are now being addressed with a new urgency and frankness, impelled by the technological developments that make flight-deck automation entirely feasible, at least from an electro-mechanical point of view.

A basic assumption

One hears, from time to time, talk of the unmanned airline cockpit. While the authors find this neither unthinkable nor technologically infeasible, we feel that, as far into the future as we can see, it would be socially and politically unacceptable. Therefore, while we do not completely dismiss the idea of an unmanned airliner, this discussion is based on the assumption that airliners will carry a human crew.* The size, functions, selection, training, and motivation of this crew, however, remain open questions. It should be noted that even the unmanned factory, so often predicted, has never come to pass.

Driving forces

Before going further, one should ask just what is the thrust behind cockpit automation. We have identified three factors.

Technology: The explosive growth of microprocessor technology has already been mentioned. Rapid improvement in performance, and decrease in size, cost, and power consumption of various electronic devices, sensors, and display media, make automation of many flight-deck (as well as ground-based) systems a reasonable alternative to traditional manual operation. This trend will continue well into the next century. One should note that technology is not a goal (as the next two factors are), but is instead a facilitating factor.

Safety: More than half of aircraft accidents are attributed to 'human error'. This term can be somewhat misleading, as one is never sure whether it means cockpit crew error, or includes other humans such as ATC controllers, weather forecasters, maintenance personnel, and dispatchers. Be that as it may, there exists ample need to reduce human error in the cockpit. Autopilots, flight directors, and alerting and warning systems are examples of automatic systems that have had a beneficial effect on pilot work-load and/or safety margins. The ground proximity warning system (GPWS) provides an excellent example. Since its introduction by Congressional mandate in 1974, there has been a dramatic reduction in terrain strike accidents, both in the United States and worldwide. It is impossible to know how many aircraft and lives have been saved by this

*For a concurring view see McLucus on the next generation of aircraft.

device. Nonetheless, it is often denounced by pilots for the frequent false alarms it generates. These false alarms are annoying, and potentially dangerous, but on balance, the GPWS would have to be viewed very favourably.

Economics: Undoubtedly, automation can bring about enormous savings through fuel conservation, if total flight time can be reduced, and more fuel-efficient climb and descent patterns can be implemented.[4, 9] Both the potential for dollar savings and the impact on airline profits are difficult to exaggerate, especially in the face of steadily rising fuel prices. In 1978 a gallon of jet fuel sold for about 38 cents (U.S.), for 70 cents by the end of 1979, and was at the beginning of 1982 costing more than one dollar. A recent analysis of the operating costs and profits of a major U.S. carrier showed that a 3% saving in jet fuel could result in a 23% increase in profits. Automation in both ATC and the cockpit could easily produce the 3% reduction in fuel consumption; even greater savings are possible on shorter runs, such as the New York–Boston shuttle. It was reported[20] that every percentage point increase in jet fuel price will cost Western Airlines $4,000,000. Likewise, we presume, every percentage point by which consumption could be reduced should save the company about the same amount. Finally, a summary[3] of 12 fuel conservation methods concluded that savings of up to 12% could be realized from their optimal use. Five per cent savings have already resulted from a partial implementation. Most of the methods it outlined would require automation to some degree in order to achieve maximum savings.

As in other industries, a large component of airline operating costs is labour. While it is questionable whether automation can reduce the number of persons in the cockpit (the authors do not wish to plunge into the two-versus-three person crew controversy), it should not be totally discounted.[19]†

Furthermore, automation may reduce direct labour costs somewhat by reducing flight times through more efficient lateral navigation, and may cut maintenance costs by more effective use of the equipment. However, in considering economics, one must also recognise that automation equipment does not come cheaply. The airline industry will be saddled with enormous capital costs to acquire the equipment, as well as operating costs for training and maintenance. But even putting the safety question aside and looking only at the economics, it appears that flight-deck automation should be a very good investment, especially in view of never-ending fuel price increases, not to mention possible shortages.

Representative Aviation Accidents and Incidents

So much for the promises of flight-deck automation. Let us now examine some of the problems, which can best be illustrated by representative aviation accidents and incidents. These accounts are confined, by necessity, to very brief summaries and comments on what is usually a very complex causal chain. The authors do not wish to over-simplify either the facts or the causal interpretations of these accidents, and the interested reader is encouraged to delve into the full reports.*

*For other examples, see Rolfe,[22] and Danaher.[5]
†The crew complement issue is, however, discussed in chapter 10.

Failure of automatic equipment

One of the concerns regarding the use of equipment for automatic control or monitoring is that it may fail to operate correctly. Consider the following incidents reported in a cockpit newsletter:

(a)   In an approach with the autopilot in control, a bend in the glide-path at 500 ft above the ground caused a very marked pitch down, resulting in excessive sink rate. The pilot, though fully aware of the situation, did not react until his position was so critical that a very low pull-up had to be made.

(b)   The altitude preselect (a device to level the aircraft at a predetermined altitude) malfunctioned. This went unnoticed by the pilots and an excessive undershoot was made (descent below desired altitude).

(c)   At level-off by use of the altitude preselect, and with the throttles in idle, the speed dropped close to the stall point before this condition was detected and rectified by power application.

(d)   While in navigation mode (autopilot steering the aircraft to maintain a track over the ground) the aircraft turned the wrong way over a checkpoint. Although the wrong turn was immediately noticed, the aircraft turned more than 45 degrees before the pilot took action.

These reports are brief, and the present authors do not have access to more details. Thus it is difficult to determine how much of the fault should be attributed to hardware failure, improper set-up of the equipment, and inappropriate expectations of how the equipment should operate. Nonetheless, the reports are typical of the day-to-day problems encountered by flight-crews.

Automation-induced error compounded by crew error

The following accident illustrates one of the special hazards of automation, one that many traditional engineers might rather not hear about. In this case, the causal chain of events was set into motion by the failure of the automated equipment, then compounded by crew error, resulting in a crash.[17] A Swift Aire Lines Nord 262 departed from Los Angeles International westbound, and shortly after gear retraction, its right propeller autofeathered. Autofeather is a device common on advanced twin-engine propeller-driven planes. It senses a loss of power in an engine and feathers the propeller (rotates the blades in line with the direction of flight to reduce drag) without human intervention. It is armed only on takeoff and initial climbout. The purpose of the autofeather is to preclude the possibility that a crew member will shut down the wrong (operating) engine in the event of power failure on takeoff. It remains for the crew to secure the dead engine, increase power on the good engine, make trim and control adjustments, and continue climbing to a safe altitude for return to the field.

Immediately after the right engine autofeathered, the crew shut down the

left (good) engine, resulting in a fatal ditching in the Pacific Ocean. Examination
of the right engine showed there had been no power loss, and the autofeather had
been due to a broken hydraulic hose in the sensing mechanism. Later investigation
revealed that the problem of inadvertent autofeathering had been encountered
previously. Thus, a device designed to automate human error out of the system
had triggered the fatal chain of events, compounded by the very human error it
was supposed to prevent.

Crew error in equipment set-up

Inertial navigation systems (INS) are automatic navigators. They are also used to
supply automatic pilots with position information to allow control of aircraft
track (the navigation mode). The latitude and longitude of the initial position of
the aircraft and a series of checkpoints ('waypoints') defining the desired track
across the earth is loaded into the INS computer by keyboard before the flight.
During the initial setup, the crew loaded their position with a northern latitude
rather than the southern latitude of their actual location. This error was detected
neither by the INS nor the crew until after takeoff. The aircraft had to return to
the departure point because the INS could not be reset in flight.

Crew response to a false alarm

Another form of automation-induced error is the false alarm, which persuades
the crew to take corrective action when in fact nothing is wrong with the system
(other than the spurious alarm). Such an error occurred during the takeoff of a
Texas International DC-9 from Denver.[16] As the aircraft accelerated to the
velocity of rotation (where the nose wheel is lifted off the runway and the aircraft assumes a nose-high pitch attitude), about 150 knots in this case, the stall
warning actuated. This was a 'stick shaker', a tactile warning system whereby the
control column begins to shake, as well as giving auditory 'clacks'. Believing that
a stall was imminent, in spite of normal airspeed and pitch attitude indications,
the crew elected to abort the takeoff resulting in a runway over-run, severe
damage to the aircraft, and non-fatal injuries to some passengers. Interestingly,
the pilots had both experienced spurious stall warnings on takeoff previously,
but they probably had little choice but to regard this as a bona fide alert.

In a 'split second' the crew faced a choice of aborting the take off, with an
almost inevitable, though perhaps non-catastrophic, accident, and continuing
the take off with a plane that might not be flyable, which could result in a much
worse accident. It might be interesting, but perhaps not profitable, to speculate
on what might have occurred if this decision function had been automated.
Suffice it to say that the decision to stop or go, as it faced the crew at that
critical moment during rotation, would have been in the hands of some distant
software designer. We leave it to the reader to decide if that is a comforting
thought.

Failure to heed automatic alarm

An Allegheny BAC 1-11 was on an approach to landing, but at an excessive airspeed. During the approach the ground proximity warning system was triggered three times (once for excessive descent rate, twice for less than 26° of flaps with gear extended and excessive descent rates). Instead of executing a missed approach, the captain continued toward landing, crossing the runway threshold at a speed of 184 knots, 61 knots above the reference speed. The aircraft landed approximately halfway down the runway and overran the far end; one person was seriously injured. The National Transportation Safety Board[18] determined that the probable cause of the accident was the captain's complete lack of awareness of airspeed, vertical speed, and aircraft performance throughout the approach and landing. A contributing factor was the co-pilot's failure to provide required call-outs of airspeed and vertical speed deviations. In its analysis, the NTSB did note that the GPWS alerts should have indicated to the crew that the approach was improper and that a missed approach was necessary. It also mentioned that none of the alerts caused the crew to take corrective action, even though company procedures dictated that they should do so.

Failure to monitor

This type of problem can be exemplified by certain 'controlled flight into terrain' accidents, in which a flight-crew, with the aircraft controllable, flies it into the ground (or water), usually without any prior awareness of impending disaster.[24] * In December 1972, an Eastern Air Lines L-1011 was approaching Miami on a clear night. During the pre-landing cockpit check, the crew encountered an unsafe landing gear indication (light failed to illuminate). ATC assigned the aircraft to a westward heading at 2000ft (mean sea level), while the crew attempted to diagnose the problem. The plane was under autopilot control. The flight-crew became preoccupied with the problem at hand (the captain and first officer had pulled the bulb appliance out of the panel to check the lamp, and were having trouble putting it back together). They did not notice that the autopilot had disengaged, and that the aircraft was in a slow descending spiral. They flew into the ground, having never detected their departure from altitude, even with full cockpit instrumentation, extra-cockpit vision, a C-chord altitude alert that sounded (and was present on the cockpit voice recorder), and an ambiguous inquiry from a radar operator in Miami who observed the descent on the alphanumeric readout on his scope.[15]

Loss of proficiency

One of the most easily imagined consequences of automation is a loss of proficiency by the operator. While there has been no specific accident or incident in which this has been cited as a contributing factor, discussions with individuals

*See chapter 5.

in the management of pilot training have noted a perceptible skill loss in pilots who use automatic equipment extensively. For example, co-pilots on wide-body jets, which have sophisticated automatic systems, accrue enough seniority to become captains on narrow-body jets, which do not have sophisticated autopilot/autothrottle systems. Those who report these skill losses go on to say that they feel they have resolved the problem by asking co-pilots to turn off the automatic systems prior to transition training so that they regain proficiency with manual systems. We have noticed that many crew members seem to have discovered this on their own and regularly turn off the autopilot, in order to retain their manual flying skills.

Beyond the possible loss of proficiency, a change in attitude may be induced by use of automation. The following excerpt from a letter from a flight training manager speaks succinctly of the issue:

'Having been actively involved in all areas of this training, one disturbing side effect of automation has appeared, i.e., a tendency to breed inactivity or complacency.

For example good conscientious First Officers (above average) with as little as 8—9 months on the highly sophisticated and automated L-101 1s have displayed this inactivity or complacency on reverting to the B-707 for initial command training.

This problem has caused us to review and increase our command training time for such First Officers. In fact we have doubled the allotted en route training time.'

Common Problem Areas

The previous discussions have concerned some very specific problems with the use of automated devices. We have analysed the above incidents and many others, and have tried to rephrase the problem statement into a more general context. This will, we hope, assist interested parties from diverse disciplines and industries to communicate in a more effective manner. Five general problem areas are described below, with some of the major issues outlined for each. As is to be expected, the boundaries of the problem areas are somewhat ill-defined, and many questions may legitimately belong to more than one category.

Automation of control tasks

This problem area has received the most attention in the past. When control tasks are automated, the operator's role becomes one of a monitor and supervisor; hence, the primary issues revolve around his ability to perform these functions, since the control task is almost always accomplished satisfactorily by the automatic system. Typical questions to be examined are:

(a)   Under what conditions will the human acting as a monitor be a better (or worse) failure detector than the human as an active controller/operator?

(b) Is there a significant 'warm-up' delay when the human changes from passive monitor to active controller? Does automation lull the operators into a state of low alertness or do they enter a state in which they are easily distracted from the monitoring task by unimportant events?

(c) What should be the form of the interaction between the operator and the automatic system? If the automatic system is changing the system configuration, should it make the change automatically and inform the operator, or make the change only after operator acknowledgement? Should the system indicate why it is making the change or not?

(d) What is the impact of different levels of equipment reliability on the operator's ability to detect, diagnose, and treat malfunctions in manual and automatic tasks? It seems plausible that equipment reliability could be an important factor. For example, if the equipment is very unreliable, then the operators will be expecting malfunctions and will be adept at handling them. If the equipment is very reliable, then there is little need for failure detection and diagnosis on the part of the operator. An intermediate level of reliability, however, may be quite insidious since it will induce an impression of high reliability, and the operator may not be able to handle the failure when it occurs.

Acquisition and retention of skills

The use of automation will probably result in a decrease in the skill level for well-learned manual tasks. Of practical importance is the rate at which these skills deteriorate and the countermeasures available to prevent unacceptable skill loss. On the other hand, the training literature suggests that part-task operation (with the other tasks automated) during the early, familiarisation phases of operation may be an effective means of total acquisition of operational skill. Thus, the major unanswered questions regarding the initial acquisition, reacquisition, and retention of skills are as follows:

(a) How quickly do manual skills deteriorate with lack of use? What factors influence the rate of loss?

(b) Can periodic practice prevent the deterioration of skill? If so, what frequency is required?

(c) Are there alternatives for practice with the actual system, for example, part-task simulators?

(d) What quality control techniques will be necessary to ensure maintenance of skills?

(e) Can automation be used to increase successfully the rate of skill acquisition in complex tasks by automating some of the subtasks? Will the operator who is learning in this mode be better at detecting anomalies in other parts of the process? Will the necessity of learning to operate the automatic equipment (perhaps a complex process itself) negate any of the gains of automating subtasks?

Monitoring of complex systems

The experimental and theoretical research on vigilance deals primarily with human perceptual processes; for example, detecting the presence of a light. Most systems, however, require much more cognitive processing to perform the monitoring task. For example, a typical pilot assessment of his fuel situation might proceed as follows: the aircraft is travelling at 200 mph and is 100 miles, or $100/200 = 0.5$ h from the destination; it is burning 100 gallons/h and therefore requires 0.5 h x 100 gal/h = 50 gallons to reach the destination; there are 40 gallons of fuel remaining, so the destination cannot be reached.

Beyond this very simple but highly realistic case, there are many situations that require cognitive functions; for example, logical, mathematical, and memory operations using multiple sources of information. The major issues in this complex monitoring are essentially those that confronted researchers in the vigilance area, but they have to be examined for the more complex situations.

(a)   Does complex monitoring performance degrade with time on watch? If so, is this decrement perceptual, cognitive, or the criterion level for responding?

(b)   What are the means for maintaining operator alertness for rare signals? Will artificial signals and alerts improve or degrade monitoring effectiveness? Will additional work-load, in addition to complex monitoring, improve or degrade performance?

(c)   What makes an automatic system more 'interpretable', that is, easier to detect and diagnose malfunctions?

Alerting and warning systems

Human behaviour with alerting and warning systems is one of the most fascinating topics in man-machine interaction. It is here that one sees both unpredictable responses. For example, it has long been recognised that people will ignore an alarm if experience has shown that the alarm may be false; we see the same behaviour with some cockpit alarms today. Important research questions for alerting and warning systems include:

(a)   What are the characteristics of an ideal (but attainable) alerting and warning system?

(b)   What attributes make a false alarm rate unacceptably high?

(c)   Why do alarms apparently go unheeded?

(d)   Under what conditions do operators rely on alerting and warning systems as primary devices rather than as back-up devices? Is this operationally sound?

(e)   Under what conditions will operators check the validity of an alarm?

(f)   Should the responsible operator be given a preview alert and opportunity for corrective action before the alarm is given to others?

(g)   A consensus seems to be building to develop alerting and warning systems that are 'smart'; among other things, they would prevent 'obvious' false alarms, and assign priorities to alarms. The logic for these systems will likely be exceedingly complicated. Will that logic be too complex for operators to perform validity checks, and thus lead to over-reliance on the system? Will the priorities *always* be appropriate? If not, will the operators recognise this?

Psychosocial aspects of automation

The psychosocial aspects of automation may prove to be the most important of all, because they influence the basic attitudes of the operator toward his task, and, we would presume, his motivation, adaptability, and responsiveness. The significance of these questions lies not in the spectre of massive unemployment due to assembly line automation, but in the effects of automation on the changing role of a few highly skilled operators.

(a) Will automation influence job satisfaction, prestige, and self concept (especially in aviation)?
(b) If there are negative psychosocial consequences of automation, what precautions and/or remedies will be effective without changing the use of automation?
(c) What does increased automation imply for operator selection? Are there clearly defined aptitudes or personality attributes which imply better monitoring (or manual) effectiveness?
(d) How should training programmes be altered to deal with possible psychosocial effects? Would a simulator help support morale? If so, what type of simulation?

Design Decisions

The words 'cockpit automation' are usually interpreted to mean autopilots, flight directors, and other equipment associated with the control of the aircraft flightpath and aircraft systems. Interpreting automation to mean the accomplishment of a task by a machine instead of a human leads to the realization that all cockpit alerting and warning systems are also forms of automation since they perform monitoring tasks. Automation of control and automation of monitoring are quite independent of one another: it is possible to have various levels of automation in one dimension (see fig. 4.1) independent of the other. Automation of control tasks implies that the operator is monitoring the computer, whereas automation of the monitoring tasks implies that the computer is monitoring the operator. Both of these dimensions will be explored in the context of design decisions after a discussion of the overall goals of the system.

System goals

Let us begin by asking what the user expects of the system. Some of the goals of the system are:

(a) To provide a flight (including ground handling) with infinitesimal accident probability.

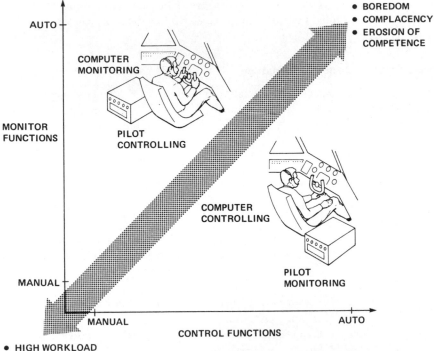

AUTO

COMPUTER
MONITORING

MONITOR
FUNCTIONS

PILOT
CONTROLLING

COMPUTER
CONTROLLING

PILOT
MONITORING

MANUAL

MANUAL   AUTO
                    CONTROL FUNCTIONS

- BOREDOM
- COMPLACENCY
- EROSION OF
  COMPETENCE

- HIGH WORKLOAD
- FATIGUE

Fig 4.1 **Two dimensions of automation**: control and monitoring. Piloting an aircraft involves both control and monitoring related to the flight path and aircraft sub-systems. This depicts the possibility of different levels of automation in the control and monitoring tasks.

(b)   To provide passengers with the smoothest possible flight (by weather avoidance, selection of the least turbulent altitudes, gradual turns and pitch changes, gradual altitude changes).

(c)   To conduct the flight as economically as possible, minimising flight time, ground delays, fuel consumption, and wear on the equipment.

(d)   To minimise impact of any flight on the ability of other aircraft to achieve the same goal (e.g., by co-operation with ATC in rapidly departing altitudes when cleared, freeing them for other aircraft).

(e)   To provide a pleasant, safe, and healthful working environment for the crew.

Now that the goals of the system have been annunciated, several things should be clear. First, the goals are exactly the same whether the systems are automated or manual. Whether flight-deck automation can help achieve these goals, and whether it is feasible and economical to do so, remains to be seen.* Second, for

*For a totally optimistic view, see Boulanger and Dai.[1]

the most part, these goals are not in conflict. There are exceptions, as clearly (b) may be in conflict with (c). The resolution of this conflict lies in evaluating the utilities to the airline, no easy job in itself. If the utilities can be made explicit, then the resolution could be automated. For example, one could envisage an on-board flight management system that would take into account the utilities of extra cost of weather avoidance versus the discomfort to passengers. The system would then, within certain constraints, navigate over a course and altitude of maximum utility. Likewise, (b) and (d) may at times be in conflict — a very rapid descent would be helpful to ATC in clearing altitudes for other traffic, but may adversely affect both passenger comfort and fuel consumption. Again, while these are not problems of automation *per se*, automation in the cockpit (and elsewere) may aid in their resolution, forcing the designer to face the question of utilities.

Design philosophies — control

So far we have specified system goals and constructed, at least, a justification for considering automation as a means of reaching these goals, along with some cautions. We must now consider design philosophies centred on the man-in-the-loop question. In simple terms, the designer must ask to what extent the human should be included in the control loop at all.[28]

This is considerably more than restating the time-honoured clichés about 'man can do these things better than machines, but machines can do these better', which were so in fashion in the early days of ergonomics. Since the authors have already ruled out unmanned airline flight (by assumption), the question must now be restated, 'under what conditions should man be part of the control loop, and what price is paid, in terms of attaining system goals, for including or excluding him?' One paradigm is that usually employed by the control systems engineer (see, for example, Johannsen).[10] This scheme envisages nested control loops with inner, high activity loops, such as aircraft attitude control, and an outward progression toward lower activity loops such as aircraft navigation. These loops must be controlled by either the pilot or the autopilot; the choice is determined by the particular mode of the autopilot in use.

During cruise, the least critical portion of the flight, designers and pilots are only too happy to turn control over to the autopilot, allowing the flight-crew to occupy themselves with other things. In other phases of the flight, use or non-use of the autopilot is largely a matter of personal style of the flight-crew.

Control by the autopilot during level flight at an assigned altitude would be satisfactory were it not for the fact that autopilots have a disconcerting way of failing 'gracefully', so gracefully that a de-coupling may not be noticed by the crew until the system is badly out of limits. Two interesting examples can be cited. First, a PAA B-707, which was cruising at 36 000 ft above the Atlantic, experienced a graceful autopilot disengagement. The aircraft went into a steep descending spiral before the crew took action, and lost 30 000 ft before recovery.[29]

A second case, the crash of an Eastern Air Lines L-1011 in the Everglades, has already been discussed in these pages.

A more demanding control task would be final approach navigation — merely a special case of lateral and vertical navigation, but one that combines relatively high bandwidth with low error tolerance. At this point, the man-in-the-loop design philosophies become controversial. An excellent example of the intrusion of basic design philosophy into equipment concepts is the controversy of the head-up display (HUD). At issue is the HUD's usefulness in aiding the pilot making a low-ceiling, low-visibility approach, below those permitted with conventional head-down displays, even when aided by autothrottles and flight directors. The two philosophies are exemplified by papers by Naish and Von Weiser[14] who were strongly supportive of retaining the man in the loop by means of providing a HUD, and by St. John[25] who wished to remove him entirely from controlling a final approach by the use of more sophisticated auto-land equipment. The argument in favour of the HUD is that it allows one crew member to remain 'head up', so that when the runway becomes visible, the transition from instruments to outside reference is facilitated. The 'head-up' pilot would then fly so as to superimpose visually the HUD runway symbology on the actual runway.

Others feel that the intervention by the pilots could introduce nothing but error to an auto-land approach — they prefer to have the autopilot/autothrottle capacity used all the way to the runway, with the pilots keeping their hands off and only monitoring (as in the extreme lower right of fig. 4.1). The middle ground would be an auto-land approach, monitored by a headup display. This procedure is gaining favour and is currently used by some European carriers.

The reader should note that at least one piece of cockpit instrumentation, the flight director, stands in contrast to the nested-loop configuration we have been describing. A flight director takes essentially outer loop decisions about navigation and computes steering commands for the pilot (or autopilot), relieving him of complex information processing requirements.

Finally, one might conceive of outermost loops where control decisions are made only occasionally: initial flight planning, or changes en route (such as weather avoidance, diversion to an alternate, or handling of critical in-flight events). Many such decisions could be automated, but presently are not. We predict that the actual decisions would always remain in the domain of the pilot for a variety of reasons, including complexity, the cost of developing and maintaining software, legal liability, and social pressures. Even in the most fully automatic mode, the equipment would process information and present alternatives to the pilot, who would weigh the results and make the command decision. The intriguing question is the many forms the crew-computer interaction might take. For example, does the automatic equipment merely compute alternatives, or should it suggest a 'best' choice to the pilot? What role could automation play in multi-attribute decisions? Let us take as an example the choice of alternate airport, should it become necessary to divert. Pertinent attributes of the candidate airports include the present weather, the forecast weather, type of instrument approach available, passenger facilities, maintenance facilities, runway length and conditions, fuel cost at the destination, surrounding terrain, and many more. Automation or not, the captain must ultimately process multi-dimensional information and make the decision, often between conflicting objective functions. Our question, once again, is how may automation assist the pilot in making his decision?

Design philosophies — monitoring

Until recently there has been little agreement on a design philosophy for automatic alerting and warning systems other than to install a warning device to alert the pilot to a condition that existed in some recent and serious accident. This, and the desire to cover all situations with alerts or warnings, has led to a proliferation of independent warning and alerting devices which many feel has reached the point of saturating the pilots' information processing capabilities.[21] For example, there are 188 warnings and caution alerts on the B-707, 455 on the B-747, 172 on the DC-8, and 418 on the DC-10. The aviation industry seems to feel that the time has come for the development of integrated alerting and warning systems.[2]

It has been stated that man is a poor monitor, yet for detecting some situations (e.g. incapacitation or aberrant behaviour of other crewmembers) man is clearly superior to any automatic monitor. If he does have monitoring difficulty in large transport aircraft, it would appear to arise from the requirement that he monitor a large number of systems and perform other duties at the same time. In spite of many laboratory studies showing the parallel processing capabilities of the human, pilots generally perform many of their tasks as single-channel processors, especially when a task is somewhat out of the ordinary. It is not uncommon, for example, to see pilots concentrate on lateral navigation during a difficult intercept manoeuvre, to the exclusion of airspeed control.

In summary, the primary necessity for automation of the monitoring functions is the single channel behaviour of the human and the increased number of devices or conditions to be monitored. Increasing the number of individual alerts and warnings is not the complete answer to the problem, however, since one anomaly may lead to a large number of alerts, many of which are superfluous or worse, misleading; thus, the industry emphasis on integrated alerting and warning systems.[21]

Strengths and weaknesses

At the risk of stumbling into the trap of 'man does this better, machines do this better', the authors close this section by summarising and generalising in Table 4.1 some of the positive and negative features of cockpit automation. The generalisations contained in Table 4.1 probably apply to the flight deck, and may apply equally well to manufacturing, ATC, medicine, telecommunications, power generation, and many non-aviation examples of highly automated systems.

Table 4.1   Generalisations about advantages and disadvantages of automating man—machine systems

Advantages	Disadvantages	Questionable	Unknown
Increased capacity and productivity	Seen as dehumanising; lower job satisfaction; consumer resistance	Overall workload reduced or increased?	Capital acquisition costs
Reduction of manual workload and fatigue	Low alertness of human operators	Total operational cost increased or decreased?	Use of common hardware (e.g. standard main-frame computers)
Relief from routine operations	Systems are fault intolerant —may lead to larger errors	Training requirements increased or decreased?	Maintenance costs
Relief from small errors	Silent failures	Reduction in crew size?	Extent of redundancy necessary and desirable
More precise handling of routine operations	Lower proficiency of operators in case of need for manual take-over		Long-range safety implications
Economical utilisation of machines (e.g energy management)	Over-reliance; complacency; willingness to uncritically accept results		Long-range impact on operators and other personnel (including physical and mental health, job satisfaction, self-esteem, attractiveness of job to others entering field)
Damping of individual differences (narrower tolerances)	False alarms		Long-range implications for collective bargaining
	Automation-induced failures		Implications for civil liability (e.g. software error resulting in an accident)
	Increase in mental workload		

Automation Guidelines

In this section we propose some guidelines for designing and using (or not using) automated systems. These guidelines should be considered over and above the usual human factors engineering requirements. The guidelines are not to be considered as specifications, since most lack the detail needed for that purpose, and conditions exist where they may not be appropriate. Moreover, there are many conflicting concepts within these guidelines. Because we have tried to make them comprehensive, some may appear to the reader to be quite obvious.

Control tasks

(a) System operation should be easily interpretable or understandable by the operator to facilitate the detection of improper operation and to facilitate the diagnosis of malfunctions.

(b) Design the automatic system to perform the task the way the user wants it done (consistent with other constraints such as safety); this may require user control of certain parameters, such as system gains (see Guideline (e)). Many users of automated systems find that the systems do not perform the function in the manner desired by the operator. For example, auto-pilots, especially older designs, have too much 'wing waggle' for passenger comfort when tracking ground based navigation stations. Thus, many air-line pilots do not use this feature, even when travelling coast to coast on non-stop flights.

(c) Design the automation to prevent peak levels of task demand from becoming excessive (this may vary from operator to operator). System monitoring is not only a legitimate, but a necessary activity of the human operator; however, it generally takes second priority to other, event-driven tasks. Keeping task demand at reasonable levels will ensure available time for monitoring.

(d) For most complex systems, it is very difficult for the computer to sense when the task demands on the operator are too high. Thus the operator must be trained and motivated to use automation as an additional resource (i.e. as a helper).

(e) Desires and needs for automation will vary with operators and with time for any one operator. Allow for different operator 'styles' (choice of automation) when feasible.

(f) Ensure that overall system performance will be insensitive to different options, or styles of operation. For example, the pilot may choose to have the autopilot either fly pilot-selected headings, or track ground-based navigation stations.

(g) Provide a means for checking the set-up and information input to automatic systems. Many automatic system failures have been and will continue to be due to set-up error, rather than hardware failures. The automatic system itself can check some of the set-up, but independent error-checking equipment/procedures should be provided when appropriate.

(h)   Extensive training is required for operators working with automated equip-
       ment, not only to ensure proper operation and set-up, but to impart a
       knowledge of correct operation (for anomaly detection) and malfunction
       procedures (for diagnosis and treatment).

Monitoring tasks

(i)   Operators should be trained, motivated, and evaluated to monitor effec-
       tively.
(j)   If automation reduces task demands to low levels, provide meaningful
       duties to maintain operator involvement and resistance to distraction.
       Many others have recommended adding tasks, but it is extremely import-
       ant that any additional duties be meaningful (not 'make-work') and directed
       toward the primary task itself.
(k)   Keep false alarm rates within acceptable limits (recognise the behavioural
       impact of excessive false alarms).
(l)   Alarms with more than one mode, or more than one condition that can
       trigger the alarm for a mode, must clearly indicate which condition is
       responsible for the alarm display.
(m)   When response time is not critical, most operators will attempt to check
       the validity of the alarm. Provide information in the proper format so that
       this validity check can be made quickly and accurately and not become a
       source of distraction. Also provide the operator with information and
       controls to diagnose the automatic system and warning system operation.
       Some of these should be easy quick checks of sensors and indicators (such
       as the familiar 'press to test' for light bulbs); larger systems may require
       logic tests.
(n)   The format of the alarm should indicate the degree of emergency. Multiple
       levels of urgency of the same condition may be beneficial.
(o)   Devise training techniques and possibly training hardware (including part-
       and whole-task simulators) to ensure that flight-crews are exposed to all
       forms of alerts and to many of the possible combinations of alerts, and
       that they understand how to deal with them.

Conclusions

There are many potential safety and economic benefits to be realized by automating cockpit functions, but the rapid pace of automation is outstripping one's
ability to comprehend all the implications for crew performance. It is unrealistic
to call for a halt to cockpit automation before the manifestations are completely
understood. We do, however, call for those designing, analysing, and installing
automatic systems in the cockpit to do so carefully; to recognise the behavioural
impact of automation; to avail themselves of present and future guidelines; and
to be watchful for symptoms that might appear in training and operational
settings. The ergonomic nature of these problems suggests that other sectors of

aviation and, indeed other industries, are or will be facing the same problems: no one is immune.

References

1. Boulanger, A., and Dai, H. N. (1975) 'New automatic systems on board aircraft'. *Proceedings of the Technical Conference*, International Air Transport Association, Istanbul, November.
2. Cooper, G. E. (1977) 'A survey of the status and philosophies relating to cockpit warning systems'. NASA Contract Report 152071, Ames Research Center, Moffett Field, Calif., June.
3. Covey, R. R., Mascetti, G. J., Roessler, W. U., and Bowles, R. (1979) 'Operational energy conservation strategies'. IEEE Conference on Decision and Control, Ft. Lauderdale, December.
4. Curry, R. E. (1979) 'Human factors of descent energy management'. IEEE Conference on Decision and Control, Ft. Lauderdale, December.
5. Danaher, J. W. (1980) 'Human error in ATC system operation'. *Human Factors*.
6. Edwards, E. (1976) 'Some aspects of automation in civil transport aircraft'. In *Monitoring Behavior and Supervisory Control* (edited by T. B. Sheridan and G. Johannsen) (New York: Plenum).
7. Edwards, E. (1977) 'Automation in civil transport aircraft'. *Applied Ergonomics*, 8, 194–198.
8. Edwards, E., and Lees, F. P. (eds.) (1974) *The Human Operator in Process Control* (New York: Halsted).
9. Feazel, M. (1980) 'Fuel pivotal in trunks' earnings slump'. *Aviation Week and Space Technology*, Feb. 18, 31–32.
10. Johannsen, G. (1976) 'Preview of man-vehicle control session'. In *Monitoring Behavior and Supervisory Control* (edited by T. B. Sheridan and G. Johannsen) (New York: Plenum).
11. de Jong, J. J., and Koster, E. P. (1974) 'The human operator in the computer-controlled refinery'. In *The Human Operator in Process Control* (edited by E. Edwards and F. R. Lees) (New York: Halsted).
12. Lovesey, E. J. (1977) 'The instrument explosion – a study of aircraft cockpit instruments'. *Applied Ergonomics*, 8, 23–30.
13. McLucus, J. L. (1978) 'Next generation of aircraft and their operating environment'. *Airline Pilot*, June, 6–9.
14. Naish, J. M., and Von Wieser, M. F. (1969) 'Human factors in the all-weather approach'. *Shell Aviation News*, 374, 2–11.
15. National Transportation Safety Board (1973) *Eastern Airlines L-1011, Miami, Fla., Dec. 29, 1972*. Report No. NTSB-AAR-73-14, Washington, June 14.
16. National Transportation Safety Board (1977) *Texas International Airlines DC-9-14, Denver, Colo., Nov. 16, 1976*. Report No. NTSB-AAR-77-10, Washington, October 27.

17. National Transportation Safety Board (1979) *Swift Aire Lines Nord 262, Marina del Rey, Calif., March 10, 1979.* Report No. NTSB-AAR-79-13, Washington, August 16.

18. National Transportation Safety Board (1979) *Allegheny Airlines, Inc. BAC 1-11, Rochester, New York, July 9, 1978.* Report No. NTSB-AAR-79-2, Washington, February 8.

19. O'Lone, R. G. (1980) '757, 767 offer two-man cockpits'. *Aviation Week and Space Technology*, March 24, 23—25.

20. Potter, R. (1980) 'European routes key for Western'. *San Jose (Calif.) Mercury*, January 10.

21. Randle, R. J., Larsen, W. E. and Williams, D. H. (1980) 'Some human factors issues in the development and evaluation of cockpit warning systems'. NASA Reference Publication 1055, Ames Research Center, Moffett Field, Calif., January.

22. Rolfe, J. M. (1972) 'Ergonomics and air safety'. *Applied Ergonomics*, 3, 75—81.

23. Ropelewski, R. R. (1979) 'L-1011 cockpit automation cuts crew workload'. *Aviation Week and Space Technology*, June 18, 46—47, 53.

24. Ruffell Smith, H. P. (1968) 'Some human factors of aircraft accidents during collision with high ground'. *Journal of the Institute of Navigation*, 21, 1—10.

25. St. John, O. B. (1968) 'All-weather landing'. *Shell Aviation News*, 364, 2—11.

26. Shackel, B. (1967) 'Ergonomics research needs in automation'. *Ergonomics*, 10, 627—632.

27. Sheridan, T. B. and Johannsen, G. (eds.) (1976) *Monitoring and Supervisory Control* (New York: Plenum).

28. Sinaiko, H. M. (1972) 'Human intervention and full automation in control systems'. *Applied Ergonomics*, 3, 3—7.

29. Wiener, E. L. (1962) 'Knowledge of results in a monitoring task'. Wright-Patterson Air Force Base, Ohio: Wright Air Development Division Technical Documentary Report No. AMRL-TDR-62-82, August.

Acknowledgement

This chapter was written while the first author was on leave from the University of Miami, in residence at the Man-Vehicle Systems Research Division, Ames Research Center, NASA. The authors gratefully acknowledge the assistance of many of the staff of that division, and many others at Ames Research Center. This chapter was first published by NASA and subsequently appeared in *Ergonomics*, 1980, Vol. 23, No. 10.

Chapter 5

Controlled Flight into Terrain Accidents: System-Induced Errors *E. L. Wiener*

It is argued then, that in the pursuit of safety an absolute reliance on automated systems may be as fraught with pitfalls as an absolute trust in human capacity. This chapter looks at some of the conflict areas of this interface, taking as a frame the recurrent phenomenon in which aircraft fully under control have flown into terrain or water, with no prior awareness on the part of the crew of the impending disaster.

The author examines such accidents, seeing them as the result of errors generated by a complex air traffic control system with ample opportunities for system-induced errors. Problems such as pilot-controller communication, flight-deck workload, noise-abatement procedures, government regulations, visual illusions and cockpit and ground-radar warning devices are discussed and here again, examples of related accidents are cited. There is room, it is clear, for the human factors profession to play a more significant role, not only in the resolution of such specific problems but in addition, of those of the whole air traffic complex.

There is an old aviation story, which may indeed be apocryphal, that in the years of the expanding Army Air Forces prior to World War II, General Arnold, concerned about the high rate of aircraft accidents, appointed a committee to study the problem. As the story goes, in the interest of impartiality, he chose a cavalry officer to head the group. At the end of the study, the committee reported back that the primary cause of military aviation accidents was the aircraft striking the ground. Today the joke is somewhat dated, and it may not have been funny even when it was current.

But now there is an ironic twist to the story: US commercial aviation, for all its incredible safety record, has undergone a rash of accidents of the form of airliners being literally flown into the ground. Two spectacular accidents, Eastern 401, an L1011 which left its assigned altitude of 2000 ft (approx. 610 m) and slowly descended into the Everglades west of Miami,[14] and Eastern 212, a DC9 which crashed 5.3 km short of the runway at Charlotte,[20] sparked considerable controversy, loss of public confidence in commercial flying, and criticism of the FAA. On 1 December 1974, TWA 514, a B727 inbound to Dulles, struck a mountain, after prematurely descending below a safe en route altitude, due to ambiguities in the pilot—controller communication terminology and navigational charts.[21] This accident was a crowning blow, perhaps one of those critical events like the Grand Canyon collision (TWA and United), which will someday be looked upon as a turning point in air traffic control. Cynics may say that this accident was critical because it occurred so close to Washington—there may be indeed some merit in that. But it also came right on the heels of the Charlotte crash, and coincidentally at a time that the FAA was reeling from criticism for its alleged mishandling of the DC10 cargo door defect, which resulted in the Turkish airline crash near Paris in March 1974. Finally, it should be said that the public, the politicians who represent them, and editorial writers found it inconceivable that air regulations and terminology were so vague that pilots and controllers could disagree on their meaning.[2] Bickering between the Airline Pilots Association (ALPA) and the Professional Air Traffic Controllers Association (PATCO) did not help. It is difficult to express the confusion and bitterness wrought by TWA 514.[23] Witness the fact that the public hearing, which usually lasts about three days, dragged on for four weeks.

TWA 514, and other CFIT accidents, can be regarded as failures of information processing. That is essentially the viewpoint of this chapter: to expose CFIT crashes as 'system-induced' errors, most of which might have been prevented by judicious consideration of human factors. The human factors profession has long recognised the concept of 'design-induced' errors. This chapter simply extends the concept to a large-scale system, whose principal components are vehicles, traffic control, and terminals. These three components are embedded in two other components: regulations and weather.

The concept of a system-induced CFIT accident can probably best be understood by looking at an example, the crash of Delta 723, a DC9, just short of the runway threshold in Boston in 1973.[15] The NTSB summary reads, in part:

The NTSB determines that the probable cause of the accident was failure of the flightcrew to monitor altitude and to recognize passage of the aircraft through the approach decision height during an unstabilized precision approach conducted in rapidly changing meteorological conditions. The unstabilized nature of the approach was due initially to the aircraft's passing the outer marker above the glide slope at an excessive airspeed and thereafter compounded the flightcrew's preoccupation with the questionable information presented by the flight director system. The poor positioning of the flight for the approach was in part the result of nonstandard air control services.

What the summary does not explain is that the reason for the non-standard clearance which rushed the flight crew beyond their capacity, and that of the plane, to enter a stabilised approach, was that the controller himself was rushed by a possible conflict of two other planes. Thus, the limitations of the man—machine system, on the ground and in the air, combined to produce this accident.

CFIT Accidents

With official concern growing, a new term was born in 1974: 'controlled flight into terrain'. The accidents were not new, only the terminology. A strict definition is not possible, but the notion behind the term is an aircraft, in normal flight regime, with no emergencies and no warning to the crew of any impending trouble, impacting the terrain (or water) at some place other than the runway. This would include a variety of very different situations: a plane close to touchdown hitting short (classically known as a 'landing short' accident) as in the case of PAA 806 (B707) at Pago Pago,[18] and Delta 723 at Boston; aircraft descending into the terrain a considerable distance from the runway, for example EAL 212; the rather bizarre case of EAL 401 which was not supposed to be descending at all; or TWA 514 which flew into a mountain 37 km from Dulles airport. The definition could include climbing aircraft, though this is unusual (see Sierra Pacific 802).[19] An exclusionary example would be the air disaster involving EAL 66, a B727 that crashed into the approach lights on JFK airport on 24 June 1975. The accident was blamed primarily on encounter with severe weather on final approach, and thus the aircraft was not in 'controlled flight'.[22]

Vigilance problems

When the author wrote his dissertation on human vigilance,[28] he quoted two reports (then CAB) of accidents occurring on the same day in 1959 which appeared to be clear cases of failure of flight crew to maintain watchfulness. In what could today be called a CFIT accident, an American Airlines Electra hit the water in normal descent configuration, on localiser, over a mile short of the runway at La Guardia, the first of the string of Electra crashes. Just a few hours prior, a PAA B707 had suffered an autopilot disengage over the Atlantic, and had slowly entered a spiralling descent without any intervention by the crew, ultimately losing 9140 m before its recovery just 1830 m over the ocean.

Since then, an alarming number of the CFITs have resembled these accidents and have caused the author, and perhaps many others, to reflect on years of study of human vigilance. Here the distinction is made, perhaps somewhat arbitrarily, between the typical 'landing short' accident in which the plane descends too low and hits short of the runway, perhaps a kilometre or two, and those accidents in which the aircraft strikes terrain a considerable distance from the airport.

But it would appear that the close-in landing short accident, as in the case of PAA 806 (1.2 km short) and DAL 723 (.9 km short) is operationally a different type of accident from EAL 212, which hit 5.3 km short. Perhaps all can be laid to crew inattention, but the first two were, during most of the approach, at least 'in the ball park', though not conforming with the standards for a stabilised approach. In EAL 212, the approach was never correct—there was a string of navigational errors, and incorrect altitudes, and what would appear to be total disregard for the progress of flight (ALPA takes exception to this). Surviving passengers report seeing trees and terrain before the crash. Actions by the pilot indicate no such sighting until literally the last second.

Even more interesting from the point of human vigilance was EAL 401. To remind readers very briefly, the L1011 began an eastward approach to Miami, the crew discovered an unsafe nose-gear indication (no light), abandoned the approach, and were cleared westbound over the Everglades at 2000 ft (approximately 610 m) while they sought to diagnose the trouble. The flight engineer and a deadheading mechanic went into the 'hell-hole' below the cockpit to (visually) inspect the gear, while the Captain and First Officer began to disassemble the warning light appliance to change the bulb. The aircraft began a slow descending turn. The two crew members in the cockpit had full instrumentation, as well as extra-cockpit cues (which can be highly deceptive at night, but certainly better than nothing), and yet completely neglected the progress of flight while preoccupied with the bulb holder. To be discussed shortly is the fact that although the premature descent was noted on radar, human communication problems and government regulations foreclosed proper intervention; again, a system-induced problem.

Several of these accidents will now be examined from the point of view of system failure, and possible remedies, including such familiar human engineering concepts as workplace design, crew workload, pilot—controller communications, reliance on automatic warning devices, and visual illusions.

System Failure

Pilot—controller communication

It hardly seems necessary to caution against the folly of a component approach to design and analysis. The main point of this chapter is that CFITs are not caused by single agents but are system generated. Perhaps this point can best be appreciated in examining communication between pilots and controllers.

Subtle changes have occurred in pilot—controller relationships in the last decade, which, this author holds, have resulted in system degradation. First, controllers, whose ranks previously were filled with World War II and Korean War pilots and military controllers, are now younger and less cockpit-oriented and have grown up in a less authoritarian age. Many were recruited 'off-the-streets' (controllers' term, not author's). Next, there is a rising militancy of ATC personnel and the creation of PATCO, with resulting labour disturbances.* And, finally, there is plain economic jealousy, a controller earning about one-third to one-fourth that of an airline captain, and for no less, perhaps more, responsibility and skill. Add to this one more dangerous element, the typical pilot's self-concept of a 'rugged individualist', whose antagonism toward any agency or person telling him what to do exceeds even that of Texas oilmen and doctors of medicine. (For the unalloyed pilots' view of controllers, see Ashworth, et al.[4]) More will be said of this when noise-abatement procedures are discussed. All of these factors have combined to strip the pilot—controller relationship of some of the camaraderie which once typified the aviation industry, and to create mutual distrust which cannot help but take its toll in system effectiveness. If anyone doubts this, let him spend some time in the cockpit and the ATC centres. One phrase the author hears over and over in both locations is 'those guys [controllers,

---

* A major strike of PATCO members resulting in dismissals and widespread disruption began in August 1981. See also chapter 10.

if pilot speaking, and vice versa] just don't understand the limitations of our equipment'. Notice that the speaker perceives the limiting factor as the equipment, not the humans.

The human communication problem could nowhere better be seen than in the exchange between pilot and controller in the case of EAL 401. The aircraft began its slow descent from the assigned altitude of 2000 ft (approximately 610 m). At 275 m the altitude was noted by the controller on his ARTS-3 radar (an advanced radar display which decodes the aircraft's transponder-altitude device and shows a computer-generated altitude readout along with other information on the 'tag' accompanying the blip). The following conversation ensued:

Miami approach
Controller: Eastern 401, how are things comin' along out there?
Pilot: Okay, we'd like to turn around and come back in.

Thirty-eight seconds later the plane crashed. Why did the controller say nothing about altitude? First, consider government regulation: the ARTS-3 manual states that the altitude portion of the tag is for the controller's use in traffic separation only, and the controller bears no responsibility for the aircraft maintaining altitude. One can feel the heavy presence of the legal profession at this point—a group not to be ignored in consideration of the 'total system'. Even so, with 175 humans and a 20-million-dollar aircraft at stake, what did the controller have to lose by speaking up and pointing out the altitude deviation to the pilot? Probably the answer lies in the social psychology of role relationship between pilot and controller. Past experience doubtlessly had taught the lower-status, certainly lower-paid, controller that he could well have expected to have his 'wrist slapped' (or more correctly, a sarcastic comment) had he mentioned the altitude to the pilot. This is analogous to a nurse who observes an obvious error on the part of a physician and wonders if he or she dare speak out. Incidentally, exactly the same problem exists between pilots and co-pilots, perhaps more in military than civilian aviation. How could the controller have handled this conflict? Perhaps by harking to the great American tradition of blaming things on machines and thereby blunting the edge of criticism. He might have prevented a tragedy and covered himself by saying: 'Eastern 401, Miami Approach Control, our ARTS-3 indicates that you have left assigned altitude 2000 [approximately 610 m] and are descending.'

This conversation points out that social—professional status and interrelationships are a vital, though elusive, portion of the man—machine ensemble, and system scientists must deal with these difficult problems. Obviously some way must be found to design into the system the freedom for lower-status operatives to point out the errors of those who enjoy higher status. Perhaps the growing militancy of those who are not at the top of the stack, in a variety of professions and industries, will produce some safety dividends.

And if militancy is not enough, the legal profession may also rear its head on behalf of the controllers. After each accident, the regulations grow in magnitude and complexity, though not necessarily in clarity. It is only reasonable that PATCO will turn to their lawyers for relief of liability or punitive action from the government. It should not surprise one to someday hear the following controller-to-pilot transmission: 'National Four-One Heavy, Albuquerque Centre: on advice of counsel, unable to approve flight level three-niner-zero.'

Before leaving this topic, two points should be mentioned. First, less than two years after EAL 401, similar issues arose in the investigation of the EAL 212 crash in Charlotte. Two ARTS-3 controllers testified that they did not observe the altitude tag near the end of the flight. Second, in the wake of TWA 514, the FAA amended its ARTS-3 procedures to state that (this language is not exact) the controller should point out altitude deviations to pilots, if it is convenient.[25]

Again, there are two issues here that should interest the system sciences:

(a)   Does the workload of the ARTS-3 controller allow him to monitor aircraft altitude for other than separation purposes?

(b)   To what extent does the fear of civil liability degrade system safety rather than help it?

Noise-abatement approaches

The problems of aircraft engine noise near airports may bear upon CFIT accidents in the future, and thus community planning and government regulation become factors in the system generation of errors. While no accident to date can be blamed on noise-abatement procedures (their role in the non-fatal accident of TWA 701 at Los Angeles [LAX] is contentious[16]) pilots argue that any deviation from optimum use of the vehicle and terminal is a compromise with air safety. It is hard to dispute this argument, but, on the other hand, one must be mindful that it is very easy for any special interest group to be contemptuous of its own environmental impact and to invoke safety as a reason why the impact should be ignored. The pilots' viewpoint, that they are being forced to pick up the tab for poor community planning, is quite valid, as far as it goes. Noise abatement enters the CFIT picture in a variety of ways: by preferential runways, which may bypass precision for non-precision navaids, or even downwind landings, as at LAX after the magic hour of 23.00.

But quite another problem is the proposed two-segment approach[8] which would require a rapid descent of aircraft (about 427 m/min) on an approximately 6° slope before intercepting the normal 3° glide slope at a point about 245 m above ground, less than 5 km from touchdown. This system is still under evaluation, but pilot reaction has been understandably negative. The author is not prepared to take sides in this controversy but only points out that a brand new type of CFIT accident may have been born: failure to transition from the steep to the normal glide slope, resulting in impact about 2.4 km from the runway. This is just what is not needed: a new form of system-induced error. Nobody can say that the two-segment approach will not work, or even that it is highly hazardous, but the thought of dramatic pitch and power adjustments close to the ground, at a point of maximum flight-deck workload and fatigue, is discomforting.

Cockpit workload

The subject now turns to cockpit design, which was once the heartland of human factors engineering, and its close cousins, workload and crew coordination. Even while recognising that accidents have multiple causation, and are system-induced, it is an unavoidable conclusion that most of the accidents are traceable to crew/cockpit problems. This chapter avoids the term 'pilot error', that judgemental relic of World War II that ignores antecedent conditions, as well as the very concept of design-induced errors.[10,27] Yet the NTSB accident summaries reveal a preponderance of phrases such as 'lack of vigilance', 'neglect of flight instruments', 'failure to monitor altitude', 'deliberate descent below flight minimums', 'pilot did not recognise need to correct for excessive descent rate', 'failure to exercise positive flight management', and many more.

One can begin by assuming that the flight crews were properly trained and qualified and did not wish to die. Although recognising the concept of sub-intentioned suicide, it seems far-fetched to advance this as an explanation of seemingly unexplainable accidents, especially in crew-served aircraft. Suffice it to say that if one pilot were entertaining an intentioned or sub-intentioned self-destruction, the remaining members of the crew would take a dim view of his actions.*

The question is what can the system sciences do to prevent future occurrences? Consider first cockpit workload. Here the author can easily take either of two contradictory viewpoints: that flying has become too easy, and that flying has become too hard. The first is the result of improved cockpit instrumentation, navigational devices, automatic flight control systems, and communications. With respect to cockpit hardware, there is little doubt that flying has become much easier in recent years. On a recent trip in a B747, the author entered the cockpit about an hour before take-off and encountered the First Officer toggling the coordinates of waypoints into the inertial navigation system (INS). (The fact that this is a poor way of entering standard data into a storage device could be the subject of another chapter.) The INS, linked to the plane's autopilot, could direct the aircraft from take-off to final approach (MIA to JFK) with minimal human intervention and could supply information such as instantaneous read-out of groundspeed, drift angle, time and distance to any waypoint or destination, merely by the flick of a switch. Coupled with an automatic ILS final approach, the INS would allow the flight to be virtually pre-programmed, from take-off to flare-out. This represents an incredible reduction in cockpit workload, but in the world of system sciences one should be aware that there is always a price tag. The author cannot back this up with hard data, but after fifteen years of studying human vigilance and operator *under*load, is convinced that over-

---

* See Japan Air Lines episode, chapter 10.

automation of control functions can be deleterious to safe human performance. Over-reliance on automatic devices, and underloading of the operator may lead to complacency and errors during those critical times when human judgement and intervention are required.[25] To a profession (flying and human factors) accustomed to dealing with operator overload, this is a radically different form of system-induced error, and one that may be exceedingly difficult to cope with. Increasingly, it will be necessary to become concerned with boredom, inattentiveness, lack of vigilance—call it what you will—as systems become more 'automatic'. The burning question of the near future will not be how much work a man can do safely, but how little.

Taking the opposite side for a moment, one can make a good case that at the same time that highly sophisticated labour-reducing equipment was added to the cockpit, flying became more complicated, for a variety of system-induced reasons. First, the amount and complexity of government and company regulations increases every year. The old aphorism that one 'has to be a lawyer' to fly may be a slight exaggeration, but it captures the spirit of a growing problem. Air traffic control procedures, noise-abatement rules, local airport regulations, required cockpit procedures, company paperwork, and even the fear of in-flight criminal attack, coupled with economic pressures and fuel-conservation measures, have all combined to make much of the cockpit workload look less like flying than a cat-and-mouse game between flight crew and the rest of the system.[23] Certain requirements can be directly traced to particular air disasters. For example, the speed limit of 250 knots below 10 000 ft (approximately 3050 m) was the result of the TWA-UAL Staten Island collision. This, in turn, generated procedures such as an 11 000 ft (approximately 3350 m) anticipatory altitude call-out during descent. More regulations and more cockpit workload may generate more or less opportunity for system-induced errors; it is hard to say. But the message is clear—it is high time to take a fresh look at the problem of cockpit workload, procedures, and fatigue. Incidentally, the same question, too hard or too easy, applies *mutatis mutandis* to the work of the air traffic controller, with the arrival of dazzling new equipment and its inevitable travelling companion, endless regulations. The growth of federal regulations in general may be seen from the following figures. In 1936, the *Federal Register*, which publishes the regulations, contained 2411 pages. By 1970 it was 20 000 pages, and five years later, over 60 000 pages! *

Crew coordination

Closely related to the cockpit workload problem is that of crew coordination. This covers some very controversial areas, including the sharing of duties, the command responsibility of the Captain when the First Officer is flying, and the touchy issue of the responsibility of the First Officer when he observes the Captain deviating from safe or legal practices, as, for example, in Delta 516, a

* By the 1980s cynics stopped counting pages and merely quoted the weight of the volume (Editors).

DC9 that crashed in Chattanooga.[17] The traditional approach to those problems has been training, standardisation, regulation, and procedure writing. But somehow these have not done the job. The cockpit voice recorder (CVR), an invaluable accident investigation tool, has revealed disturbing casualness in the cockpit, the most extreme case known to the author being the EAL 212 crash at Charlotte[20] (NTSB rpt, 20 & App. E). ALPA does not agree.[6] CFIT accidents have spawned a series of proposals which were rather stringent, compared to past methods of dealing with crew coordination. These included confidential peer reporting among pilots and the use of CVR tapes and flight data recorders (FDR) after non-accident flights as measures of crew performance, proposals understandably greeted with vociferous denunciation by the flightdeck unions. Whether these measures might prove to be effective quality control measures is still difficult to say.

But let no one, pilot, passenger, or scientist, mistake one fact: if public fear and outrage over CFIT accidents (especially those that *appear* to result from cockpit neglect) continues, the government will take increasingly harsh measures. The concept of system-induced errors is too complex, or too subtle, for a frightened public, or its elected representatives, to comprehend. The day of a pilot as absolute monarch of the flight deck may be drawing to a close, and in fairness it should be added, for better or worse.

Warning devices: cockpit

An appealing, though perhaps somewhat simplistic, answer to vigilance and attention problems is to install warning devices which are assumed to be attention-demanding. One must recognise these from the outset for what they are: one form of sensory stimulation replacing or amplifying another, and the extent to which they are useful is determined primarily by their novelty. There is never a guarantee that any stimulus, regardless of its psychophysical dimensions, will be correctly attended to, 'correctly' because one of the usual ways of dealing with warning devices, particularly in the auditory mode, is to shut them off. Ground proximity warning systems (GPWS)[9] in the cockpit may be well intentioned, and may indeed prevent some CFIT accidents, but human factors specialists would do well to regard them with a measure of scepticism. Altitude warning systems are not new—in fact, in the EAL 401 accident, the warning chime, signalling a 76 m deviation from altitude, could clearly be heard on the CVR recording, yet it did nothing to alert a crew preoccupied with other duties. Part of the problem, with respect to novelty, is that there may be too many warning signals already. Consider the following testimony from the public hearing on EAL 212:

Q (Board): Is the usefulness of the altitude warning system degraded by too frequent appearance?
A (surviving First Officer): Yes.
Q: Also for terrain warning?
A: Yes.

(The quotations of the testimony of the surviving co-pilot of EAL 212 are from the notes of the author who attended the public hearing, not from an official transcript.)

Note that in this aircraft (DC9) an altitude alerting light comes on 228 m above (in descent) a target altitude and stays on until 76 m above when a beeper comes on, and at 30 m (above ground level) a light reading 'ALT' and beeper appear. Human factors specialists who belittle 'knobs and dials' should study this accident. The testimony of the surviving pilot is replete with examples of confusion in reading and interpreting the various altimeters.

In December 1975, the FAA held hearings in Atlanta to consider the revocation of the licence of James Daniels, the surviving co-pilot of EAL 212. As his primary line of defence, Mr Daniels blamed the design of the drum and pointer altimeter, which he claimed was easy to misread by 1000 feet (305 m).[5] This is substantially the view point of ALPA which denied that the flight was conducted in an unprofessional manner, and petitioned the NTSB to either modify the probable cause or reopen the investigation (letter from J. J. O'Donnell, President of ALPA, to NTSB, 21 May 1976). The following statement from the petition should interest the reader: '. . .we reiterate our concern that the human factors associated with this and many other accidents represent an important subject which has been ignored in the past by the NTSB. If we continue to overlook this subject area, we most assuredly are exposed to a repetition of tragedies such as this.'

Warning devices: radar

Following the EAL 401, EAL 212, and TWA 514 accidents, the altitude monitoring responsibility of ARTS-3 controllers was reconsidered by FAA. A new device was proposed which is essentially a reverse of the cockpit GPWS. Radar coverage is divided into 3.2 km squares, and data on the minimum safe altitude for each square are stored in the computer which drives the ARTS-3. If any aircraft is below an allowable tolerance, the tag will blink, and a horn will sound. Also, the future path of the aircraft for 30 seconds will be predicted, with similar warnings. This may be quite helpful in assisting the ATC controllers in their increasing responsibility for altitude monitoring. It is speculative whether it could have prevented any known CFITs, other than perhaps TWA 514. Controllers interviewed by the author were extremely sceptical and felt that there would be excessive false warnings.[24] It is noteworthy that when the crash of DAL 723 damaged approach lights, setting off alarms in Logan Tower, they were ignored by the tower operators, due to a history of frequent false alarms.

Visual illusions*

Much has been written about visual illusions in flight, especially on final approach where pilots judge their position by a stored model of what the runway trapezoid

---

* See Stanley Roscoe on the psychology of vision, chapter 8.

or approach lights should look like. This image is subject to perceptual distortions by environmental factors such as darkness, rain, or haze, or by context such as surrounding terrain, snow on the ground, or the approach and runway configurations.[7,12,13] The terminals, including the contextual features mentioned above, may contribute to system-induced errors. For example, controversy has surrounded the visual approach slope indicator (VASI), which visually provides the pilot with vertical guidance during final approach. The VASI is useful in two very different applications:

(a)   during transition from the ILS to extra-cockpit indications in the final segment of a precision approach, a likely spot for close-in CFIT accidents (see Delta 516 and PAA 806); or

(b)   as the primary source of vertical position information on non-precision instrument approaches, or at airports which have no instrument approaches at all.

Following the Iberian Airlines DC10 accident, and again after DAL 516, the NTSB recommended to FAA that VASIs be installed on precision runways to avoid the hazardous final phase. The FAA's reply was that their intent was to devote their limited VASI funds to non-precision runways (see letter appended to NTSB report on DAL 516). This is an allocation problem in operations research terms: whether to invest heavily in partially redundant devices for the most frequently used runways, or install apparatus on poorly equipped, less used runways.

It is also arguable as to whether conversion from ILS to VASI is a desirable flying technique on precision approaches—there is a full range of pilot opinion on the question. But the point is that if cockpit instrumentation is insufficient, neglected, or ignored to the preference of extra-cockpit visual reference during the final phases of approach, another opportunity for system-induced error is created. The development of Category III approaches in which the plane is electronically guided all the way down to flare may relieve this problem, but caution is recommended for anyone advancing this argument. First, for years Category III approaches will be limited to a few, high-density airports. If VASIs, which are relatively inexpensive and require negligible maintenance, pose a resource allocation problem, one can hardly imagine many airports, or more than one runway at those airports, being equipped with the electronics necessary for Category III. And second, one should have learned by now that problems cannot be 'electronised' away. Expensive equipment usually trades one type of human factors problem for another, and visual illusions in flight will be a problem as long as there is visual image processing.

Confusing terminology and charts

What better way to produce a system-induced error than to have terminology and printed information that is ambiguous, even to highly qualified professionals?

Again, the author sees this problem less as one of government regulation than of human engineering. The Air Force once lost a C124 on a missed approach because of two opposite interpretations of the command 'take off power' (remove the power versus increase power to take-off level). The investigation of TWA 514 reveals that the same confusion in terminology that led to its crash had been encountered and reported previously. It seems incredible that pilots and controllers could have differing interpretations about the term 'cleared for an approach', in particular whether it meant the plane could immediately descend to certain minimum altitudes. And it was surprising to many that controllers and pilots could have different information on their charts. But what is equally incredible to this author is that the human factors profession has not been enlisted to bring its special expertise in human information processing to bear on this problem. The NTSB report on TWA 514 is a textbook on system-induced errors.

Conclusion

An unwieldy system of vehicles, traffic control, and terminals has emerged as a result of piecemeal design, and this system will continue to generate CFIT accidents. Ideally, it would be a good thing to tear the system down and rebuild it *de novo*, but that is not the way problems are remedied in a democratic society. If it were, one could lay out the welcome mat for an endless number of systems to be torn down and rebuilt. So ATC must be improved the same way it was created, by patchwork. Throughout the system one finds a crying need for help, even in patchwork, from human factors specialists. The human factors profession was born precisely because even simpler aviation systems had grown too complex for the men operating them, but has had its inevitable difficulties in becoming fully accepted. In fairness to all segments of the industry, the problem of airline disasters must be kept in perspective. Flying by US scheduled commercial carriers is now, and remains, one of the safest ways of getting from one place to another.

The purpose of this chapter is not to assess blame for CFITs—there is enough blame to go around. Consider ALPA, which is constitutionally unwilling to accept the notion that airline pilots can cause accidents.[26] Then consider the FAA, which is mired in politics, sluggish, and seemingly unable to make changes and recognise hazardous conditions until accidents and their resultant political pressures impel them; and the National Transportation Safety Board, whose so-called human factors sections of accident investigations are medically oriented, rather bland accounts of accident survivability and physical conditions of the crew, with little or no recognition of the man-machine or information-processing aspects of human factors that may have prevented the accidents. Clearly, the meaning that NTSB attaches to the term 'human factors' has little to do with the activities and expertise of the society by the same name and, while it is NTSB's turn to get the gaff, they might take a close look at the information exchange problems in their public hearings. This author was shocked at the poor quality of the EAL 212 hearing, and even the *Charlotte Observer* commented editorially on its conduct.[2] And finally, the human factors profession could profit from some self-examination for its patronising attitude toward the very kind of practical problems that brought the profession into existence in the first place, an attitude exemplified by the disparaging term 'knobs and dials', which seems to convey the belief that consideration of workplace design, workload, and instrumentation is somehow beneath its latter-day dignity.

Acknowledgements

The author is indebted to the many persons interviewed in preparation of this chapter, pilots and flight engineers, FAA controllers, and others in the aviation industry and in government. Thanks are due also to the University of North Carolina at Chapel Hill and the University of Southern California where the author wrote the original form of this chapter during his sabbatical leave.

This chapter is from *Human Factors*, 1977, Vol. 19, pp. 171–81. Copyright 1977 by the Human Factors Society Inc., and reproduced by permission.

References

1. Anonymous (1974) 'Crash questions not asked, not answered'. Editorial in *Charlotte Observer*, 18 November.
2. Anonymous (1975) 'When airliners meet mountains'. Editorial in *Los Angeles Times*, 6 February.
3. Anonymous (1975) 'Pilots shun new FAA reporting program'. *Aviation Week and Space Technology*, 16 June, **102**, 73.
4. Ashworth, A., Bassett, C. E., Buck, R. N., McBain, D., Moran, W. P. and Soderlind, P. (1975) *Special Air Safety Advisory Group (SASAG) Report to FAA* 30 July. Published by FAA, no document number or publication place. Reprinted in two instalments in *Air Line Pilot*, April 1976, 23–30 and May 1976, 13–19, 38–40.
5. Cowan, A. (1975) 'EAL pilot misread altimeter'. *Charlotte Observer*, 4 December.
6. Cowan, A. (1976) 'Findings in Charlotte crash disputed by pilots' group'. *Charlotte Observer*, 22 May.
7. DeCelles, J. L., Burke, E. J. and O'Brien, J. E. (1975) 'Warning–approach lights in sight', *Air Line Pilot*, February, **44**, 28–38.
8. Geiger, W. J. (1974) 'The two-segment approach'. *Flight*, September, **63**, 24–25, 88.
9. Geiger, W. J. (1975) 'An operational look at GPWS'. *Flight*, March, **64**, 23–25, 55.
10. Gilstrap, R. W. (1975) 'Equal dignity for humans'. *Air Line Pilot*, July, **44**, 12–13.
11. Hotz, R. (1975) 'Spotlight on safety'. Editorial in *Aviation Week and Space Technology*, 13 January, **102**, 9.

12.   Kraft, C. L. and Elworth, C. L. (1968) 'How high is up?' *Interceptor*, October, 1–12. Ent. AFB, Colorado: USAF Aerospace Defense Command.

13.   Kraft, C. L. and Elworth, C. L. (1969) 'Flight deck work load and night visual approach performance'. Renton, Washington: Boeing Company Document No. D6-22996.

14.   National Transportation Safety Board (1973) *Eastern Airlines L1011, Miami, Fla., Dec. 29, 1972*. Report No. NTSB-AAR-73-14, Washington, 14 June (Flight 401).

15.   National Transportation Safety Board (1974) *Delta Air Lines DC9-31, Boston, Mass., July 31, 1973*. Report No. NTSB-AAR-74-3, Washington, 7 March (Flight 723).

16.   National Transportation Safety Board (1974) *Trans World Airways Boeing 707-131B, Los Angeles, January 16, 1974*. Report No. NTSB-AAR-74-10, Washington, 14 August (Flight 701).

17.   National Transportation Safety Board (1974) *Delta Air Lines DC9-32, Chattanooga, Tenn., Nov. 27, 1973*. Report No. NTSB-AAR-74-13, Washington, 8 November (Flight 516).

18.   National Transportation Safety Board (1974) *Pan American World Airways Boeing 707-321B, Pago Pago, American Samoa, Jan. 30, 1974*. Report No. NTSB-AAR-74-15, Washington, 8 November (Flight 806).

19.   National Transportation Safety Board (1975) *Sierra Pacific Airlines Convair 340/440, near Bishop, Cal., March 13, 1974*. Report No. NTSB-AAR-75-1, Washington, 10 January (Flight 802).

20.   National Transportation Safety Board (1975) *Eastern Air Lines Douglas DC9-31, Charlotte, N.C., September 11, 1974*. Report No. NTSB-AAR-75-9, Washington, 23 May (Flight 212).

21.   National Transportation Safety Board (1975) *Trans World Airlines Boeing 727-231, Berryville, Virginia, December 1, 1974*. Report No. NTSB-AAR-75-16, Washington, 26 November (Flight 514).

22.   National Transportation Safety Board (1976) *Eastern Airlines Boeing 727-225, Kennedy International Airport, June 24, 1975*. Report No. NTSB-AAR-76-8, Washington, 12 March (Flight 66).

23.   O'Donnell, J. J. (1975) 'Seek the "why?" of aircraft accidents'. *Air Line Pilot*, April, **44**, 6–9, 43.

24.   Schneider, C. E. (1975) 'Controller functions due more scrutiny'. *Aviation Week and Space Technology*, 14 April, **102**, 23–24.

25.   Schneider, C. E. (1975) 'Extensive changes set at FAA'. *Aviation Week and Space Technology*, 5 May, **102**, 23–23.

26.   Speiser, S. M. (1965) 'Airline passenger death cases'. *Trials, American Jurisprudence*, **8**.

27.   Stone, R. B. (1975) 'Pilot error and other accident enabling factors'. *Proceedings of the 19th Annual Meeting of the Human Factors Society* Dallas, October, 92–4.

28.   Wiener, E. L. (1962) 'Knowledge of results in a monitoring task'. Wright Patterson AFB, Ohio: Technical Report AMRL-TDR-62-82, August.

Chapter 6

Mid-air Collisions: The Accidents, The Systems and the Realpolitik *E. L. Wiener*

The need for that greater emphasis on human factors propounded by Earl L. Wiener is now brought into high relief in this, the first of two chapters which consider some of the deficiencies of air traffic control.

The world's worst ever mid-air collision occurred over Zagreb, Yugoslavia on 10 September 1976 resulting in the deaths of 176 people. In 1977 two jumbo jets collided on the runway at Tenerife, Canary Islands. One year later there were two further mid-air collisions, one at Memphis and, shortly afterwards, one at San Diego. These accidents have called into question the adequacy of air traffic control systems and have revealed numerous problems which may lead to human error. Following the San Diego collision in September 1978 involving an air-carrier Boeing 727 and a Cessna 172 light aircraft there was a public demand for action, and among the many proposed solutions were higher control of 'visual flight rules' aircraft and expansion of the positive control airspace. This began a political battle involving general aviation, the Federal Aviation Administration and the US Congress. These pressures are noted here, in an examination of collisions from a human factors perspective: these accidents are seen to result from an air traffic control system which emphasises airspace allocation and political compromise, rather than dealing directly with the variety of problems facing pilots and controllers operating within the National Airspace System.

Nothing excites the mind of the American public like a plane crash. If it is a collision, all the better. The press has a heyday, the authors of future books comb through the human wreckage even while the National Transportation Safety Board (NTSB) investigators are still 'kicking tin', and plaintiffs' lawyers arrive at the scene with a rapidity that suggests a power bordering on precognition.* Politicians are also fascinated. In the wake of every major airline disaster, Congress goes into high gear. Within days of the American Airlines DC10 crash in Chicago in May 1979, no less than five Congressional committees announced their intention to hold hearings on the accident, the airworthiness of the DC10, and the Federal Aviation Administration's (FAA's) inspection and certification procedures.†

Congressional concern for the 200 or so persons killed each year in US air carrier accidents may be contrasted with their attitude toward tobacco, which is

---

* Alas, one of the Editors is a lawyer.
† See also M. Strickler, chapter 2, p. 26, showing the effect of political events on safety developments.

annually responsible for 300 000 American deaths. For plane crashes Congress holds hearings; for tobacco they grant subsidies.

This chapter describes two mid-air collisions occurring in 1978, one at Memphis, one at San Diego, and further examines the air traffic control (ATC) system and procedures in operation at the time of the accidents, the human factors implications, and the political aftermath.

The statistics of mid-air collisions

As tragic and dramatic as the accidents may be, aircraft collisions are not statistically a major safety hazard for airline operations. For air carriers, the collision hazard cannot begin to compare with 'controlled flight into terrain' accidents. In the twenty-one years covered by the NTSB's 1957–77 study,[28] there were twenty-four mid-air collisions involving US air carriers (see Table 6.1). Many did not result in fatalities to the airline passengers and crews. In the ten years prior to 1978, there were twelve mid-air collisions involving US air carriers, and only six of these involved air carrier fatalities. Although general aviation aircraft are involved in far more mid-air collisions, these accidents are still a minor part of the safety problem. In 1977 there were 4286 accidents involving general aviation: only thirty-four were mid-air collisions. The accident rate for general aviation overall was 11.0 accidents per 100 000 aircraft hours, but was 0.088 for mid-air collisions.[26] They accounted for 3.5% of the Air Force's accidents in three years reported by Zeller,[41] and that includes formation collisions.

However, it should not be assumed from these data that the system is working well, but only that somehow collisions are avoided. Data on near mid-air collisions (NMACs), which will be presented later, indicate that there are more close calls than one would like to think about. Fortunately, few result in accidents.

Table 6.1   Mid-air collisions 1957–77 by segment of aviation involved (data abstracted by author from NTSB Report).[28] Table based on 528 accidents of which 286 involved fatalities.

	Aviation Segment		
	Air Carrier	General Aviation	Military
Air Carrier	2	17	5
General Aviation		465	39
Military			*

* Accidents involving only military aircraft are not investigated by NTSB.

The Accidents

Beyond Tenerife

The accident on the ground at Tenerife, Canary Islands, in March, 1977, was the nightmare come true, a collision of two heavily loaded jumbo jets (747s). The interested reader has his choice of three conflicting versions of the same accident:

(a)   the official report issued by the Spanish government, assisted in their investigation by the NTSB (Spanish Ministry of Transport, 1978);
(b)   a version by the Air Line Pilots Association (ALPA);[33]
(c)   the Dutch version, disputing much of what appeared in the official text (Dutch Aircraft Accident Inquiry Board, 1979).

A further discussion of runway incursions can be found in Billings and O'Hara.[12]

Memphis—radar is not enough

As briefly as possible, the facts of the Memphis accident follow.[27] A Falcon jet, N121GW, departed Memphis (MEM) on a training flight, instrument flight rules (IFR), remaining in the MEM traffic to practise instrument approaches. Two hours into the flight, the fatal leg began. Falcon 21GW made a go-around from Runway 17R with a clearance to climb to 2000 ft, turning right to heading 320° for the downwind leg to 17R (see Fig. 6.1). At that time, a Cessna 150, N6423K, was returning, visual flight rules (VFR), to MEM from a training flight to the west. The local control of traffic within a 5 nautical mile radius of MEM was shared by two controllers in the tower: LCI handled the quadrants east and west, LC2 the north and south quadrants. The controllers could communicate directly with each other, and they shared two BRITE radar scopes in the tower. Since it was a Terminal Radar Service Area (TRSA), radar vector service was

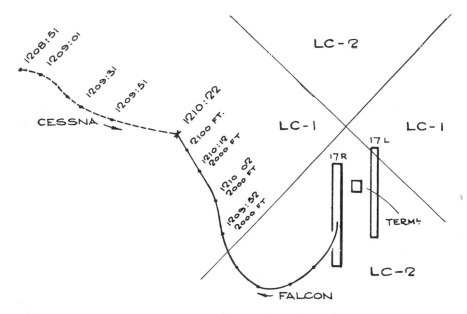

Fig. 6.1   Ground track of aircraft in Memphis collision. (Redrawn by author from NTSB report)

provided by Memphis Approach Control (APC)—controllers designated as AR2 and AR6.

Falcon 21GW was under the control of AR6 and LC2 (north–south) as it worked the pattern. After the go-around, LC2 issued the clearance, inspected his BRITE scope, and, seeing no traffic west, transferred control to AR6. By this time the Falcon was west of the field in LCI's sector. AR6 knew nothing of the in-bound Cessna. Now the crucial step: when LC2 transferred control of the Falcon to AR6, he made no effort to coordinate with LC1, he merely 'visually coordinated' by looking at the BRITE and did not see the primary return from the Cessna. AR6 assumed that all necessary coordination had taken place.

Meanwhile, AR2, which had been handling the Cessna, called LC1 and transferred its control to him. LC1 gave entry instructions and turned his attention to another aircraft in his east sector. When he accepted the Cessna, he checked the BRITE and saw no other traffic west. He testified later that he was unaware of the presence of the Falcon in his sector. His attention was abruptly brought back to his west sector when LC2 asked him if he had traffic west. LC1 looked into his BRITE, saw the targets 1–2 nautical miles apart, and attempted to issue an instruction to Cessna 23K. A few words into his transmission, he observed a fireball to the west.

What were the salients of this accident from a human factors viewpoint? A few are given here.

(a) *Vigilance*. At least three controllers examined their scopes and did not see 'other' aircraft, only the one they were controlling. Also, the pilots had every opportunity to visually sight each other.

(b) *Workload and workplace design*. The controllers in the tower, though their work stations were only about 3 m apart, failed to communicate to each other the presence of their respective aircraft. The NTSB report indicated some disagreement about whether the workload at the time was moderate or heavy. A third position (CC), whose responsibility was to coordinate between controllers, was vacant. The controller had left, as he was allowed to do during light workloads.

(c) *Radar advisory service*. In a TRSA this can be deceptive. While ideally it should provide sequencing, advisories, and, in some cases, separation, present human-radar systems simply are not capable of doing so reliably (the accident speaks for itself). It is still mandatory that pilots, on clearances of any type, 'see and avoid' other aircraft when operating under visual meterological conditions (VMC). The very concept is questionable, as there are so many limitations on the visual ability of the pilots, as well as heavy cockpit workloads that make extra-cockpit scanning a low priority item. Furthermore, operations in a radar environment contain an inherent danger: the assumption by the flight crews that they are being offered flawless, radar-based separation and, hence, can relax their scanning vigil.

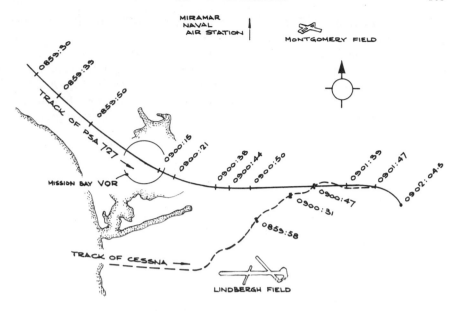

Fig. 6.2 Ground track of aircraft in San Diego collision (from AOPA Pilot, March 1979. copyright, Aircraft Owners and Pilots Association.)

These very questions of inter-controller communication, of the 'see and avoid' doctrine, and of relaxed vigilance in (or under) a TRSA, would again arise four months later in the skies over San Diego.

San Diego: 'I think he's passed off to our right'

On the fatal morning, a Cessna 172, N7711G, departed Montgomery Field (MGY), VFR, flying south-west to San Diego's Lindbergh Field (SAN) for practice Instrument Landing System (ILS) approaches.[15,39] Lindbergh Field lay below the SAN TRSA, whose floor was at 4000 ft. Aircraft in this area received Stage II radar service, meaning that radar sequencing and advisory service, but not separation, was available to participating pilots. Nearby Miramar Naval Air Station had a full Stage III TRSA.

The wind was calm, the active runway 27, but the ILS runway was 09, so 11G was working east-bound approaches (see Fig 6.2). After the second practice approach to ILS 09, 11G departed north-east bound, with instructions from SAN Tower to contact Approach Control, located at Navy Miramar. At 08.59:50, two minutes prior to the collision, they did so, and were cleared by APC to maintain VFR and climb on heading 070, not to exceed 3500 ft.

PSA 182, a Boeing 727, was south-bound from Los Angeles, IFR, destination SAN. At 08.53 they reported to APC at 11 000 ft and were cleared down to 7000 ft. At 08.57, PSA 182 reported descending through 9500 for 7000 ft, airport in sight. APC then made the crucial move, clearing 182 for a visual approach to Runway 27. Under this type of clearance. ATC authorises an IFR flight to proceed to the airport essentially as if it were a VFR flight—turning and descending at will, rather than with directions from ATC. Such a clearance is generally thought to reduce workload both on the ground and on the flight deck. There could be little dispute as to reducing the controllers' workload, but in the cockpit, the workload might not be reduced at all if the crew were to actually perform the required visual scanning. In reality, any workload reduction probably comes at the cost of extra-cockpit vigilance.

Furthermore, the Federal Air Regulations (FARs) make it clear that pilots are responsible to 'see and avoid' other aircraft when flying in VMC conditions, regardless of their flight plan. In short, ATC is always responsible for providing positive separation between IFR aircraft and, in a Terminal Control Area (TCA), provides the same separation for VFR aircraft. In a TRSA, though the regulations may be clear, the operational necessities are not. It may be added, parenthetically, that it seems regrettable that there is so little commerce between regulation writers and human factors specialists. Time and again accidents can be traced to a lack of understanding about just what a regulation requires an operator to do. In short, regulation writing should be regarded as an enterprise fully as deserving of human factors participation as the design of hardware.

At 08.59:39, as 11G was climbing out of its final ILS approach, APC issued the first of three warnings that PSA would receive about the Cessna. In order that the reader can fully comprehend what occurred in the last two minutes, some (not all) of the radio transmissions and cockpit voice recorder (CVR) conversations are given below.

08.59:30 APC to 182	Traffic is twelve o'clock, one mile, north bound.	
08.59:35 182 to APC	We're looking.	
08.59:39 APC to 182	PSA 182, additional traffic's, ah, twelve o'clock, three miles, just north of the field, north-east bound, a Cessna 172 climbing VFR out of 1400.	
08.59:50 182 to APC	OK, we've got that other twelve.	
08.59 APC to 11G	*Issuance of clearance.*	
09.00 APC to 182	PSA 182, traffic's at twelve o'clock, three miles, out of 1700.	
09.00:22 182 to APC	Traffic in sight.	

This was the fatal transmission. 182 was closing on 11G, and APC had been led to believe that the crew had him in sight. Under the visual clearance, it is clearly the overtaking aircraft's burden to keep the slower aircraft in sight and, in the event that it loses sight of it to inform ATC. APC's reply: 'Okay, sir, maintain visual separation, contact Lindbergh Tower, etc.' At 09.00:38, PSA received its fourth and final warning, this time from the tower.

09.00:38 SAN to 182	PSA 182, Lindbergh Tower, ah, traffic twelve o'clock one mile, a Cessna.
09.00:44 182 to SAN	Okay, we had it there a minute ago.
09.00:50 182 to SAN	I think he's passed off to our right.

09.00:42 Cockpit	Is that the one (we're) looking for? Yeah, but I don't see him now.
09.00:52 Cockpit	He was right over here a minute ago.
09.01:11 Cockpit	Are we clear of that Cessna?
09.01:11 Cockpit	Supposed to be.
09.01:11 Cockpit	I guess.
09.01:11 Cockpit	I hope.
09.01:21 Cockpit	Oh, yeah, before we turned down-wind I saw him about one o'clock, probably behind us now.
09.01:38 Cockpit	There's one underneath.
09.01:47 Cockpit	*Sound of impact.*

Just before the 09.00:38 transmission, PSA left APC frequency and switched to Lindbergh Tower frequency. At 09.01:38 (19 s before collision) a conflict alert sounded at the Miramar Radar Facility. This is a computer-based system that takes transponder and altitude encoder returns and computes a cylindrical space with a 2.5 nautical mile radius around each aircraft. If the space of one aircraft is projected to intrude upon another within 2 min. an alert is sounded in the centre. The controller must then devise a solution and warn one of the pilots or some other controller (see Smith).[36] The APC controller had been told that 182 already had 11G in sight, and, besides, he could contact 182 only through Lindbergh Tower. He issued an ironic and futile warning to Cessna 11G at a very ironic moment—09.01:47, 'Traffic in your vicinity, a PSA jet, has you in sight.'

As he began his 09.01:47 transmission, the CVR aboard PSA was recording the sound of impact. An elaborate network of people and machines had failed.

The Systems and the Realpolitik

The aftermath of SAN—blaming the victim

Hardly had the wreckage been cleared from the streets of San Diego before everyone had the answer: keep 'small planes' out of terminal areas. Never mind the fact that 11G had been doing exactly what it was supposed to be doing when it was struck. One can quibble forever about the possible role of a number of errors preceding the accident. One minute prior to the collision, the Cessna had turned 20° right (to 090) of its assigned heading: APC had failed to observe the 4000 ft crossing restriction abeam MGY when it cleared PSA to descend; and the local controller in Lindbergh Tower was not wearing his required corrective glasses.

What unfolded after the accident, as many remedies were proposed, was a classic example of what has been called 'blaming the victim'.[34] While the public outcry and political opportunism were predictable, the poor quality of press coverage may not have been anticipated. The examples are endless. The usually excellent *Los Angeles Times* wrote, 'The smaller plane reportedly struck the right wing of the jet' (true in a sense—see the NTSB report). Accompanying this was an artist's rendition which showed how this could be done, with a caption reading, 'Cessna 172 hits right wingtip of Boeing 727' (not 'reportedly' this time). A popular aviation magazine reported (the author cannot vouch for this) that a television commentator, obviously blaming the accident on the Cessna pilots, demonstrated on camera the use of an instrument hood. He put the hood on backwards, peering out at the camera through the adjustment holes in the head strap. *Newsweek* magazine ran a generally accurate three-dimensional drawing of the flight trajectories, even stating that the PSA overtook the Cessna, but in an inset showing the collision, gave the reader quite the opposite impression. It appears from the inset that the Cessna flew into the 727's right wing from behind and right.[30]

The FAA—NPRM 78-19

The political wheels began to turn. Almost immediately, FAA was under attack from the public, the Congress, the airline pilots, and the airline industry. Blaming the victim became the order of the day. By December, FAA had proposed a number of restrictions on the National Airspace System (NAS), including dropping the floor for positive controlled airspace (PCA) from 18 000 to 12 500 ft west of the Mississippi and to 10 000 ft east and in most of California. VFR aircraft flying between 12 500 and 18 000 would operate under 'controlled visual flight rules', requiring compliance with clearances similar to those issued to IFR flights.[37] In December 1978, the FAA published its controversial Notice of Proposed Rule Making (NPRM) 78-19, which specified the new NAS plans and, furthermore, its intention to increase the number of TCAs from 21 to 65 and the TRSAs from 67 to 147 by the year 1983. Three weeks after the accident, NTSB had recommended that SAN be made a full Stage III TRSA. FAA went a step further—NPRM 78-19 proposed to make San Diego a TCA, as well as Memphis. So the squeeze was on the general aviation pilot.

The basis for choosing which terminal areas would become TRSAs and TCAs left no doubt about who was to be 'protected'. The designation was based not on aircraft traffic, but on passenger traffic. Any terminal area enplaning 0.25 per cent of the total airline passengers in a year would be a TCA. Previously the figure had been 1 per cent. Now 97 per cent of the airline passengers would be 'protected'. This decision rule probably puzzles those with training in systems design. For one thing, the percentage of passengers may be roughly correlated with air carrier movements, but it is clearly oblivious to general aviation and military flights.

The response of the general aviation pilots and their associations was also predictable. 'The Government's Major Airspace Grab', the *AOPA Pilot* titled its article (February 1979). Charles Spence of the Aircraft Owners and Pilots Association (AOPA) made their position clear: 'If there is a proliferation of TCAs, we will violently (sic) oppose them'.[24] The VFR pilots screamed in outrage. A letter writing campaign to Congress was begun, and letters also poured in to aviation magazines. One pilot wrote, 'I am becoming so concerned with the insensitivity of the FAA to the rights of citizens who are pilots that I am seriously thinking of ending my pilot career'.[2]

When they got over their initial outrage, AOPA members offered some very interesting criticism of NPRM 78-19, arguments that should find a sympathetic ear among human factors professionals who might otherwise have little use for the general aviation pilot. Their arguments were that the new restrictions might have the opposite of their intended effect, since they would require heavier workload on both pilots and controllers, would result in a proliferation of already confusing regulations, and would increase the variety of types of clearances a controller would have to handle. Also there would be heavier communications loads, personnel requirements, hardware investments (for FAA and aircraft owners), flight time wasted, fuel expended, flights clustering along the boundaries of TCAs, and so forth. (A pilot flying VFR from Washington to Boston would pass through seven TCAs in the roughly 350 m.) Soon Congress was to discover that AOPA and its allies were not to be ignored. And in the midst of the furor, general aviation received some help from an unlikely source: NASA. But more about that later.

The Halls of Congress—HR 3942

The beleaguered FAA was soon to learn a fundamental lesson about the politics of mid-air collisions: in a democratic society, there are two (or more) sides to be heard. AOPA was soon joined by powerful allies, including the Commuter Airline Association, the General Aviation Manufacturers Association, the National Business Aircraft Association, the National Air Transportation Association, and the Helicopter Association of America. Their common cause—the defeat of the proposals of NPRM 78-19. Some even proposed their own plans for carving up the National Airspace.[31] The trauma of San Diego had faded, and the VFR pilots began to be heard, as AOPA mounted a very effective campaign. By September 1979, over 43 000 comments had been filed in response to 78-19. The release of the transcripts of the radio recordings in early 1979 clearly helped their case.

The political impact of an organisation with 230 000 members and powerful allies in other organisations was not to be lost to their elected representatives. Note that these are 230 000 people who can afford to own and fly private planes, not 230 000 migrant agricultural workers. Besides, many Congressmen felt that they had 'heard it before' from the FAA and that NPRM 78-19 would inevitably be followed by requests for enormous funding increases. By the end of the summer of 1979, the countervailing pressures to 78-19 were building, and Congress was threatening to block its implementation. The readers of this chapter may find it difficult to comprehend or appreciate the labyrinthine relationships between Congressmen, pressure groups, and regulatory agencies.

A champion of the general aviation pilots emerged in Representative William Harsha (R-OH). His method: to attach an amendment to the House aviation noise bill (HR 3942) denying to FAA any funds for implementation of the proposals of 78-19. Other politicians spoke up. Rep. Allen Ertel (D-PA) said:

I am particularly gratified that HR 3942 prevents FAA from implementing its proposed airspace rule making. The FAA's proposals were a gross and precipitous over-reaction to the tragic mid-air collision over San Diego. These proposals would have paralyzed general aviation without providing protection against accidents similar to that in San Diego.

Rep. Gene Snyder (R-KY) sounded more like one of us than one of them when he stated:

These proposals were not only an over-reaction to the San Diego collision, but they would adversely affect safety by overloading the air traffic control system and by compressing more traffic along the periphery of the PCAs and TCAs. In addition, they would result in increased fuel consumption and longer delays for all users of the nation's airspace.

Other Congressional comments included the very reasonable view of Rep. Barry Goldwater, Jr. (R-CA).[2]

By summer's end, the Harsha Amendment had cleared the House Public Works and Transportation Committee. By this time the FAA must have wondered what the world had come to—less than a year after PSA 182 and N7711G had plunged to the streets of San Diego and an outraged public was demanding protection from 'small planes', FAA officials found themselves under fire for doing too much, rather than too little. Blaming the victim, they might say.

FAA began to vacillate. In September 1979, it essentially cancelled the proposals of NPRM 78-19, announcing that proposals for controlled visual flight had been withdrawn, and six of the forty-four cities slated to become TCAs had been dropped from the list.[6,16] The basis for selecting the six is not clear; Jacksonville was dropped, but Syracuse remained. In the future, TCAs and TRSAs would be installed on the basis of a site-by-site examination, rather than the airline passenger formula. This makes better sense from a system design viewpoint, but it has an interesting second-order effect: it allows AOPA and its colleagues to marshal local support to fight each TRSA/TCA proposal, rather than opposing the entire plan nationally.

FAA Administrator Langhorne Bond exhibited a certain flair for understatement when he wrote Rep. Harsha, 'I can assure you that the FAA's final rules will reflect the comment we have received'.[5] At a party in September, Bond caught the eye of AOPA president John Baker, pulled out a white handkerchief, and waved the traditional flag of surrender.[39] The realpolitik had spoken.

Enter NASA

After a long absence, the human factors profession is welcomed to centre stage. Politics aside, at least for the moment, the basic systems question must now be confronted. Simply put, do the various terminal radar environments do the job? Or could they be doing the opposite of what they are designed to do? Fortunately, the number of mid-air collisions is too small to furnish an answer. Instead, near mid-air collisions (NMACs) must be examined. Enter NASA's Aviation Safety Reporting System (ASRS). In brief, ASRS is a data gathering system by which persons from all segments of aviation (mostly pilots and controllers, of course) can submit reports of incidents, near accidents, situations that should be corrected, and the like, without fear of retribution.* In April 1976, the system was transferred from FAA to NASA, in order to ensure the reporters of immunity from prosecution. In the summer of 1979, ASRS, which was just beginning to become effective, almost collapsed when Mr Bond announced some limitations on the immunity. Fortunately, he later relented.[4,40]

ASRS has conducted two studies of interest here. In the first,[9] the authors noted that of the first 2300 reports received, 360 (16 per cent) involved TRSA and TCA operations. Seventy per cent of those reported potential conflicts between aircraft, and 37 per cent reported NMACs. The fourth quarterly report in 1977 was devoted to a special study of 136 reported incidents in TRSAs and TCAs. The report is too complex and too valuable to attempt to summarise here. It is sufficient to say that a number of what would clearly be recognised as human factors problems emerged. To list a few: misunderstanding clearances; entering TCAs without clearances (for whatever reason); deliberately breaching the system; unclear and misleading instructions and symbology on charts; communication with non-English-speaking pilots; high pilot workload; high controller workload; and many more. Many of AOPA's very objections had been confirmed.

Granting that ASRS reports are voluntary and may contain unknown response biases, a problem that will be confronted in discussing the NMAC study, the system provides a rare insight into actual pilot and controller behaviour and into operational problems encountered by aviation personnel. Granting as well that incident reports, like accident reports, tend to accentuate the negative, it is important to realise that they provide the human factors profession with a valuable data base for understanding terminal area problems. In the second ASRS study, NASA provided the first insight into the fundamental question of the relative safety of radar environments versus other terminal areas. This time the luck was on the side of AOPA and other opponents of the post-SAN remedies.

The ASRS staff tabulated NMACs (defined as a report of passing within 500 ft horizontally or vertically of another aircraft). Note that these are pilots' estimates, not measurements. The tabulations for TRSAs, TCAs, and non-radar environments were compared to FAA data on the number of aircraft movements in these types of airspace, allowing computation of NMACs per million aircraft movements. These are shown in Table 6.2. The results are startling. Again the reader is cautioned that this is a tabulation of reports, not occurrences, and that response biases may inevitably creep in. For example, a pilot may be more likely to report what he perceives as another aircraft too close in a radar environment because he expects to be guaranteed separation. An aircraft seen in exactly the same position in a non-radar terminal area might be perceived as 'part of the game'. Numerous other explanations may be and have been proposed to explain

* For details of the operation of ASRS see NASA Tech Memo No TMX-3445.[11]

Table 6.2   ASRS reports of near mid-air collisions in terminal airspace, May—November 1978. Intake (Billings *et al.*[10])

Category	TRSAs	TCAs	Other Terminal Airspace
All NMACs	120	76	231
Estimated NMACs/year	222	140	426
FAA airport Traffic volume (FY 1977)*	16.2	7.8	52.4
NMACs reported /Million Operations/year	14	18	8

* In millions.

these results, including differences in the types of pilots, aircraft, and operations in the different airspace, and this author has suggested that the mere availability of ASRS reporting forms to pilots encountering NMACs during a flight may vary with the type of terminal airspace.

But the ASRS staff has been more than cautious on that point—their report is laced with caveats. While we must not rush to judgement that it is riskier to fly in radar environments than non-radar areas, it would be equally foolish to ignore or denigrate the ASRS study. It is amusing to note that a preliminary report of this study was entered into the *Congressional Record* by a Congressman, much to the chagrin of the ASRS staff. Their chagrin was heightened when the report was immediately picked up and run in the April 1979, *AOPA Pilot* ('Questioning the system', 1979) and used as ammunition by the AOPA long before ASRS authors felt that the study was ready for public consumption, let alone to be a weapon in the battle between AOPA and FAA.

Labour-intensive solutions

One basic point must be emphasised. The imposition of positive control is a labour-intensive solution, coming right at a time in systems development when operators, both on the ground and in the air, do not need any additional work-loads. For the controller, it means at the very least more flight plans to deal with, more radio communication, more varieties of clearances and more controller-to-controller communication. For the pilot, it means also more radio work, more chart reading, more precise navigation, and more regulations to cope with. What is supremely important is that it demands of the pilot more time with his or her 'head in the cockpit', instead of employing the only currently operational airborne collision avoidance device, the human eye. One should look with caution at any solution which is, to coin a phrase, 'cockpit intensive'.

Problem Areas

To list all of the areas where human factors engineering could contribute to the collision avoidance problem would read like the index of a beginning text on the subject. Let us consider only a few.

Visibility

Extra-cockpit visibility has not enjoyed high priority with aircraft designers. There will be little improvement until designers are willing to break with tradition and design a cockpit that is more than a fuselage with small windows, opting instead for something like the bubble canopies of fighter aircraft. Why not? Traditional design fills up much of what could be forward scanning area with knobs and dials. They have to go somewhere, the designer says. Perhaps the microprocessor revolution will offer a way out. With more compact CRT-type displays and smaller, digital controls available, the opportunity is at hand for a major rethinking of cockpit design.

A 727 pilot's view of the visibility problem was given by L. Morgan in *Flying*.[25]

Cockpit displays

The cockpit display of traffic information (CDTI) and distributed management of air traffic control is discussed by Hart and Loomis,[20] and Kreifeldt.[23] Just what duties of the ground-based controller could be moved to the cockpit, and whether it is desirable to do so, should be the subject of considerable research in the years to come. A rather strong view in favour of increased pilot participation in traffic separation is expressed by Gravat.[19] It is not clear just how the CDTI will be used in conjunction with other collision avoidance displays. Once again we seem to be committing original sin by adding 'boxes' to the cockpit one at a time. The problem is not whether traffic control can be moved to the cockpit, but whether it should be. The question can ultimately be answered only by very expensive full-scale simulation of both aircraft and ATC simultaneously. In the meantime, the author stands by his caution about cockpit-intensive solutions, but promises to keep an open mind about the matter. There is one big difference between control on the ground and in the air: one can always add another operator on the ground.

Communications: software

The imprecise use of language continues to plague aviation. This appears frequently in accident reports, as well as in the incident reports of the ASRS. Much work remains in the often tedious, unglamorous, but vitally necessary task of developing a standard ATC lexicon free of ambiguities. One must never forget the last transmission of the Captain of the KLM 747 as he started down the runway at Tenerife: 'We are at take-off'.

Communications: hardware

It seems inconceivable that one cannot find a solution to radio frequency allocation that would never place an aircraft out of reach of controllers who have
knowledge of impending tragedy. It is futile to develop a sophisticated computer-
based conflict alert system if the controller cannot contact a pilot when the
alarm goes off. A very simple and low-cost solution might be to require every
aircraft to carry a receiver on a fixed ATC frequency. The only transmitters
would be located in ATC centres and would be used strictly for extreme emergencies to contact aircraft not on the regular operating frequency. If Miramar and
N7711G had possessed such a capability (a hundred or so dollars per plane at
most), this might have been a different chapter. It seems too simple to be true.

Cockpit discipline

The author has pointed out elsewhere something confirmed by many NTSB
reports, namely, that cockpit discipline and professionalism remain unsolved and
difficult areas. One often hears this problem written off as 'complacency', a
nondescript word if there ever was one: yet the author eagerly awaits an operational definition of the term. The problem nonetheless exists, though it may be
beyond present methodologies. Researchers wishing to look into this touchy
matter should not be surprised if they fail to find a welcome mat at the cockpit
door.

Conclusions

Where does collision avoidance stand today? There are two answers. First, it
stands confused. The current system could be said to be excellent by most
standards of accident prevention; but by the harsh and absolute standards of
aviation, tolerant of nothing short of perfection, it is beginning to show signs of
trouble for the third time since World War II. One does not have to wait for
collisions to see this; ASRS reports give ample proof.

Second, the aviation community stands on the threshold of a new generation
of highly sophisticated ATC hardware. In the next decade, the Discrete Address
Beacon System/Automatic Traffic Advisory and Resolution Service (DABS/
ATARS) system will be in place (see Senne[35] and Klass[21]) presumably backed
up by an airborne collision avoidance system. These may or may not provide the
answer. Unfortunately, there is still far too little known about the human factors
of automation. Many human factors people harbour a hard-earned mistrust for
anyone who claims that any system is going to automate human error away.*
What is more, if all the proposed systems are implemented, the flight crew may
be, at some moment, bombarded with anti-collision information and guidance,
some of it possibly conflicting.

* See chapter 4.

Furthermore, it is regrettably possible that Congress will step in and dictate a cockpit collision avoidance system.[21] If anyone thinks that the hall of Congress is the place to do systems engineering, just let him review the lamentable history of the Emergency Locator Transmitter (ELT) and the Ground Proximity Warning System (GPWS), both legislated pieces of equipment. The very last place in the world that cockpit equipment should be specified is the US Congress.

Epilogue

By December 1979, disturbing stories of near mid-air collisions and ATC computer breakdowns were appearing almost daily. Two NMACs involved airliners over the San Diego area. In January, an NMAC between a Navy helicopter and an American Airlines plane was reported, but disputed by the Navy pilot. By the end of January, NMAC articles were appearing so frequently in newspapers and magazines that the author stopped cutting them out.

Perhaps even more disturbing, accounts of frequent and occasionally long-duration computer outages (over 1 minute) began to appear.[8] The computer at Albuquerque was down over 14 hours. Indianapolis Center experienced sixty-eight outages during October. In February the author visited a radar approach control facility. The controllers said, 'You should have been here yesterday—we had a total power failure. Computers, scopes, communications, the whole works —for over 15 minutes.' Fortunately, the centre was able to take over APC's function during the outage. The public and political reactions to stories of NMACs and computer failures would probably have been more severe were it not for the fact that these reports were eclipsed by two DC10 crashes (Mexico City and Antarctica). It may or may not have calmed some fears when NTSB vice-chairman, Elwood Driver, testified before a Congressional subcommittee that up to that date (December 1979) no accident investigated by the Board could be attributed to computer or radar failure.[13]

While the Professional Air Traffic Controllers Organization (PATCO) and FAA were differing over questions of computer reliability[22] NTSB and FAA were engaged in a protracted debate over what to do about San Diego terminal control.

In December 1979, FAA issued an NPRM to establish a TCA in San Diego.[17] It contains seventeen separate airspace segments with various altitudes. If one were to set out to design a navigational nightmare for the general aviation pilot, he could scarcely improve on this proposal. AOPA had its own proposal for SAN. A comparison between the plans appears in the January 1980 issue of *AOPA Pilot*. On 15 May 1980, the plan was implemented. Orlando, Fort Lauderdale, Memphis, and Portland were next on the list.

Acknowledgement

This chapter was written while the author was on leave at the Man-Vehicle Systems Research Division of NASA—Ames Research Center. The chapter does not represent an official NASA viewpoint or project. The author gratefully acknowledges the support of NASA and persons at Ames too numerous to list.

References

1. *AOPA Pilot*, August 1979, 32–33.
2. *AOPA Pilot*, September 1979.
3. *AOPA Pilot*, January 1980.
4. *Aviation Week and Space Technology*, 7 May 1979.
5. *Aviation Week and Space Technology*, 3 September 1979.
6. *Aviation Week and Space Technology*, 17 September 1979.
7. *Aviation Week and Space Technology*, 26 November 1979.
8. *Aviation Week and Space Technology*, 3 December 1979.
9. Billings, C. E. (ed.) (1977) *NASA Aviation Safety Reporting System: Fourth quarterly report*, Moffett Field, CA., NASA-Ames, NASA Tech. Memo 78433.
10. Billings, C. E., Grayson, R., Hecht, W., and Curry, R. E. (1980) 'A study of near midair collisions in US airspace', in *NASA Aviation Safety Reporting System: Eleventh quarterly report*, Moffett Field, CA., NASA-Ames, NASA Tech. Memo 81225.
11. Billings, C. E., Lauber, J. K., Funkhouser, H., Lyman, G., and Huff, E. M. (1976) *NASA Aviation Safety Reporting System quarterly report No. 76-1*, Moffett Field, CA., NASA-Ames, NASA Tech. Memo. No. TM X-3445, September.
12. Billings, C. E. and O'Hara, D. B. 'Human factors associated with runway incursions' (1978) in *NASA Aviation Safety Reporting System: Eighth quarterly report*, Moffett Field, CA: NASA-Ames, NASA Tech. Memo. 78540.
13. Driver, E. T. (1979) 'Statement before Subcommittee on Aviation of the Committee on Public Works and Transportation'. Washington, 11 December.
14. Dutch Aircraft Accident Inquiry Board (1979) *Verdict of aircraft accident inquiry board regarding the accident at Los Rodeos Airport, Tenerife (Spain)*. Dutch Government, The Hague, July.
15. Federal Aviation Administration (1978) *FAA practices, procedures and actions at San Diego, Calif., September 25, 1978*. FAA, Evaluation Report, no number, Washington, 21 December.
16. Federal Aviation Administration (1979) 'Controlled visual flight rules. Withdrawal of en route proposals.' *Federal Register*, 13 September 44 (179), 53416-19.
17. Federal Aviation Administration (1979) 'Proposed Group II terminal control area—San Diego'. *Federal Register*, 6 December, 44 (236) 70181-88.
18. 'The Government's Major Airspace Grab' (1979) *AOPA Pilot*, February.
19. Gravat, J. (1978) 'Transfer of information: Not a fair exchange'. *Air Line Pilot*, February, 6–8.

20.   Hart, S. G., and Loomis, L. L., (1980) 'Evaluation of the potential format and content of a cockpit display of traffic information'. *Human Factors*, **22**, 591–604.

21.   Klass, P. J. (1979) 'Collision avoidance plan views diverge'. *Aviation Week and Space Technology*, 23 July.

22.   Klass, P. J., (1980) 'PATCO, FAA debate ATC system safety'. *Aviation Week and Space Technology*, 7 January.

23.   Kreifeldt, J. G., (1980) 'Cockpit displayed information and distributed management in air traffic control'. *Human Factors*.

24.   *Miami Herald*, 22 December 1978.

25.   Morgan, L., (1979) 'Collision avoidance from the captain's chair'. *Flying*, January, 70–3.

26.   National Transportation Safety Board (1978) *Annual review of aircraft accident data*. Washington, NTSB, Report No. NTSB-ARG-78-2, 16 November.

27.   National Transportation Safety Board (1978) *Midair collision involving a Falcon jet and a Cessna 150, Memphis, Tenn., May 18, 1978*. Washington, NTSB , Report No. NTSB-AAR-78-14, November.

28.   National Transportation Safety Board (1978) *Briefs of accidents involving midair collisions*. Washington, NTSB, Report No. NTSB-AAM-78-13, December.

29.   National Transportation Safety Board (1979) *Pacific Southwest Airlines B-727 and Gibbs Flite Service Center Cessna 172, San Diego, Calif., September 25, 1978*. Washington, NTSB, Report No. NTSB-AAR-79-5, April.

30.   *Newsweek*, 9 October 1978.

31.   North, D. M. (1979) 'General aviation urges VFR alternatives', *Aviation Week and Space Technology*, 26 March.

32.   'Questioning the system. Special report on the fallacy of positive control', *AOPA Pilot*, (1979) April, 49–56.

33.   Roitsch, P. A., Babcock, G. L., and Edmunds, W. W. *Human factors report on the Tenerife accident*, Washington: Air Line Pilots Association, no date.

34.   Ryan, W. (1971) *Blaming the victim*, Vintage Books, New York.

35.   Senne, K. (1977) 'What happened to IPC? They renamed it ATARS', *Journal of Air Traffic Control*, July–September, 12–15.

36.   Smith, B. A. (1978) 'Control factor in crash investigated', *Aviation Week and Space Technology*, 19 October.

37.   Smith, B. A. (1978) 'FAA eyes tighter terminal area control', *Aviation Week and Space Technology*, 6 November.

38.   Spanish Ministry of Transport and Communications (1978) *Report of collision between PAA B-747 and KLM B-747 at Tenerife, March 27, 1977*. Translation published in *Aviation Week and Space Technology*, 20 and 27 November 1978.

39.   *Wall Street Journal*, 12 November 1979.

40.   Winant, J. H. (1979) 'The revamping of ASRS', *Journal of Air Traffic Control*, July–September, **21**, 2.

41.   Zeller, A. F. (1972) 'Human error in the seventies', *Aerospace Medicine*, May, 492–7.

Chapter 7

Human Factors in Air Traffic Control
R. C. W. Weston

We have seen in the preceding chapters a number of examples of incidents in which the role of the air traffic controller has proved critical. In particular there are the graphic accounts of the events leading up to mid-air collisions at Memphis and San Diego, in Chapter 6. Pilot-oriented research may inevitably attach insufficient weight to the influence of the controller's own environment: this contribution is, therefore, a salutory glimpse of some of the difficulties and pressures in this sector which determine the quality, efficacy and ultimately, safety of the service on which the pilot depends.

The essential role of air traffic control has been described simply as converting traffic demand into traffic flow. In this simple statement is encompassed a wide range of functions and skills, not all of which are common to every ATC task, but all of which depend heavily on the human element—the air traffic controller.

With the complex air space structure and high air traffic levels associated with most developed countries, the demands and pressures on the controller are formidable. Aviation has come a long way since the days when safe separation between aircraft was based purely on the 'see and be seen' principle. Then, responsibility was placed fairly and squarely on the pilot. But with aircraft closing speeds in excess of 1000 m.p.h., the total impracticability of reliance upon such a system today is obvious. The need to safeguard passengers, crew and aircraft is now met by an extensive and sophisticated ground-based infra-structure, in which air traffic controllers issue mandatory instructions to pilots. The aim of the service, imprinted on the mind of every controller and enshrined in the foundations of the system, is simple—to ensure a safe, orderly and expeditious flow of air traffic. Of course, it remains a paramount duty of the flight crew to keep a good look-out at all times, although the limited field of view from the flight deck of most modern aircraft imposes considerable limitations in this regard. In addition, the prevalence of 'instrument meteorological conditions' for much of the year in many busy areas, such as western Europe, further limits the effectiveness of a good look-out. Thus, whilst the aircraft captain still bears the ultimate responsibility for the safety of his aircraft, in terms of maintaining safe separation from the other traffic, this authority is exercised by the air traffic controller for all practical purposes. The exercise of this authority demands considerable confidence by the pilot in the disembodied voice of the controller and in the integrity of the system of which he is a part; it is the task of the controller and the air traffic control network to justify that confidence.

The air traffic controller, therefore, is an essential element in the maintenance of air safety and, as a human being, he can make mistakes. The very nature of the function he performs is such that any omission or misjudgement on his part can have disastrous consequences, as a number of air disasters in recent years have shown only too clearly. There is a distinct analogy to be drawn here with the 'pilot error' verdict, for 'controller error' can all too easily be used to describe what is essentially failure of the system. The one advantage the controller has over the pilot in such circumstances is that the controller usually lives to tell the tale—even if experience suggests that precious few people are willing to listen.

If the ultimate motivation of self-preservation cannot be said to govern a controller's action, only the most cynical and uninformed would suggest that this has any co-relation with the frequency with which 'controller error' may occur. All controllers live in fear of their actions causing, or contributing towards, an accident. They, more than anyone (pilots included), are only too well aware of how narrow the dividing line between safety and disaster can become in air traffic control terms. Every day, controllers face situations in which the failings of the system, and their personal limitations are too readily apparent, although only a minority of such cases progress to the point at which pilots become aware of the deficiency. But the constant reminder of these limitations, the feeling of 'there but for the grace of God. . .', scares controllers. Of course, they tend to make light of such feelings, for it is not in the make-up of the average controller to confess his personal tensions and dramas. Society, and a sense of manliness demands that such emotions be glossed over*—but they are there.

The Weakest Link

In managing the air traffic flow in a safe, orderly and expeditious manner the controller has available certain tools of the trade. In the more sophisticated ATC environments these may consist of the best that modern technology can provide by way of computer-based radar and flight data processing and display systems. At the other end of the spectrum, they may consist of no more than a few essential telephone lines, paper 'flight progress strips' on which to record flight details, and a large amount of intuition. Generally speaking the degree of sophistication at the ATC network is dictated by the nature, quantity and complexity of the traffic operating, although in certain parts of the world the investment in such facilities fails to balance the equation. The essential requirement, of course, is the maintenance of safety, and failure to provide adequate facilities should in theory have an adverse effect only on expedition; in practical terms however safety is affected also. For example, certain popular European holiday resorts are served by airports which are not equipped with surveillance radar. This requires aircraft to carry out a procedural let-down and approach, a much slower, time-consuming method than that attainable by radar sequencing. Although the

---

* See Dr Allnutt, chapter 1, p. 14 on this conflict of manhood v. society.

procedural approach is perfectly safe when flown accurately, if there is high
ground in the vicinity there may be little margin for error. As recent events have
shown, momentary disorientation of the flight crew or a misunderstood ATC
instruction can lead to disaster—a situation which could be prevented or detected
by the availability of radar. But whatever ATC environment we consider, however
complex and sophisticated the infrastructure, it can only be as effective and safe
as the weakest link—communication.

We have established the essential role of the controller in ensuring the safe
separation of aircraft at all stages of their flight. To accomplish this task, he
passes instructions to pilots, from starting engines to shutting down at destination,
by radio telephony or RT. Clearly, in such an environment, every step must be
taken to try to eliminate any possibility of misunderstanding. To this end, agreed
'standard phraseologies' are laid down by the International Civil Aviation
Organisation (ICAO), the majority of which are used worldwide for civil and
military operations. Of course, there are local variations, and there are many
situations for which it is not possible to lay down specific phraseology. Nevertheless, the standard phraseologies and procedures provide the backbone of the
system of communication.

As a double check, pilots are required to 'readback' to controllers certain
instructions, such as climb, descent and routeing clearances, and certain
information, such as altimeter pressure settings by which the altitude of an
aircraft is measured. Thus there is a greater possibility that the passing, or hearing,
of incorrect information will be detected. For instance, it is easy to appreciate
how, over a busy or none-too-clear RT channel, an instruction to an aircraft to
'climb to Flight Level 80' (8000 ft on the 'standard' altimeter pressure setting)
could be heard as 'climb to Flight Level 280' (28 000 ft), the consequences of
which could be disastrous if allowed to go undetected. The possibility of such
mis-hearings, or misunderstandings, is further exacerbated by the problem of
'expectancy' and by the highly political question of language.

Expectancy

Dr Allnutt has already examined expectancy from the psychologist's viewpoint
in chapter 1. However, the subject is of such importance that it is worth some
further discussion from the controller's viewpoint.

We are all, to a certain extent, creatures of habit. We know, from experience,
that certain events tend to follow as a natural consequence of certain actions.
Such anticipation is a perfectly normal and natural part of the reactions of any
pilot or controller. But therein lies the danger, for it is all too easy to hear what
one expects to hear rather than what is said; the higher the degree of expectancy,
the more likely this is to happen. For instance, the Standard Instrument Departure
procedure (or SID) from a major airport requires aircraft following a certain
route to climb to 4000 ft. After take-off, these aircraft contact the departure
radar controller, responsible for the subsequent climb of the aircraft when clear
of in-bound traffic, and announce 'XY 123 climbing to 4000 ft'. The radar
controller knows from his data display the moment the aircraft is airborne and

is planning his tactical strategy to expedite the aircraft's climb to cruising altitude. However, should one pilot mis-read the altitude restriction applicable to his SID, and announce on frequency 'XY 123 climbing to 5000 ft', the controller *may* hear the aircraft as climbing to 4000 ft because that is the requirement of his clearance—all aircraft routeing that way climb to 4000 ft. Thus the pilot's error may go undetected, at least initially, with the distinct possibility of conflict with other aircraft.

Language

Communication, of course, is all about language, and language in the international aviation context means English. Not that the English language is used exclusively for air traffic control purposes by any means, but, if you speak English, you can fly anywhere; not so with any other language. Naturally, the degree of proficiency in English amongst controllers and pilots to whom it is not a native language varies enormously. While the hazards inherent in the passing and execution of instructions between air traffic control and pilots, one of whom is of doubtful proficiency in English, are obvious, clearly the scope for misunderstanding is that much greater when neither controller nor pilot is especially proficient in the language. Despite the limited vocabulary necessary to master 'standard phraseology', the dangers inherent in poor understanding are all too clear. Thus, many countries use a language other than English for communications in such circumstances, whilst English remains available for aircraft requiring it. It can be argued that the possibilities of misunderstanding, and perhaps potentially unsafe actions, are thereby minimised. Of course, there are two sides to every argument.

Pilots, not unnaturally, have a distinct interest in what is going on around them. From the RT communications they hear, they can often build up a 'mental picture' of the whereabouts of other aircraft in the same general vicinity. Of course, this may be of little value in busy areas where communication is largely one-way (controller to pilot) and where aircraft are operating on more than one frequency within a given area. Additionally, the extent of radar coverage of such areas has greatly reduced the amount of 'position reporting' which is required with more procedural methods of control, thereby reducing further the data on other flights available to pilots. However, most pilots would agree that a little information is better than none. Certainly, there are many reports, especially from more 'backward' ATC environments, where pilot monitoring of the RT has been instrumental in detecting conflicts. But, in most environments, if only part of the RT communication is carried out in English, the chances of detecting possible hazards are greatly reduced. In the mid-air collision between a British Airways Trident and a DC9 of Inex Adria over Zagreb in 1976, the crew of the Trident may have been unaware of the imminent danger of collision because the Yugoslav controller spoke to the Yugoslav DC9 in the Croatian tongue.*

* The critical transmissions are noted in the United Kingdom Department of Trade, Accidents Investigation Branch, *Aircraft Accident Report 5/77*. Human factors bearing on this incident are examined in R. Weston and R. Hurst *Zagreb One Four—Cleared to Collide?* Granada Publishing, St Albans, UK (1982).

Unhappily, the question of language has now become something of a political football, especially in Canada where attempts to introduce bi-lingual ATC have been vigorously contested.* As always when political considerations are introduced, arguments tend to be based more on emotion than on a rational examination of the pros and cons, which is especially sad when air safety can be the only loser.

Managing the Flow: Human and Technological Resources

Although the first steps towards providing something more than an Aldis lamp or Verey pistol to signal to aircraft for clearance to land had pre-dated World War II, air traffic control as we know it today dates from the end of hostilities. With the outbreak of peace, and the steady growth of civil air transport, the need arose for a regulated system of separating passenger-carrying flights at all stages from take-off to touch-down. Equipment provided in the early days was minimal, consisting basically of paper 'flight progress strips', upon which abbreviated details of aircraft flight plans were recorded, and landline and ground/air communications facilities. In the busier terminal areas, radar was introduced to improve the safety of the system and, most noticeably, enable far greater expedition of traffic than could be obtained using 'procedural' methods (i.e. separation by time or altitude). Aircraft speeds were slow, traffic demands generally were not high, and a small number of controllers, almost exclusively ex-air crew, laid the foundations of the present system.

Such was the growth of traffic that it was not long before equipment manufacturers were developing technology to help the controller—new ATC radars were introduced to replace former wartime military facilities—and a rapid expansion of air traffic control networks got under way. But the provision of more advanced facilities, the ability to squeeze more aircraft into a given portion of airspace, inevitably increased the demands upon the controller. Thus it became clear that the physical and mental limits of the individual were the overriding factor in determining system capacity, whilst maintaining the required standards of safety. Naturally, some equipment enabled the controller to work more efficiently, and thereby raised the 'threshold' of saturation, whilst other equipment made its own demands upon the controller with no benefit to system capacity.

Sectorisation

In the 'en-route' environment, air traffic control facilities are 'sectorised' to limit the number of aircraft under the control of one controller (i.e. the route structure is divided into sections, each the responsibility of a different controller using a discrete VHF RT channel). A natural reaction to overloading has always been to sectorise further (i.e. subdivide the airspace between more controllers) but there

* But not successfully. See reference chapter 10.

is a limit to how far this practice can be taken. If aircraft are to transit safely between sectors, exceptionally close coordination and liaison is required. Although ATC procedures are designed to minimise this requirement as far as possible (by the use of standard routes, agreed flight levels etc., at transfer points), and modern techniques of automatic data transfer can assist greatly, there is still a finite limit to the controller's capacity to coordinate. This, together with the requirement for a sector to be a viable size if the controller is to employ tactical methods of control, effectively limits the degree of sectorisation which is feasible. For instance, if a sector is becoming overloaded, to subdivide it (i.e. double the controller manning and duplicate all the technical facilities) may increase the system capacity by only, say, 20 per cent due to the increased complexity of coordination. Further subdivision may be impossible if the airspace allocated to a controller is not to become so limited in size as to prevent him actually having the tactical freedom to control anything—not to mention an unacceptable number of changes of RT channel for pilots.

Equipment and the human element

So, if saturating the system with more controllers is not the answer, what is? The answer must be to provide equipment and facilities which enable the controller to raise his, and therefore the system's, saturation level. That does not simply mean more, or advanced, equipment—it means equipment which will actually increase system capacity. It is here that professional human factors expertise must be integrated with professional air traffic control expertise to ensure that the systems designers and engineers produce what is needed for the job. For whilst there are variations between countries, there is ample evidence of equipment being procured for financial or overtly political considerations—and frequently it is not the right equipment for the job. In many countries, there is little or no controller or human factors input at any stage of the specification, design or procurement process—a state of affairs hardly conducive to producing a safe and efficient ATC system.

To the operational controller, there is no mystique about human factors—to him it extends from the efficient design and layout of his equipment to the role he plays in the control 'loop'. To consider a simple case, a controller may be required to control on a number of sectors or operational positions. Each function, each position, is the subject of a specific rating and validation on his licence. He is trained, examined and regularly checked on each function. It is normal for an operational position to have discrete landline communication with, perhaps, twenty to thirty other sectors, airfields etc., with whom there is a direct interface. If the controller then moves to the next sector operating position, he may find that a large percentage of his landline facilities will be to the same control positions as on the previous sector. But will each position be represented by the same button on the thirty-line keyboard his is faced with? The chances are that they are not, even though they could be.

Now, if this sounds nothing more than a minor irritation, picture the controller operating a busy sector, issuing climb, descent and heading instructions to perhaps fifteen aircraft carrying anything from 1000 to 6000 passengers. The RT will be heavily loaded (say 90 per cent) allowing only 10 per cent of his time for thinking, planning, liaising, etc. He writes whilst he talks, updating his traffic display as required. But to give a radar handover to airfield A or sector B, he has to take his eyes from his radar display and scan thirty labelled buttons for the correct landline, using badly needed thinking time. Given a modicum of human factors consideration, that landline could be in the same relative position on all relevant sectors, enabling the controller to select the correct button by second nature.

In the formative days of ATC, when equipment was frequently a hand-down from a redundant military requirement, the poor ergonomics were accepted. Pressure was not so great, understanding of ergonomics was not so well defined and, arguably, the personnel had been well-prepared by wartime experiences to accept that half a loaf was better than no bread. But in the era of purpose-designed equipment, vast investment in the air transport industry and the pressures of intensive traffic demand, controllers rightly expect adequate attention to be paid to ergonomics. Sometimes, basic ergonomic deficiencies result from the rapid advance of technology. For instance, in the early 1960s large, horizontal radar displays were introduced in the USA, although all the evidence showed that a radar screen should be in a near-vertical position for ideal viewing characteristics. However, large horizontal displays were chosen to enable small markers, called shrimp-boats, to be moved across the face of the tube. These markers carried the aircraft identification and were moved manually in association with the appropriate radar 'blip'. No sooner had the displays been introduced than the development of secondary radar enabled each radar 'blip' to be labelled electronically on the radar screen with the aircraft's identification and, later, altitude. By now the UK, too, had committed itself to the American concept and, ever since, controllers have been cursed with a display system which is an ergonomic disaster, the concept and *raison d'être* of which was overtaken by technology even before it was introduced.

In many ways, it seems to run contrary to human nature to be satisfied with one's equipment and facilities, especially when performing a demanding task such as controlling air traffic. But it is certain that the concern expressed by controllers worldwide is not simply a manifestation of this syndrome. They are under pressure operationally, and frequently administratively too; they see a vast investment by the airline industry in new aircraft and engineering facilities and they cannot understand why, in relative terms, the investment in ATC facilities amounts to 'peanuts'. It is a combination of factors which contributes its fair share to industrial unrest in the profession.

Developing the system

Of course, the effectiveness of any equipment or facility is dependent largely upon the manner in which it is utilised. Even in those more enlightened countries where human factors input at the design stage helps to produce ergonomically sound equipment, there is frequently a lack of human factors input into planning the most effective means of utilising it. In simple terms, this may be a case of who does what—the division of tasks between the 'executive' controller on a sector and his 'planning' or 'support' controller or assistant. In more complex cases, a human factors input may help achieve the optimum structure and *modus operandi* of an entire ATC system, a factor all too frequently overlooked. There is no shortage of expertise or enthusiasm although there is often a marked reluctance to commit hard cash to human factors research in ATC. Nevertheless, over the years a considerable fund of knowledge and experience has been built up as a result of research work in the USA and the UK. It is a matter of great regret that, when funds are tight, it is so easy to opt for the quick, cheap, off-the-shelf solution which, given even the smallest element of human factors input at an early stage, could transform the subsequent operational effectiveness of the equipment or system. Air traffic control, like aviation itself, is not a static enterprise; it is continually changing, developing, adapting, advancing. But this evolutionary process brings its own pitfalls to even the most well-ordered ATC system, for whatever the value of human factors input at the equipment and system design stage, this can soon be negated by subsequent developments. It is not only major changes that are of concern, for relatively minor changes can result in quite disproportionate effects on the control task. For instance, in a carefully planned and laid out control tower, the subsequent installation of an additional item of equipment may obstruct the aerodrome controller's view of part of the runway or approach path from his normal operating position—an additional requirement for coordination by a radar controller which may, in certain circumstances, impose a significant increase in workload at a moment when he is least able to cope with it. So, unless the proposed changes are examined from the human factors viewpoint, both in terms of physical characteristics and the effect upon operational functions, they can easily undo any good that has been achieved by careful design and task analysis in the initial stages.

Human reactions

Traditionally, air traffic control has been considered a demanding but rewarding profession, at least in terms of job satisfaction. Despite the inevitable constraints of rules and regulations, the very nature of the job offers a challenge; to meet that challenge may require a controller to call on all his skills and experience. In accomplishing his tasks safely and efficiently lies the inherent satisfaction of the job.

In general terms, the more demanding the traffic situation, the more challenging the job and the greater the satisfaction to be derived therefrom. Of course, there is a limit to how far this theory may be taken, for when the traffic demand reaches a certain level, when the controller feels he is on the point of being overloaded, any element of self-fulfilment becomes subservient to self-survival if not sheer panic. But, normally, controllers who may outwardly profess to aspire to a quiet life, can be seen 'hunting' for traffic. This manifests itself in the rapidity with which controllers seek to combine sectors in quieter periods, thus enabling one controller to remain reasonably busy instead of two or three having little to do.

It is reasonable to ask whether such actions are in the best interests of safety, for surely the lower the traffic demand upon a controller, the less the likelihood of error? In practice, however, from an examination of near-miss incidents it soon becomes apparent that a significant number involving controller error happen under conditions of light traffic loading. In other words, take away the stimulus of a traffic situation which demands the controller's attention and concentration and you probably raise the chance of controller error. Of course, it is essential to keep such a philosophy in context, for at the other extreme— controller overloading—the implications are much more serious.

The picture and controller overload

It is not easy to describe the mental processes by which a controller works. Basically, he builds up a mental picture of the traffic situation from the data displayed to him on his radar display and flight progress strips, and information he receives over the RT and by telephone from other controllers. He then applies his own knowledge of aircraft performance and the requirements of the particular sector, or position he is operating, in forward planning—a complex task which has been likened to a game of three-dimensional chess. The busier the traffic situation, the less time is available for planning the tactical strategy necessary to deal with a given traffic situation. Eventually, the point is reached where the controller is struggling to react to situations as they arise with little or no time available to anticipate or plan for a specific pattern of events. Herein lies the real danger, the controller's nightmare of 'losing the picture'.

Generally speaking, controllers do not control their own workload. Techniques of scheduling and flow control are, as yet, totally inadequate to ensure that certain portions of airspace do not, at times, become overloaded. In fact, of course, although it is common to talk of 'sector overload', what is really meant is 'controller overload', although it is true that the structure and complexity of the airspace environment have a direct bearing on the point at which this overload occurs. Indeed, whilst some countries are more realistic than others, there is a feeling amongst controllers worldwide that theoretical studies of system capacity fail to take due account of controller capacity, which is ultimately the limiting factor. And, inevitably, the capacity of a particular controller will be dependent upon his training, experience, mental dexterity, reactions under pressure and other factors. Thus, whilst close monitoring and checking of controller performance can reasonably ensure the maintenance of a certain minimum standard, no two controllers will ever be precisely the same—hence the point at which a controller will begin to 'lose the picture' cannot be predicted with any accuracy.

There is no generally accepted explanation of how and why 'picture loss' occurs. Perhaps the best description is that the controller 'builds' his picture rather like a pyramid of cards—suddenly, with the addition of one more card, the whole thing collapses. That final card may be the arrival on frequency of yet another aircraft, or it may be an unexpected happening such as an aircraft taking an incorrect route, or an aircraft responding to an instruction addressed to another aircraft. The effect is quite startling—the vast bank of short-term, transient information stored in the controller's brain is dumped, he loses the picture. If he can cope with the trauma of the incident, and many cannot, the controller has to start from scratch again, slowly building up the picture from the information presented to him. In a simulator exercise, it is possible to 'freeze' the situation while he does this, but a real-life case of picture loss presents real danger to all aircraft involved. Many pilots will know of situations where they have been able to read into the controller's voice that he is nearing, or has reached, overload. The undoubted extra vigilance that such a situation inspires on the flight deck is a necessary reaction by all pilots to an unnerving and serious situation.

One of the difficulties in trying to predict at what point a sector, and hence a controller, will become overloaded is that there are simply too many variables. If it were simply a matter of numbers of aircraft, there would be no problem—but every controller knows of situations where he has been able to handle twenty flights reasonably comfortably whilst at other times less than half that number have led to overload. Indeed, most controllers and pilots will know of situations where a single pilot, perhaps seeking a lengthy and complicated re-route, or having difficulty understanding an ATC instruction, has monopolised RT time and controller effort to such an extent that a very low traffic density has approached the overload condition.

Pilots have a great responsibility, both to themselves and to other pilots, to do their bit to prevent unnecessary workload for the controller. Of course, there are times when workload is high on the flight deck, but failure to maintain an adequate listening watch on the requisite ATC channel can be a serious hazard and yet remains one of the most common causes of controller complaint. Indeed, the failure to elicit a response from an aircraft can distract a controller from more immediate and important tasks to a degree quite out of proportion with the gravity of the situation. Many near-miss and incident reports, which have apportioned blame to the controller, have commented that the controller was for some time distracted by a relatively trivial incident, such as the failure of an aircraft to respond to RT calls.

Performance assumption

Controllers are required to have a reasonable knowledge and understanding of aircraft performance criteria. They do not and cannot, know such characteristics in detail. This broad-brush understanding is based on the aircraft type, stage length, ambient air temperature, requested flight level and knowledge of the operational characteristics employed by particular airlines—the latter normally being learned purely by experience. The control strategies employed are ideally based on the fail-safe principle—that is to say, in simple terms, issuing a clearance to an aircraft which will be safe, even if the controller's attention is subsequently distracted by other traffic demands. In other words, if aircraft A wishes to climb from Flight Level 100 to Flight Level 310, with aircraft B approaching from the opposite direction at Flight Level 240 approximately, say, 150 miles away, the prudent radar controller will clear aircraft A to climb to Flight Level 230, thereby ensuring that, without further controller invervention, the minimum vertical separation standard of 1000 ft will not be infringed. Subsequently, he will monitor the climb performance of aircraft A *vis-à-vis* the progress of aircraft B until the former aircraft is approaching its cleared altitude, at which stage the controller is faced with two main alternatives:

(a)   Do nothing—in which case aircraft A will level off at Flight Level 230 and maintain until aircraft B has passed, at which stage the controller will clear aircraft A for further climb.

(b)   Clear aircraft A for further climb above aircraft B.

The circumstances in which he may opt for alternative (b) can be described as:

(i)   If aircraft A's rate of climb has been such that the controller is satisfied that it will be well above aircraft B's altitude whilst the aircraft are still a considerable distance apart; or

(ii)   If aircraft A and B are 'locked' on radar headings to ensure adequate lateral separation (normally 5 mm) until aircraft A has climbed at least 1000 ft above aircraft B.

Although such fail-safe control strategies form the basis of a controller's tactics, the busier and more complex the traffic situation, the more heavily is the controller likely to be forced into a certain number of performance assumptions if any aircraft is to climb or descend at all. These assumptions are minimised by the use of radar headings, a subject of some disagreement with many pilots who feel their constant use removes navigational responsibility for the flight from the flight deck. But while no controller would plan on an assumption of a specific level of aircraft performance, knowing only too well the variations that arise in operational practice, he is surely entitled to assume that the aircraft performance will not be grossly abnormal, unless he is advised to the contrary. But operators and pilots all too frequently pay scant regard to such factors.

    For instance, a few years ago a major world airline introduced a newer version of a wide-body aircraft. After a number of ATC incidents, which only controller vigilance had prevented deteriorating into near-misses, it transpired that the flight management system fitted to the aircraft required it to level off in the descent at Flight Level 120 and maintain that altitude for two minutes or so before resuming descent. No one, either operator or flight crews, had thought to tell air traffic control of this requirement until quizzed by anxious controllers who, bending over backwards to provide the continuous descent pleaded for by most pilots, were caught unaware by the aircraft levelling off at

Flight Level 120. The moral is quite simple—if you wish to climb at 100 ft per minute, or descend at 10 000 ft per minute, or level off during a descent to allow speed to decay—tell the controller. All things are possible, given adequate warning.

Fatigue

The topic of fatigue — its nature and effects — has already been discussed by Dr Allnutt in chapter 1; many of his observations apply equally to controllers. Essentially, the report of the Bader committee* differentiated between tiredness and fatigue in terms of arousal to a stimulus—fatigue being defined as that level of reduced performance from which there is no certainty that a person can be aroused in an emergency even when considerable stimulus is present. But from the purely practical viewpoint, the dangers of an omission or error of judgement caused simply by tiredness are just as great and rather more likely to be tested, than the individuals' ability to react to the stimulus of an emergency when fatigued.

Of course, there are basic differences in the work situation of pilots and controllers which limit the validity of any direct comparison; however, the similarities are too obvious to be ignored. Thus, whilst controllers do not suffer the change of time zone which afflicts long-haul pilots, they have very similar problems of irregular working hours and eating habits which can totally disrupt the body's normal circadian rhythms. And there are aspects in which the controller perhaps fares less well than pilots—for instance, manning a busy sector can stimulate physical and mental reactions for hours at a time to the sort of levels pilots normally reach only at the more crucial phases of flight, take-off and landing. And whilst pilots have achieved a degree of legal control of duty hours, as a result of the Bader committee's recommendations, controllers are not so fortunate.

The more enlightened employers of controllers, be they governments, independent agencies or airport authorities, recognise the vital role they play in the maintenance of safety standards, and roster controllers with this in mind. However, there are still employers in the so-called developed nations who pay scant regard to such considerations. How can one justify an approach radar controller, at an airport handling scheduled airline traffic, coming on duty at 07.00 having slept in the tower for three hours after finishing a fourteen and a half hour duty at 03.30? Such indefensible practices may be very much in a minority but that they can happen at all must be of concern to all who care about air safety. In a near-miss investigation a few years ago in the UK, it transpired that the approach radar controller who took the blame had been manning his radar console for four hours without a break, during which time he had handled 108 movements. Now no one can prove that, under less taxing working conditions, he would have reacted differently—but it must be a

* Set up in the United Kingdom (in 1972) to enquire into Flight Time Limitations.

possibility. The medical and human factors advice available suggests that a fatigue break of thirty minutes every two hours is the minimum acceptable for a busy radar position. Whilst responsible employers provide manning levels commensurate with this requirement, others are content to ignore such advice until legislation compels otherwise.

In 1979, after a 'Meeting of Experts' on ATC called in Geneva, the International Labour Office issued a list of conclusions on a wide range of factors affecting the employment of controllers. It is worth quoting from conclusions 18–21, as they encompass many of the points just considered.

18.   Controllers are directly involved in the safety of civil aviation and have problems which are unique to their profession, and their concern with safety could broadly be compared with that of pilots.
19.   Hours of work, length of shifts, duration of uninterrupted work at air traffic control positions and other parameters of work schedules have a direct impact on air safety. It is therefore necessary to establish guidelines for work schedules to reduce fatigue of air traffic controllers.
20.   Long working hours and inadequate rest periods for controllers are potential threats to the safety of aviation. . .
21.   Maximum working hours per day, per week and per month with minimum rest periods should be laid down for controllers by the governments of all states in consultation with the trade unions and other representative organisations concerned. These should preferably be enforceable by law. . .

Why, therefore, one may ask, in the face of such recommendations from an independent international body, are governments apparently so unwilling to act? In the UK, at least, it appears that the reason is the Civil Aviation Authority's professed intention to regulate 'with a light touch'; other countries presumably have different reasons. Whatever the motives, however misguided the attitudes, one thing is clear—they do nothing to advance the cause of aviation safety.

Automation—The Mixed Blessing

Earlier, this chapter considered the limitation on system capacity imposed by the ability of the controller to handle the traffic offering. Clearly, if automated techniques allow the controller more thinking time, there may be scope for increasing system capacity. But such improvement is by no means certain, for automation brings with it its own problems.

Perhaps the most obvious area for the application of modern technology is in the handling of flight data, and it is in this sphere that the initial steps were introduced in most countries. The 'storing' of repetitive flight plans, the calculation of elapsed times en route between subsequent navigational fixes, and the printing of essential flight data on 'strips' for controllers are all tasks which have been largely automated, saving much in the area of support functions, but have little impact on performance of the control function. Radar displays, too, have benefited from modern data processing techniques which enable synthetic displays to be produced from radar data remoted from distant locations. The clean and neat symbology now available contrasts markedly with the former display of 'raw' radar video, whilst the widespread use of secondary radar has enabled aircraft responses on the radar display to be 'labelled' with a discrete code (usually converted by the display system to the aircraft's call-sign) and altitude read-out transmitted directly from the aircraft's altimeter. Thus the controller no longer needs to keep in his head the identity of each radar 'blip' on his screen, an essential requirement hitherto, and no longer must constantly interrogate pilots by RT for altitude reports, particularly crucial when aircraft are climbing or descending. These benefits have undoubtedly increased the traffic handling capacity of controllers very considerably.

However, no system is infallible and the tendency of modern processing and display systems to 'swap' labels between targets in certain circumstances, display false targets from secondary radar reflections and cause 'jitter' on aircraft tracks, leads to their being treated with a certain degree of circumspection by most controllers. But a whole generation of controllers is now appearing who have known no other form of display, thereby increasing current doubts about the ability of controllers to cope with system failure when a reversion to the techniques of old is required.

The traffic display

Much thought is currently being expended on ways of automating controllers' traffic display. Currently, this normally consists of flight progress strips, pieces of paper measuring about 8 in x 8 in, mounted in a plastic holder and displayed adjacent to the controller's radar console. These strips contain the essential data a controller needs to know on flights within, or shortly to enter, his area of responsibility. They are updated by the controller as required to indicate clearances and other instructions given to aircraft. Unfortunately, they can be unwieldy in busy times—there is simply not enough room within easy reach of the controller to display all the relevant traffic details. They require an excessive time, in computer terms, to be printed and require arranging, by the controller, into the required display sequence (normally time order). But they have their advantages too—they are versatile, can be amended and re-distributed easily, provide a readily available 'hard copy' for incident investigations and so on. Thus they have been retained in use long after electronic data displays could have been expected to have replaced them. However, there is one other important reason why the flight progress strip is hard to replace electronically. The present system can be updated at the stroke of a pen—to update an electronic data display requires the entry of the appropriate keyboard message by a controller for whom time is at a premium.

Defining the role

There is no escaping the fact that increased use of automation in ATC is inevitable. If controllers themselves seem less than enthusiastic at the prospect, it is in no way due to a 'Luddite' approach—rather it is an expression of concern that inadequate forethought may lead to a fundamental, and detrimental, change in the role of the controller, coupled with a degree of conservatism which is right and proper amongst those whose prime concern is safety. Where automated systems have been introduced, and have materially improved the ability of the controller to perform his tasks efficiently whilst not threatening his basic role, they have been readily accepted. But what makes controllers particularly wary is the clear impression that automation is sometimes introduced because it is available and not necessarily because it offers an improved way of tackling a particular problem. It is this pressure to put the cart before the horse—to see what modern technology can provide and then find tasks for it—that causes concern.

Even where the benefits to be derived from the introduction of automation are readily apparent, inadequate thought is sometimes given to the limitations of the facility and to the consequential effects on both controller tasks and other elements of the system. It is here that professional human factors advice is essential, for the introduction of automation into a complex system, operated by highly trained, highly skilled personnel, requires careful consideration of its most effective method of utilisation and the manner of its introduction. Such thoughts seem far from the minds of administrations in certain parts of the world who, under pressure politically or from airlines to improve basic deficiencies in their ATC system, seize on automation as an opportunity to show they are doing something. The hurried purchase of 'off the shelf' equipment, with little or no analysis of the technical requirement or appreciation of the human element, cannot compensate for basic system deficiencies (lack of radar, shortage of trained staff etc.). It may be expedient politically, but it does the cause of automation, system efficiency and air safety no good whatsoever.

From the controller's viewpoint, therefore, the introduction of automation presents two challenges—to the technical integrity of the system and to the essential task and role of the controller. Given adequate attention to functional requirement, design, system integration and shake-down, and training of both controllers and technical support staff, the former can be overcome. The second element requires the adoption of a philosophy that the role of automation in air traffic control is to extend the skills of the controller, not to replace them.

The man/machine interface

The problem of keyboard input by controllers has already been mentioned in terms of updating data displays—a sphere where the automated system compares poorly, in terms of workload, with the manual, or handwritten, update. So if controllers are to be required to shift attention from their primary source of data, in most cases a radar screen, then there must be significant benefits to be derived from so doing. In the absence of such benefits, it is natural that controllers will resent the intrusion of another peripheral task, however much training and experience reduces the conscious effort involved. Whilst much research work has been done into man/machine interfaces in general, and in air traffic control in particular, clearly there is a long way to go. If current research work into speech update of computers eventually produces a viable system, many of these problems may be overcome.

An aid—not a solution

Perhaps the most clear-cut advantage of automated systems is their predictive ability. In ATC terms, this means the ability to 'look ahead' in a complex traffic situation, to give advance warning of conflicts and to examine the validity of potential re-clearances. Although initial experiences of such features have not been altogether happy, there can be little doubt that the bugbears of the system will eventually be overcome, thereby providing a useful extension of the controller's skills and providing a positive back-up to his judgement when making decisions. For the back-up nature of the role is important in accordance with the philosophy discussed earlier. The controller will still plan, and exercise his control function, with a view to avoiding conflict, just as a pilot flies his aircraft with the intention of avoiding the terrain; the conflict warning capability will provide a useful 'long-stop', just as the GPWS (ground proximity warning system) provides an alert to the pilot in danger of inadvertently approaching high ground.

Of course, not only can automation assist the controller in applying his skills in the most efficient and safe manner, but by removing many of his more mundane tasks it can give him more of that precious commodity, time—time to think, time to plan, time to control. It is unfortunate that, in western Europe at least, the fragmented development and introduction of automation amongst the various states has inhibited the automatic transfer of flight data between centres, a task well-suited to the computer. But a much more fundamental change is in the offing, for moves are now afoot to utilise the ground—air data link capability of forthcoming systems to replace that most tenuous link in the control loop— the RT.

Communications: a case for a broader outlook

There is no doubt that a busy RT channel can occupy an excessive proportion of a controller's attention, reducing or almost eliminating the time available for planning and coordination. Equally, the requirement to monitor constantly imposes a significant workload on the flight crew. The theory of the data link is that messages and instructions between the controller and the pilot will be transmitted, not by a general voice broadcast as at present, but by a discretely addressed computer-generated message, initiated by the pilot or controller. The messages would be received only by the aircraft to whom they were addressed, or the controller, and displayed on a suitable electronic display or, perhaps, printed out. Superficially, the system has considerable advantages, especially in terms of overcoming most of the problems of communication discussed earlier. Over the past few years the methods of message display on the flight deck and the effect on pilot workload have been the subject of research in the UK and elsewhere. However, only as an afterthought was it realised that a requirement to generate messages in this manner, perhaps acceptable on a flight deck, could pose enormous problems for a controller dealing with say, twenty aircraft. Whilst research continues, it is clear that major advances will be required if the controller is not to be reduced entirely to a button-pressing automaton, with even less time available for planning and decision-making. This is, perhaps, indicative of the separate approach to human factor problems on the flight deck and on the ground which has bedevilled the industry for too long. In terms of air traffic control, both ends of the system must be seen as part of a whole, and treated as such.

There are other aspects to this question which should not be overlooked. The human voice can convey much more than the basic text of the message indicates —inflexion, pitch and intonation can put, if not a different meaning, at least a different emphasis on a message. Any pilot will surely react that much quicker to instructions from a controller to climb, descend, turn or whatever when the urgency of the instruction is apparent from the controller's voice. Even if there is not the imminent possibility of conflict, the indication of high controller workload which can be read into the sharp exchanges of a busy RT channel will ensure a prompt reaction by most pilots.

There can be little doubt, too, that the verbal RT exchanges play no small part in the mental process by which the controller builds up the traffic picture. Just as children find it easier to learn multiplication tables or Latin declensions by saying them aloud, so the RT exchanges fix the evolving traffic situation in the controller's mind. Such elements would be missing from a data link—a prime example of a situation where human factors considerations are of vital importance to any discussion of the relative merits of a new system.

The Complementary Role—The Complementary Aim

In terms of maintaining the safety and integrity of the system, the roles of pilot and controller are inextricably linked. Each have problems specific to the environment in which they operate but, as this book clearly illustrates, they share many of the same doubts, frustrations and, at times, injustices. Only in recent years has air traffic control been exposed to the full glare of publicity, the instant judgements and uninformed speculation which so often follow a major aircraft accident.

Increasingly, air traffic controllers' actions are being questioned and examined in isolation; when scapegoats are needed, the controller comes a close second to the pilot.

In considering the problems of the controller, the pressures upon him, and his role in present and future systems, one must not seek in any way to over-dramatise the situation. But as a vital part of the control, and therefore safety, 'loop', the controller's problems are the pilot's problems. If only from instincts of self-preservation, pilots must be just as concerned with the underlying reasons for so-called 'controller error' as for 'pilot error'. Both are fighting the same battle, for a rational assessment of the actions, and the reasons for those actions, of all who may be implicated in an aircraft accident. In advocating this approach, both professions owe it to themselves, and to the public, not to be drawn into unseemly battles and squabbling to 'clear their yard-arm' in the aftermath of an accident. To do so can only prejudice their major aim—the advancement of air safety through greater understanding.

Chapter 8
Neglected Human Factors *S. N. Roscoe*

Other chapters have made reference to pilot judgement and the hazards of visual illusions. Stanley Roscoe is especially concerned with these areas of investigation and devotes the penultimate chapter of this book to a consideration of related problems. These range from difficulties experienced during landing approaches to the influence of cockpit design on pilot visibility and therefore, on the risk of collision.

The incidence of false perception indicates the need for protective training, for an understanding of the many elements which contribute to the situation and, where necessary, for redesign of the cockpit environment.

This chapter deals with a family of 'pilot errors' that are never explained in accident reports, the causes of which have been ignored or intentionally obscured by aircraft manufacturers, regulatory and investigative authorities, the aviation scientific community, and by pilots themselves.

During the history of experimental psychology a vast literature has emerged on our ability to detect things and our so-called constancies in judging their shapes, sizes, and distances. Among the many human factors in aviation, these abilities are particularly critical. Yet there is surprisingly little communication between investigators of the psychology of vision, the designers of aeroplanes, and the operational types who select and train flight crews. How we judge position and motion relative to airport runways and other surface objects and how we detect other aeroplanes, especially those on collision courses, are among the most seriously neglected human factors in aviation system design, training, and operation.

Judging Size and Distance

In 1950 at the University of Illinois it was discovered that aeroplane pilots making landing approaches by periscope come in high and land long and hard, unless the image of the scene is magnified by about 20–30 per cent[29,38] (see Fig. 8.1). In 1973 Everett Palmer at the NASA-Ames Research Center in California experimentally confirmed the common observation that pilots also make high approaches and long, hard landings in flight simulators with contact visual systems.[26] Similar misjudgements occur with helmet-mounted imaging displays. Why is it that either real or virtual images projected at unity magnification cause objects such as airport runways to appear smaller and farther away than when viewed directly?

In 1975 Robert Randle of NASA-Ames Research Center and the author set

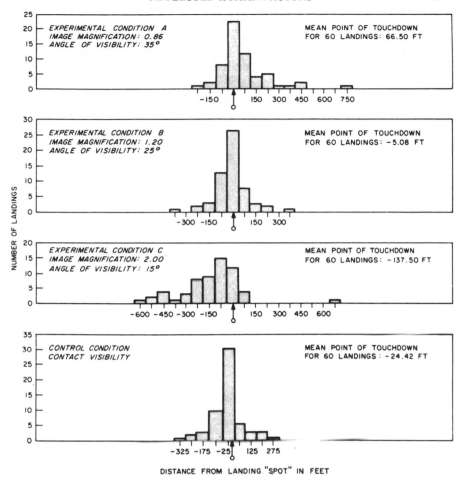

Fig. 8.1   Distributions of points of touchdown for 60 landings (10 by each of 6 pilots) in four experimental conditions, three involving periscope magnification factors of 0.86, 1.20, and 2.00 and the fourth providing contact visibility. With x2 magnification pilots touch down short of the aim-point and unexpectedly; with image minification they round out high and land long and hard; at x1.2 the distribution of touchdown points is virtually indistinguishable from that for contact visibility.[38]

out to find answers with the expert help of Robert Hennessy, now of the US National Research Council, and a gaggle of graduate research assistants at San José State University 1975–77, the University of Illinois in 1977–79, and New Mexico State University in 1979–81. Together we discovered a correlation of 0.9 or greater between the apparent, or perceived, size of objects subtending a given visual angle and an observer's visual accommodation—the distance to which the eyes are focused[33,34] (see Fig. 8.2). This finding runs directly counter to accepted theory.

Perhaps it is not surprising that a relationship between perceived size and eye focus for distances well beyond the near limit of 'optical infinity' went undiscovered for so long. Stimulus distances normally included in laboratory experiments do not approach those from which pilots view the world below them in flight. Indeed, few laboratory experiments in which eye focus was actually measured have involved distances of more than a few metres. But now that a strong relationship between the distance of eye focus and apparent size has been established, other mysteries of visual perception and illusion in flight become fair game for reassessment.

For example: Why do pilots making landing approaches over water at night toward a brightly lighted city consistently come in low[13] and sometimes land in the bay short of the runway? This has happened in Tokyo, San Francisco, Los Angeles, Salt Lake City, and elsewhere. Why is it that military pilots making ground attack runs so often fail to pull up in time and fly into the terrain in clear daylight? And why, in a group of pilots with 'normal' vision, will some spot 'bogies' so much sooner than others?

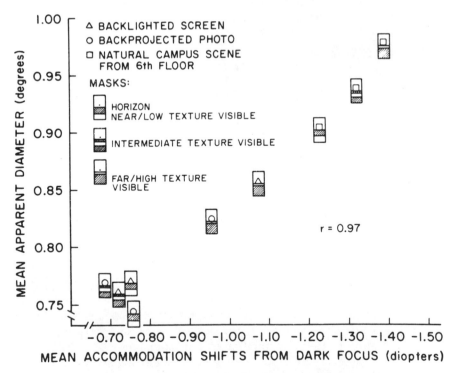

Fig. 8.2 Mean apparent diameter of the simulated moon as a function of mean accommodation shift from individual dark-focus distances for eight observers viewing the moon against three different backgrounds (scenes), each differentially obscured by a series of three masks that induced further shifts in visual accommodation and apparent size. (Hull, Gill, and Roscoe, in press)

Background

Before suggesting answers to such questions, some background is in order. By 1970 Randle had developed a classical Pavlovian conditioning technique, employing automatic biofeedback of focusing responses to study the extent of possible voluntary control of accommodation. Randle's initial purpose was to teach children how to avoid becoming myopic. Then during the early 1970s, Hennessy, working with his mentor, Herschel Leibowitz, and fellow graduate student, Fred Owens, at the Pennsylvania State University, greatly extended our understanding of the 'anomalous' empty-field, night, and instrument myopias, and clarified the role of the dark focus, or relaxed accommodation, of the eye.*

Then, between 1975 and 1981 at Ames Research Center, the University of Illinois, and New Mexico State University, twenty-three experiments were conducted involving the relationships among visual stimulus variables, eye accommodation, and associated perceptual responses.* There is no longer any question that this line of investigation is of great importance to aviation. Among the many findings, the following stand out as contributing to our understanding of why pilots often misjudge sizes and distances and fail to see and avoid other aircraft in flight.

(a) Judgements of size and, by inference, the distance, of objects in natural outdoor vistas are strongly dependent on the distance to which the eyes are focused ($r > 0.9$).

(b) Accommodation to natural vistas depends in a complicated way on the dark focus† of the individual, the retinal locus and spatial frequency of visible texture,[1] and the sharpness of focus needed for the discrimination of object identity, for example, reading a sign.[40]

(c) The wide individual differences in dark focus range from perhaps 15 D (7 cm) in extremely myopic people to as distant as − 4 D (far beyond 'optical infinity') in the extremely hyperopic. The more distant the individual's dark focus, the greater his or her tendency to focus *beyond* an acuity target to maximise apparent size for the discrimination of detail[40] (see Fig. 8.3).

(d) Some individuals can be trained more readily than others to control the focal distance of their eyes voluntarily. There is some evidence that such trainability depends in part on the individual's dark focus and that both the selection and training of pilots should take such characteristics into account.

The moon illusion revisited

A convenient way to study perceptual responses to the distant vistas seen in

---

* Though not cited individually here, reports of these experiments are included in the references at the end of this chapter.

† The distance at which the eyes focus in an empty field such as a clear sky is very close to the distance at which they come to rest in the dark.

contact flight is to use a technique developed by Lloyd Kaufman and Irvin Rock[12] to quantify the moon illusion. By superimposing a collimated disk of light on any natural outdoor or laboratory scene and providing an adjustable-diameter comparison disk nearby, surprisingly consistent estimates of the

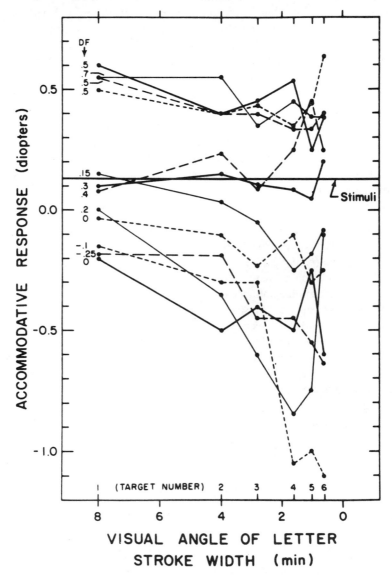

Fig. 8.3   Individual visual accommodation responses to Snellen letters of various sizes presented at a fixed distance of 7.6 metres under constant illumination of 1.3 ftL. As the letters become smaller and harder to read, observers with more distant dark focus levels accommodate farther and farther *beyond* the targets for maximum acuity; observers with nearer dark focus levels do not exhibit this zoom-lens effect.

apparent size of the simulated 'moon' can be obtained. An adaptation of the Kaufman and Rock technique (known affectionately as 'the moon machine') has been used in a series of experiments to correlate measured eye accommodation, judgements of apparent size, and characteristics of both natural and artificial visual scenes.[34]

These experiments have shown that with both natural and artificial scenes, whether in daylight or at night, when viewing conditions cause the eyes to focus near, the moon shrinks, and when they cause distant focus, the moon grows.[1,10,11,12,42]

Whatever the causal explanation may turn out to be, this invariant relationship appears to be the key to many of the misjudgements experienced by pilots. Such misjudgements can cause pilots to land in the water at night, fly into the terrain or overshoot a runway in the daylight, or fail to see and avoid another aeroplane on a collision course.

Critical Variables

Viewing conditions that induce shifts in focus either outward or inward from the dark focus include subject, cockpit design, task, and environment variables as well as the distribution of visible texture.

Subject variables

Differences in perceptual abilities among people qualifying as having normal '20/20' vision are staggering.[40] Some are surprisingly near-sighted while some have the ability to focus − 4 D beyond 'optical infinity', much like a zoom lens of a TV camera. A US Air Force recruit, when told by Nicholas Simonelli that he had remarkable vision, said, 'Yes, Suh, I can tell the colour of a frog's eyes at 100 paces'. The recruit was not bragging; his acuity was of the order of 20/10 and his dark focus and far point well into the negative range.

Eye accommodation is a tug-of-war between the stimulus and the dark focus, with the stimulus normally pulling just hard enough to be seen and recognised. Simonelli refers to this as the 'acuity demand' of a stimulus. As we talk, drive a car, or fly low over the terrain, our accommodation is determined largely by Gibson's[7] well-known 'texture gradient'. The retina unconsciously performs some kind of an averaging routine on the textural elements to reduce the blur, and the fact that much of the scene necessarily remains blurred normally goes unnoticed so long as the acuity demand remains low.

In daylight the gradient extends uninterrupted from the nose and other parts of the body to the near foreground and on out to the distant horizon. But from the cockpit at night, and even in daylight at higher altitudes, the gradient is not uninterrupted. Between nearby cockpit surfaces and the outside visible texture the gradient is interrupted by empty space. Even clouds are effectively textureless in that they present little acuity demand, and at night the outside texture is limited to a thin horizontal band of point light sources. Now this is where individual differences in dark focus can cause giant misperceptions.

If a pilot's dark focus is at about arms' length, normal for young healthy eyes, he will experience empty-field myopia in daylight, as well as night myopia. Empty-field myopia is reinforced by the stimulus pull of window posts and frames, some of which are even nearer than arms' length. For example, at New Mexico State University we found that pilots focused at almost exactly the distance of window posts viewed against a sky background, even when a post was no wider than the two and a half inch distance between the eyes, thereby supposedly causing no binocular obstruction to outside vision (Roscoe and Hull, in preparation).

Even though other traffic may be clearly visible, the effect of induced myopia is to blur the retinal image, reduce effective contrast and make objects harder to see and apparently both smaller and farther away.[14,33,34] Targets can still be detected, particularly if they flash or glisten, or if they present an extended distinctive shape, such as a long, thin contrail, or if they move. However, another aeroplane on a collision course doesn't move, it only grows, slowly at first and then very rapidly, and it must subtend a visual angle of more than 8 minutes before it can be readily detected when badly out of focus.[18]

Now for a different danger. If a pilot's dark focus is quite distant, possibly beyond optical infinity, and his attention is directed to the lights of a coastal airport and the city rising beyond, the visual scene can appear greatly magnified. The nearer lights of the runway threshold will expand downward from the horizontal band of city lights, thereby making it appear that the aeroplane is high on final approach. The pilot may compensate by reducing power and drop below the proper glide-slope. At some point the low position will suddenly become apparent, and normally the pilot will add sufficient thrust to land safely; but with engines spooled down, thrust may come too late to avert the water landing.

Cockpit design variables

The pilot's legal requirement to 'see and avoid' as a means of maintaining traffic separation in clear weather is at best an anachronism. At high subsonic speeds, head-on closing rates approach 1000 knots. That is about 17 nautical miles per minute, or one mile every four seconds. To avoid another aeroplane on a near head-on collision course, it must be picked up at a minimum of about three miles. Fortunately, at en route flight levels, aeroplanes typically leave contrails that can be seen for many times that distance, so despite the undependability of the see and avoid concept, seeing and avoiding continues to save many lives every year.

Consequently, while few pilots count on seeing and avoiding, everyone does the best he can. Everyone, that is, except the manufacturers of aeroplanes, the regulatory agencies who certificate them, and the investigative agencies who determine the probable causes of mid-air collisions. Strong words? Perhaps, but objectively accurate in view of the routine certification of aeroplanes that do not meet nominal minimum cockpit visibility standards, and the fact that officially

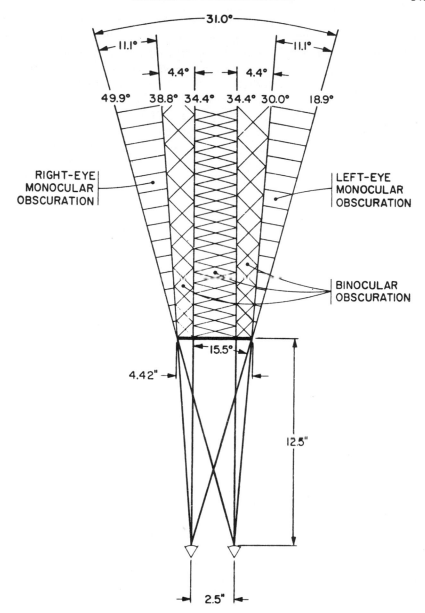

Fig. 8.4 Visibility diagram showing sectors of monocular and binocular obscuration caused by a window post of 4.42 in projected width, 12.5 in from pilot's eyes.

approved deviations from such standards are never cited as contributing causes of pilot errors in mid-air collisions on clear, bright, sunny days.

Title 14 of the US Code of Federal Regulations, as revised in 1963, stated in part that no windshield post in the cockpit of a transport category aircraft shall 'exceed 2.5 inches total obstruction in projected width on the pilot's eyes when located within a sector of 20 degrees and 60 degrees azimuth to the left of the pilot's forward vision. . .' This standard is based on the fact that two and a half inches is the average distance between human eyes, and any window obstruction of greater projected width necessarily makes it possible for another aeroplane on a stationary collision course to be completely obscured to both eyes. Nevertheless, this standard is frequently violated in the design of transport category aircraft.

One current commercial transport, for example, has a window post starting 30° to the left of the pilot's forward vision (and another to the right of the co-pilot) that exceeds the inter-ocular distance by approximately two inches. It creates a binocular obscuration of almost 9°, as shown in Fig. 8.4, and a total sector of obstruction to one eye or the other of 31°. Fig. 8.5 illustrates the zones of monocular and binocular visibility from the pilot's nominal eye position, and compares these with the nominal standard. The solid black areas are supposed to be free of binocular obscuration.

Oversized window posts can, in fact, be found in a number of current commercial aircraft. To investigate this problem, we measured the effects of simulated window posts 2½ ins and 4⅝ ins wide, and 12 ins in front of the eyes, on the probability of detecting simulated contrails at various elevations projecting various angular distances from the right or left edge of such a post (Roscoe and Hull, in preparation). With a 2½ ins post, the probability of detection in a single fixation of ⅓ second ranged from 0.79 to 0.97 as the angular length of a contrail increased from 6° to 16° to the right or left of forward vision, as illustrated in Fig. 8.6.

With the 4⅝ ins post (2⅛ ins greater than the inter-pupillary distance), the probabilities of detection for corresponding contrails, also shown in Fig. 8.6, plunged to 0.10 for 6° (barely visible to one eye or the other at the right or left edge of the post) and gradually increased to 0.29 for 7°, 0.55 for 9°, 0.68 for 12°, and 0.65 for 16°. In addition to the total binocular obscuration caused by

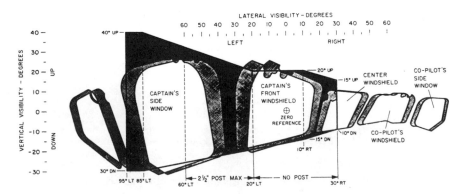

Fig. 8.5   Comparison of visibility with US Federal Aviation Administration nominal visibility standard. Solid dark areas indicate binocular visibility obscuration where none should exist; shaded areas indicate monocular obscuration.

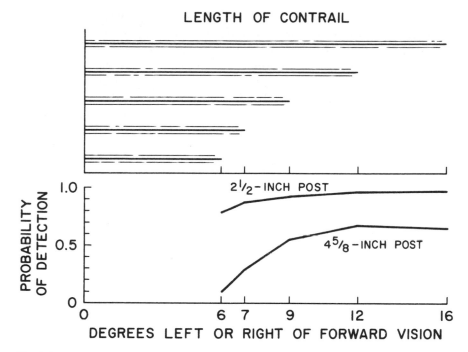

Fig. 8.6   Probability of detecting simulated contrails of varying angular subtense against a uniform background as a function of the obscuration caused by window posts of 2½ ins and 4⅝ ins projected widths at 12 ins from the pilot's eyes. (Hull and Roscoe, in preparation)

an oversized window post, the probability of detection of a contrail in the sectors of monocular visibility on either side is greatly reduced. Few pilots are aware of the danger caused by wide window posts a few inches from the eyes.

Task variables

Pilots with normal visual functions can expect outward shifts in accommodation when task demands create elevated workloads and stresses. Several experiments have demonstrated accommodation shifts with interposed mental activities[19,5] (see Fig. 8.7). Bob Randle and John Petitt found that accommodation shifted outward between measurements, 20 secs and 10 secs before touchdown on simulated landing approaches by reference to a computer-animated night visual scene. We have no comfortable explanation.[28]

However, outward accommodation is at least partially mediated by the sympathetic branch of the autonomic nervous system[1,4,5] —that is the one that makes us run faster and fight harder. It also helps us see the distant enemy in the shadow of a rock and the stag behind a bush. It increases our acuity by magnifying what we see, just as outward focus magnifies the moon. Can it be that the flow of sympathetic adrenalin in the attack pilot expands his visual world, makes the ground appear lower, and causes him to pull up too late? When a periscope's magnification is set too high, pilots are often surprised by a touchdown far short of the runway (recall Fig. 8.1). Randle, Petitt, and the author also found that pilots do not accommodate accurately to changing focus demands induced by ophthalmic lenses. They responded slightly better to a direct view of the computer-animated display than to collimated virtual images as presented on head-up displays, thus bringing into question the supposed advantage of preparing the eyes to see the runway when it suddenly appears on low visibility approaches. Optically collimating an image tends to release our focus from the distant stimulus and allows it to lapse toward the dark focus distance.

Environmental variables

This discussion might have been headed, 'St Thomas Revisited'. Surely one of the most puzzling and dramatic aviation mysteries surrounds the crash of an American Airlines B727 at Harry S. Truman Field, St Thomas, Virgin Islands, in

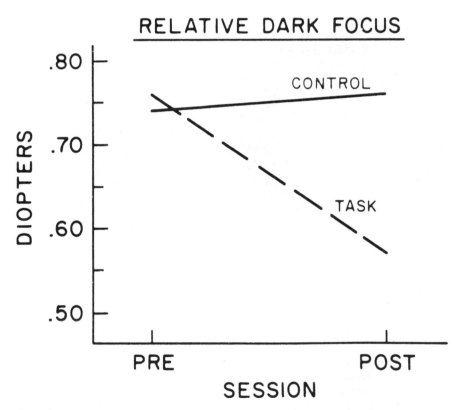

Fig. 8.7   Relative dark focus (absolute dark focus minus far-point focus in diopters) before and after task subjects performed a short-term memory task (delayed digit cancelling) for four minutes and control subjects rested for four minutes.

1976. Captain Arthur Bujnowski had made 154 uneventful landings on the same short, wide runway with similar daylight visibility and light, gusting winds. But on 27 April 1976, Art Bujnowski made a normal 'slotted' approach, levelled off a few feet above the runway, and floated beyond the point of no return. The flaming crash and resulting smoke cost the lives of thirty-five passengers and two flight attendants.[20,31,35]

Art Bujnowski is a pilot's pilot, a skilful, calm, no-nonsense ex-Captain, now in forced retirement in Connecticut and permanently grounded. But three minutes before his ill-fated landing in 1976 he was in extreme pain from blocked ears due to an abnormal increase in cockpit and cabin pressure caused by mismanagement of the air compressor during a rapid descent. Other crew members and passengers were in similar pain. Intense stimulation of the inner ears causes an accommodative spasm of the eyes at about arms' length on average.[3]

Neither Bujnowski nor his co-pilot could see the clearly visible VASI lights on final approach, and both testified they expected the aeroplane to touch down, as doctrine called for, 1000 feet from the runway threshold. But it did not touch down, and with about 1500 feet of runway remaining, the co-pilot finally said, 'You're still high, Art'. The same comment is often made by a safety pilot in the right seat while a pilot-subject rounds out high and floats with a periscope set at x1 magnification. The visual field is compressed with near accommodation, and the runway appears higher than it is. As Art Bujnowski remembered:

'. . .all I could see were cottages and stores or whatever they were. But it seemed like the activity was right there at eye level, . . .'

(Transcript of NTSB public hearing, p. 360)

Real-world application

Randle's demonstration of the possibility of conditioning the accommodation reflex by the application of biofeedback calls for systematic investigation of the trainability of individuals varying in dark focus distances and other oculo-motor abilities. Basic data in this area are fragmentary but promising, and effective conditioning techniques are needed involving only simple, inexpensive equipment that can be used by instructors or technicians with limited training, or even by the individual pilot. There has been some success using a simple vernier optometer constructed from cross-polarised strips of inexpensive filter material.[41]

The effective focal distance of the eyes can be manipulated either voluntarily, following bio-conditioning, or involuntarily, by having pilots wear polyfocal glasses as is done by United Air Lines.[8] Acuity in resolving distant stimuli is enhanced by focusing at a distance greater than that of the stimulus to be discriminated (recall Fig. 8.3). It is possible that detection of distant 'point' targets, such as other aircraft, also can be enhanced by inducing accommodation to distances at or 'beyond' optical infinity for individuals capable of unusually distant focus.

Each of the so-called anomalous myopias and the associated micropsias* are encountered in varying degrees by pilots flying aeroplanes, particularly those with head-up displays. Similar myopic responses and micropsic perceptions occur in aeroplane simulators with contact visual systems. Recall that it was concern with the bias errors in landing with imaging flight displays that stimulated interest in this line of research in the first place. It is evident that pilots do learn to compensate partially for such biased perceptions. The possibility of training individuals to recognise conditions in which to expect macropsic† as well as micropsic misperceptions and to compensate for them voluntarily is out there like Mt Everest (or Mt St Helens).

Conclusion

Misjudgements of position in flight and failures to detect other airborne traffic are casualties of the eternal tug-of-war between visible texture and the pilot's dark focus. The eye is lazy and resists the pull of a distant stimulus, preferring to rest at a relatively short focal distance as it does in the dark or when looking at the sky. Judgements of apparent size are highly correlated with visual accommodation distance, and the difficulty of detecting aeroplanes on stationary collision courses is greatly aggravated when focus is trapped by a structure close to the eyes. Subject, cockpit design, task, and environment variables all interact to determine what we think we see.

References

1. Benel, R. A. (1979) *Visual Accommodation, the Mandelbaum Effect, and Apparent Size*. New Mexico State University, Behavioral Engineering Laboratory, Technical Report BEL-79-1/AFOSR-79-5, Las Cruces, New Mexico.
2. Benel, R. A. and Benel, D. C. R. (1979) *Accommodation in Untextured Stimulus Fields*. University of Illinois at Urbana-Champaign, Department of Psychology, Technical Report Eng Psy-79-1/AFOSR-79-1, Champaign, Illinois.
3. Clark, B., Randle, R. J. and Stewart, J. D. (1975) 'Vestibular-Ocular Accommodation Reflex in Man'. *Aviation, Space, and Environmental Medicine* 46, 1336-9.
4. Cogan, D. G. (1937) 'Accommodation and the Autonomic Nervous System'. *Archives of Ophthalmology* 18, 739-66.
5. Gawron, V. J. (1979) *Eye Accommodation, Personality, and Autonomic Balance*. New Mexico State University, Behavioral Engineering Laboratory, Technical Report BEL-79-2/AFOSR-79-6, Las Cruces, New Mexico.
6. Gawron, V. J. (1980) *Differences Among Myopes, Emmetropes, and Hyperopes*. New Mexico State University, Behavioral Engineering Laboratory, Technical Report BEL-80-1/AFOSR-80-1, Las Cruces, New Mexico.

* Reduced apparent size.
† Increased apparent size.

7. Gibson, J. J. (1950) *The Perception of the Visual World*, Houghton Mifflin, Boston.
8. Harper, C. R. and Kidera, G. J. (1968) 'Flight Deck Vision and the Aging Eye'. *Aerospace Medicine* **39**, 1119–22.
9. Hennessy, R. T. (1975) 'Instrument Myopia'. *Journal of the Optical Society of America* **65**, 1114–20.
10. Hull, J. C., Gill, R. T. and Roscoe, S. N. (1979) *Locus of the Stimulus to Visual Accommodation: Where in the World, or Where in the Eye?* New Mexico State University, Behavioral Engineering Laboratory, Technical Report BEL-79-5/AFOSR-79-9, Las Cruces, New Mexico.
11. Iavecchia, H. J., Iavecchia, H. P. and Roscoe, S. N. (1978) *The Moon Illusion: Apparent Size and Visual Accommodation Distance*. University of Illinois at Urbana-Champaign, Department of Psychology, Technical Report Eng Psy-78-4/AFOSR-78-3, Champaign, Illinois.
12. Kaufman, L. and Rock, I. (1962) 'The Moon Illusion'. *Scientific American* **207**, 260–8.
13. Kraft, C. L. (1978) 'A Psychophysical Contribution to Air Safety: Simulator Studies of Visual Illusions in Night Visual Approaches', in Pick, H. A., Jr (ed.), *Psychology: From Research to Practice*. Plenum Press, New York.
14. Kraft, C. L., Farrell, R. J. and Boucek, G. P., Jr (1970) *Visual Performance from the 737 Cab as a Function of Pilot's Position within the Cab*. The Boeing Company, Unnumbered internal report, Seattle.
15. Leibowitz, H. W. and Owens, D. A. (1975) 'Anomalous Myopias and the Intermediate Dark Focus of Accommodation'. *Science* **189**, 646–8.
16. Leibowitz, H. W. and Owens, D. A. (1975) 'Night Myopia and the Intermediate Dark Focus of Accommodation'. *Journal of Optical Society of America* **65**, 1121–8.
17. Leibowitz, H. W., Hennessy, R. T. and Owens, D. A. (1975) 'The Intermediate Resting Position of Accommodation and Some Implications for Space Perception'. *Psychologia* **18**(3), 162–70.
18. Luria, S. M. (1980) 'Target Size and Correction for Empty-Field Myopia'. *Journal of the Optical Society of America* **70**, 1153–4.
19. Malmstrom, F. V. (1979) 'Effects of Concurrent Mental Activity on Static and Dynamic Accommodation Responses'. Ph.D. dissertation, Oklahoma State University, 1978, *Dissertation Abstracts International*, **39B**, 61–2.
20. National Transportation Safety Board (NTSB) (1976) *Aircraft Accident Report: American Airlines, Inc., Boeing 727-95, N1963; St Thomas, Virgin Islands, April 27, 1976*. United States Government Printing Office, Report NTSB-AAR-77-1, Washington, DC.
21. Owens, D. A. (1977) 'Factors Influencing Steady-State Accommodation'. Ph.D. dissertation, Pennsylvania State University, 1976, *Dissertation Abstracts International* **37B**, 5863.
22. Owens, D. A. (1979) 'The Mandelbaum Effect: Evidence for an Accommodative Bias toward Intermediate Viewing Distances'. *Journal of the Optical Society of America* **69**, 646–52.

23. Owens, D. A. and Leibowitz, H. W. (1975) 'The Fixation Point as a Stimulus for Accommodation'. *Vision Research* **15**, 1161–3.
24. Owens, D. A. and Leibowitz, H. W. (1976) 'Oculomotor Adjustments in Darkness and the Specific Distance Tendency'. *Perception and Psychophysics* **20**(1), 2–9.
25. Owens, D. A. and Leibowitz, H. W. (1976) 'Night Myopia: Cause and a Possible Basis for Amelioration'. *American Journal of Optometry and Physiological Optics* **53**, 709–17.
26. Palmer, E. and Cronn, F. W. (1973) 'Touchdown Performance with a Computer Graphics Night Visual Attachment'. *Proceedings of the AIAA Visual and Motion Simulation Conference*. American Institute of Aeronautics and Astronautics, New York.
27. Randle, R. J. (1970) 'Volitional Control of Visual Accommodation'. *AGARD Proceedings No. 82 on Adaptation and Acclimatization in Aerospace Medicine*. North Atlantic Treaty Organisation, Neuilly-sur-Seine, France.
28. Randle, R. J., Roscoe, S. N. and Petitt, J. (1980) *Effects of Accommodation and Magnification on Aimpoint Estimation in a Simulated Landing Task*. National Aeronautics and Space Administration, Technical Paper NASA-TP-1635, Washington, DC.
29. Roscoe, S. N. (1951) 'Aircraft Pilot Performance as a Function of the Extent and Magnification of the Visible Horizon'. Ph.D. dissertation, University of Illinois at Urbana-Champaign, 1950, *Dissertation Abstracts International*, **11**, 173.
30. Roscoe, S. N. (1975) 'Ground-Referenced Visual Orientation in Flight Control Tasks: Judgments of Size and Distance', in *Vision R & D Program Review*. Naval Air Systems Command and Office of Naval Research, Washington, DC, 145–74. (Originally issued by the University of Illinois as Technical Report ARL 75-7/ONR-75-1, 1975.)
31. Roscoe, S. N. (1976) 'Appendix I: Human Factors and Crew Performance in the St Thomas Accident', in *Accident Investigation Post-Hearing Submission to the National Transportation Safety Board, B-727 Accident, St Thomas, Virgin Islands, April 27, 1976*. Allied Pilots Association, Arlington, Texas.
32. Roscoe, S. N. (1977) *How Big the Moon, How Fat the Eye?* University of Illinois at Urbana-Champaign, Aviation Research Laboratory, Technical Report ARL-77-9/AFOSR-77-8, Savoy, Illinois.
33. Roscoe, S. N. (1979) 'When Day is Done and Shadows Fall, We Miss the Airport Most of All'. *Human Factors* **21**, 721–31.
34. Roscoe, S. N. (1979) *Ground-Referenced Visual Orientation with Imaging Displays. Final Report*. University of Illinois at Urbana-Champaign, Department of Psychology, Technical Report Eng Psy-79-4/AFOSR-79-4, Champaign, Illinois.
35. Roscoe, S. N. (1980) *Aviation Psychology*. Iowa State University Press, Ames, Iowa.

36. Roscoe, S. N. (1980) 'Bigness Is in the Eye of the Beholder'. *Proceedings of the Seventh Symposium on Psychology in the Department of Defense.* United States Air Force Academy, Colorado Springs, 39—80.

37. Roscoe, S. N. and Benel, D. A. (1978) *Is the Eye Smart or the Brain Forgiving?* University of Illinois at Urbana-Champaign, Department of Psychology, Technical Report Eng Psy-78-1/AFOSR-78-1, Champaign, Illinois.

38. Roscoe, S. N., Hasler, S. G. and Dougherty, D. J. (1966) 'Flight by Periscope: Making Takeoffs and Landings; the Influence of Image Magnification, Practice, and Various Conditions of Flight'. *Human Factors* 8, 13—40. (Originally issued in 1952 by the Office of Naval Research as Human Engineering Report 71-16-9, classified CONFIDENTIAL.)

39. Roscoe, S. N., Olzak, L. and Randle, R. J. (1976) 'Ground-Referenced Visual Orientation with Imaging Displays: Monocular versus Binocular Accommodation and Judgments of Relative Size'. *Proceedings of the AGARD Acrospace Medical Specialists Meeting, Athens, Greece.* North Atlantic Treaty Organisation, Neuilly-sur-Seine, France.

40. Simonelli, N. M. (1979) *The Dark Focus of Visual Accommodation: Its Existence, Its Measurement, Its Effects.* New Mexico State University, Behavioral Engineering Laboratory, Technical Report BEL-79-3/AFOSR-79-7, Las Cruces, New Mexico.

41. Simonelli, N. M. (1980) 'Polarized Vernier Optometer'. *Behavior Research Methods and Instrumentation* 12, 293—6.

42. Simonelli, N. M. and Roscoe, S. N. (1979) *Apparent Size and Visual Accommodation Under Day and Night Conditions.* University of Illinois, Department of Psychology, Technical Report Eng Psy-79-3/AFOSR-79-3, Champaign, Illinois.

Chapter 9
Research Perspective *S. N. Roscoe*

The contributors to this book have shown many facets of the problem of aviation safety. They have also emphasised that the syndrome so loosely and erroneously described as 'pilot error' is not the consequence of individual aberration but, in fact, is a function of two determinants: how far the technology of aviation itself has developed and how incompatible in essence are so many of its demands on human capability.

The whole future of aviation safety rests on the recognition of these facts and therefore on those who work towards the solutions required to overcome their implications. It is intelligent to establish the pathways such research should explore and in this next chapter Stanley Roscoe charts the most potentially rewarding course.

Modern aircraft feature computer-aided communication, navigation, guidance, control, and display systems that provide area navigation, vertical guidance, speed control, and energy management. Improved traffic control computers, displays, and control procedures are being developed, a new microwave landing system (MLS) is being implemented, and a satellite global positioning system (GPS) and communication aids are waiting in orbit. These technological and operational advances will affect all types of flying; their benefits and demands will not be felt exclusively by the aeronautically sophisticated.

Research Needs

Predictably the situation just described involves complex changes in the roles of people and machines both on the ground and in the air. Understandably various elements of the aviation community are concerned about the long-standing human factors problems that are being elevated to critical levels and will surely get worse before they can be solved. However, before presenting a programme of research on human factors in aviation, let us examine why such a programme should be considered at all and what can reasonably be expected to result from its implementation.

There appear to be two principal reasons for the growing feeling of urgency in developing a comprehensive programme of research on human factors in aviation. The first concerns the changing roles of flight crews and air traffic controllers with increasing computer-based automation and the impact of these changes on the people themselves—not only on pilots and controllers but also on passengers and support personnel. The second is the growing recognition among responsible people that both airborne and ground instrumentation—including simulators and other training devices as well as displays, controls, and communication equipment —frequently fail to provide necessary and sufficient information in a suitable form for current operations, and that this need not and should not be the case for the future.

Function allocation to people and machines

Whether on the ground or in the air, some functions can be handled better by computers than by pilots and controllers, but the converse is also true. Nevertheless, the best ways to take advantage of the capabilities of each are not always evident and generally not clearly resolvable on the basis of current scientific knowledge. Furthermore, how well each can handle any given function depends greatly on how performance of the function is designed into the system—how computers are programmed, how pilots and controllers are selected and trained, and what types of displays and controls are provided to support their uniquely human abilities.

Other things being equal, as they seldom are, if people are to be most effective in complex system operations, they have to be kept busy. Humans are poor watch-keepers, or monitors, when called on to perform only when something goes wrong or when the unexpected occurs. Computers, on the other hand, are excellent monitors and are capable of fast, accurate, and reliable responses in any situation that occurs predictably. The 'Catch 22' is that the uniquely human capability to handle the unpredictable can be depended on only if the human is awake, alert, and ready to take effective action, and these conditions can be maintained only if the human is routinely involved and currently proficient.

Human factors in aviation system design

The burden of human factors research in aviation is to provide a practical scientific basis for designing equipment and procedures, and training and certification programmes, to optimise human performance of those functions assigned to pilots, controllers, and maintenance personnel. Whenever an airplane cockpit, a traffic control centre, or an operational or maintenance procedure is designed, the designer has to make many decisions, whether consciously or otherwise, that will affect the performance of operational and/or maintenance personnel. Some relevant design principles have been established and embodied in minimum standards for certification, but these are generally not well stated, documented, or understood.

Furthermore, in a subtle, not consciously intentional way, pilots provide a stubborn resistance to innovation in the cockpit—particularly older pilots in high places and company test pilots and training managers. There is a giant pride associated with breaking a wild horse or the masterful manoeuvring of an unruly aeroplane at the edges of its performance envelope. The 'right stuff' is required and, like manhood, must be defended. If the horse or the aeroplane were to be made too gentle in advance, lesser stuff might appear right enough.

Human factors in aviation training and certification

Similar problems exist in the area of operator training, certification, and currency maintenance and assurance. Some principles of effective training and transfer of learning have been developed through research and operational experience. But once again these have not been well documented and are not well understood by many who are responsible for specifying the characteristics of training devices or for developing training programmes. Clearly the major airlines have made the best use of advanced technology in training, but even here much improvement is possible and needed, and the benefits of their experience need to be passed along to the rest of the aviation community.

The airlines, for example, could make greater use of their simulators in preparing individual pilots for specific operations, particularly emergency operations at marginal airports or on marginal approaches to otherwise normal airports. Better use could be made of simulators and computer-based training scenarios that are pregnant with opportunities for bad decisions. Such scenarios can also serve to validate or revise procedural doctrines for specific marginal or emergency operations. Finally, crew members need to be trained to recognise and circumvent situations in which they may be subject to illusory or otherwise degraded judgements and responses.

Approach

How should a programme of research on human factors in aviation be organised and implemented to ensure timely availability of workable solutions for the problems just described?

As a first suggestion, the problems can be approached in either a horizontal or a vertical fashion, and each has its place. By the horizontal approach we mean the development and validation of general principles of design for human effectiveness—principles that can be applied across the board whenever an operator is called on to perform a certain class of functions or tasks. By the vertical approach we mean the application, testing, and validation of horizontally derived principles during the advanced development of specific systems and prior to their operational certification. While this may cost time and money up front, it will surely pay off later.

As a general rule, horizontally oriented research tends to be done by universities and by a few small contract research groups. In contrast, the time and energies of research personnel in government laboratories and industry tend to be consumed by projects of a more typically vertical nature. The research programmes at the University of Illinois on principles of display frequency separation, flight path prediction, and visual time compression are representative of the former type.[4] The cooperative FAA/NASA programmes on Terminal

Configured Vehicles (TCV) and the Cockpit Display of Traffic Information (CDTI) are examples of the latter type.*

Display and control design principles

Recurring problems in instrument design stem from the fact that whenever any particular function has to be implemented the designer has to make a number of decisions; he may or may not be aware that he is making decisions, and very frequently he fails to consider that the same alternatives have been dealt with many times before over many other drawing boards. Few laboratory directors, project engineers, training managers, or pilots realise just how many important design decisions are made in precisely this way. Nevertheless, this process has gone on and on throughout the history of aviation system development.†

What are the sorts of decisions made over and over by different designers at their drawing boards? A few examples and some of the alternatives involved are listed below:

(a) Size, scale factor, and sensitivity of a display.
(b) Direction of sensing: fly-to, fly-from, or frequency-separated.
(c) Visibility and reachability.
(d) Combinations of indications within a display.
(e) Display modes: alpha-numeric, symbolic, pictorial.
(f) Arrangement of controls and displays within a panel or console.
(g) Feel of controls; damping, detents, feedback.
(h) Coding and function of switches, knobs, levers.
(i) Grouping of functionally related operations.
(j) Logic and coding of caution and warning indications

During the less than half-century since human factors engineering was recognised as at least a semi-scientific discipline, countless horizontal and vertical research programmes have dealt with such issues as those embodied in the list above. Nevertheless, different decisions have been made by different designers regarding similar applications of each of the items listed. Possibly because individual applications differ in subtle ways, the proper selection among design alternatives is not always evident even to the most experienced people in the field.

None of the required decisions would be particularly difficult if experts could agree on the correct choice among alternatives in each case or if there were available a sufficient body of objective data describing the consequences of any decision. It is a fact, however, that the experts do not agree. Some like the moving card, others like the moving pointer; some believe in 'symbolic', others

* In the TCV programme, advanced airborne computing, display, and control systems for terminal-area operations are tested from a simulated cockpit in the cabin of a real Boeing 737. One such system displays other traffic in the vicinity on a map-type CDTI thereby allowing flight crews to assume and exercise greater authority and responsibility for spacing and conflict avoidance.

† Our discussion of this topic draws heavily on a report prepared in 1954 for the US Air Force by Professor A. C. Williams, Jr, and his students at the University of Illinois. Since then great progress has been made, but somehow the real problems never seem to change.

in 'pictorial' displays, and so it goes. On the other hand, there is experimental evidence on many of these issues, but it is not complete and, in addition, lacks generality. When new problems arise that are somewhat different from the old ones that have been solved experimentally, it is not certain that the old solutions are applicable.

Solving each new problem or each new version of an old problem by experiment is simply not feasible. There is neither enough time, money, nor manpower to accomplish such a programme. Nor is it satisfactory, in the absence of experimental evidence or unanimous opinion, to be confronted with the necessity for making what often appear to be arbitrary decisions. Often this necessity is avoided by authorising development of several alternative versions of the same system in the hope that one will prove satisfactory. When this is done the designer knows in advance that a large proportion of his money is necessarily being wasted.

The hope that a largely horizontal programme of research might ultimately reduce the designer's uncertainty appears to follow as a natural consequence of the present dilemma. A horizontal programme, as a complement to existing vertical programmes, carries with it the notion of generality of results, and this is what is needed. The horizontal approach implies in effect: let us not be totally diverted by the particular problems that arise from day to day, but let us consider the problem as a whole and attempt to arrive at general rules for displays and controls that can be applied successfully in any subsequent instance.

While advocated, and from time to time initiated by one governmental agency or another, no comprehensive horizontal approach has ever been sustained. Such an undertaking appears to be inherently unstable. Either the people involved succumb to the pressures to solve current problems 'yesterday', usually by invoking some inscrutable wizardry, or they withdraw into their hobby shops and are heard from, if at all, only through their publications in scholarly journals. In both cases efforts quickly become too narrowly focused, either on the specific problems of individual aeroplanes or on specific experimental variables so abstract that all touch with reality is lost and generalisation is impossible.

In a sense this state of affairs might be considered merely a management problem. Surely there are qualified investigators who would prefer to avoid either trap and develop a comprehensive science of aviation engineering psychology. The apparent reason this management problem remains unsolved is that the pay-off would come long after those with the authority to support such an undertaking were retired or casualties of a subsequent election. Happier times for their successors are not high on the list of incentives that shape the actions of Generals, Admirals, and Administrators, or for that matter, Air Marshals.

Training and transfer principles

Human factors problems associated with the training, certification, and refreshment of pilots, controllers, and support personnel have much in common with those encountered in equipment and procedures design, but there are also notable differences. In common is the situation that much of what is known and can be stated as principles is not necessarily known to the people responsible for operational applications. In contrast, however, this is not so much a problem for research as it is a challenge to spread the word to managers, administrators, and individual operators, including instructional system developers and professional instructors.

For example, the potential effectiveness of flight simulators in pilot training and certification is well documented, and in the case of airline operations, widely and legally accepted. However, simulators do not command similar respect and use in general aviation, air taxi, and commuter operations. Admittedly there is less economic pressure to replace flight training in less expensive aeroplanes, but the factors contributing to the relatively ineffective use of simulators in primary and intermediate training phases are complicated and subtle. To be cost effective, simulators must save their operators money by costing less to own and operate than the flight time they replace.

Possibly because of the outstanding success of airlines in using complex and costly flight simulators for training, the belief is widely held that simulators have to look, feel, move, and smell like aeroplanes to be effective. In a subtle way the airlines have been caught in their own trap. To persuade their professional pilots to accept the complete substitution of simulators for aeroplanes in the training and certification process, they have emphasised the total fidelity of simulators to their counterpart aeroplanes. The pilots, in turn, have so embraced the notion that a simulator has to be a tethered aeroplane that they are now insisting on simulators of higher and higher apparent fidelity.

This circular sequence of events and positions offers mixed blessings. Clearly the importance of certain types of simulator fidelity has been well established both through research and operational experience, and this conclusion is gaining wide acceptance. Unfortunately it is also evident that efforts to achieve ultimate apparent fidelity of simulators can be counterproductive.* Not only is the cost far out of line with any possible benefits, but also the training effectiveness of such devices can suffer. Research has shown that certain intentional departures from literal duplication of aircraft characteristics can make possible training strategies far more effective than those currently employed.

Evidence for these strong and, to some people, heretical statements can be found in research on augmented feedback in training;[2] on unrealistically exaggerated response lags and instabilities;[10] on intentionally reduced visual cues in contact flight training; and on elevated workloads creating 'larger than life' stresses—analogous to swinging a leaded bat before stepping to the plate.† Similarly the unwarranted emphasis on ultimate apparent fidelity tends to discourage development and imaginative use of simpler and more flexible and

* Compare with suggested parameters for simulators, chapter 2, p. 38.
† By comparison, the regular wooden American baseball bat feels lighter to the batter, and easier to control.

reliable part-task devices and computer-based teaching scenarios that can yield
even more effective training at a greatly reduced cost.[1]

Reasons for the current state of our aviation training technology are not hard
to discover. While the US Department of Defense has invested vast sums in
training–research simulators, virtually all of the research has been of a vertical
rather than a horizontal nature. Because transfer of training experiments are
difficult to conduct and also very expensive, such experiments typically involve
comparison of two, three, or four training conditions treated as qualitative
factors because they are actually composites of quantitative factors too numerous
and confounded to unravel and manipulate individually. This approach is
essentially vertical in that total simulator configurations are developed and then
comparatively evaluated.

Results of such comparisons lack generality of application because they
reflect only the combined effects of particular sets of values of the many
component variables individually important in simulator design and use. To get
at the main effects and interactions, statistically speaking, of the many independent design and use variables, a different research strategy is called for, one that
is essentially horizontal rather than vertical. Fortunately a research paradigm
new to the aviation community, but long used in the chemical industry, has been
advanced by Dr Charles Simon.*

Economical multi-factor research

Simon's 'holistic' philosophy for the conduct of behavioural experiments
emphasises the importance of accounting for as many potentially critical variables
as possible, whether equipment, environment, subject, or temporal. The key
word in this definition is 'critical'. Whatever their number, if critical variables are
held constant in an experiment, unless the fixed values are close to operational
reality, findings can be grossly inaccurate when applied to real-world situations.
Properly implemented, the holistic approach will yield data that are more precise,
less biased, and more generalisable to the field, at far less cost than traditional
elemental reductionist approaches.

The practicality of applying this innovative research strategy to human
operator performance and training is no longer a matter for speculation.
Experiments conducted at the University of Illinois, though faulty in many
respects, showed that economical multi-factor experimental designs and multiple
regression analyses could be applied to human behavioural research. Such designs
were employed more successfully at NASA-Ames Research Center in a study of
pilot judgement of projected touch-down points on simulated landing approaches
by reference to computer-generated visual displays,[3] and at the US Naval Training
Equipment Center in Florida in a study of carrier-landing performance as a
function of ten experimental variables.[11]

Even more directly applicable, a transfer of training experiment at New

* Dr Simon's numerous technical reports are not cited individually here, but they are
included in the references at the end of this chapter.

Mexico State University included five simulator design variables, one training variable, and three transfer-vehicle configurations. The experiment, completed in less than two months, involved only eighty trainees, forty-eight of whom received training in individually unique simulator configurations. The experiment yielded regression equations for the main effects and first-order interactions of the six experimental variables for each of the three transfer-vehicle configurations. The specific findings, dealing with a simple lateral-steering task, have little direct application to aviation but demonstrate that meaningful multi-factor transfer experiments can be conducted effectively and economically.[10]

Fringe benefits

The benefits of a comprehensive, horizontal aviation research programme are not limited to the application of research findings and technological advances, although these can be expected to be substantial. The functions of such a programme arc to educate as well as discover, and the production of scientists and engineers who specialise in solving human problems encountered in aviation system design, training, and operation carries a high priority. Individuals formally trained and with research experience in these areas are in extremely short supply and are badly needed by the aviation community.

Agenda for the Eighties

The following is a categorical tabulation of research problems and issues that might be resolved if such people were in good supply and supported. The items listed represent the sifted and consolidated consensus of responsible members of the US aviation community who attended a workshop on 'Human Factors in Aviation' held at the Federal Aviation Administration's Civil Aeromedical Institute in Oklahoma City in July 1981.

Category: ATC automation
Issues: The paramount concern of the aviation community centres on the evolving automation of air traffic control. How are functions to be redistributed between ground and airborne elements and, in each, between people and automatic devices? For any given distribution, how are functions to be implemented? How are sectors, airways, approach and departure routeings to be redefined? How will new display technologies be applied, and what, for example, will be the impact of colour displays on controllers with defective colour vision? To resolve these questions, better means are needed for modelling, experimentally testing, and predicting the effects of various alternatives on system efficiency and safety, as well as on the resulting role of the controller, including means of identifying the skills and knowledge and underlying traits and abilities needed for successful performance.

Category: Psychological factors in ATC

Issues: Job-related psychological and psychosomatic problems have long
been associated with controlling air traffic, and these in turn may
affect controller performance. The nature and causal effects of the
controller's task are subjects of much speculation and little objective
assessment; more objective methods are needed. Positive as well as
adverse feedback concerning actual performance quality is needed
to induce job satisfaction rather than dissatisfaction and possibly
reduce the incidence of neuroses, ulcers, stress-related blunders,
and general inefficiency. But such an approach to relieving psychological and psychosomatic problems and improving controller
morale depends first on the discovery and validation of reasonably
objective methods of assessing performance and the establishment
of causal relationships.

Category: Flight-deck function allocation

Issues: What would be the consequences of the various possible distributions
of responsibility and authority between automatic sensing,
computing, and control devices and the flight crew, and also
among the crew members themselves? How, for example, will
collision avoidance, traffic information, metering and spacing, and
microwave landing functions be integrated in the cockpit? Who or
what normally does the in-flight deciding and controlling as opposed
to monitoring with control-by-exception authority? Who is in
command, and to what degree? How is human proficiency maintained in each case? The objective is expressed by the term 'optimum
flight-deck resource management'.

Category: Flight-deck information presentation

Issues: Closely related to the distribution of flight-deck responsibilities
and authority is the determination of what information is to be
presented and how. The advent of improved sensing, computing,
and display devices allows many new degrees of design freedom,
but to avoid chaos, the need for standardisation of basic presentation
principles without inhibiting creative innovation is greater than
ever. Above all, the situation calls for the integrated presentation
of related information rather than the proliferation of cockpit
instrumentation.

Category: Economical training alternatives

Issues: The concept of 'training economy through simulation' has been
sold effectively and widely accepted. However, full-mission
simulator costs are too high for much of the training required, and
less costly alternatives are urgently needed. Not only are part-task
devices, procedural trainers, and computer-based instructional
systems less costly, but also some of these are more flexible and

potentially applicable to types of training not normally provided at all, such as risky decision-making, routine good judgement, and cockpit workload and stress management.

Category: Workload measurement and management

Issues: Cockpit workload levels, subjectively judged, vary tremendously from one type of aircraft to another, and for any given type they vary as a function of the type of flight operation and of its phase. Within a given flight there may be long intervals in which workload is actually too low to sustain pilot alertness punctuated by briefer intervals of work exceeding normal attention capacity. Related problems include the lack of entirely satisfactory workload measures, vague and generally too lenient performance criteria for certification, uncertainty concerning the changes in flying tasks with increasing automation, and the need for explicit training of flight crews in cockpit workload management.

Category: Proficiency maintenance and assurance

Issues: The skill, knowledge, and decisional demands of flying change rapidly with changing regulations, procedures, and equipment, and there is inadequate assurance that all legally certificated pilots can fly safely under any but the most routine conditions. Complicating factors, in addition to marginal currency, include subtle deterioration with ageing, minor strokes, or traumatically stressful life events (such as divorce or death of a spouse), and even such common practices as flying a variety of aircraft types but some only rarely. Unfortunately, re-certification testing is insufficiently sensitive to flush out these latent causes of disaster. Tests involving time-sharing of attention, short-term memory, flexibility in responding to changing situational demands, and possibly the electro-physiological recording and analysis of potentials evoked during performance of such tasks, need to be developed and validated as criteria for continued certification beyond the age of 60 and for mandatory grounding at any age.

Category: Physiological stressors

Issues: Everybody talks about 'jet lag', but nobody understands it, and consequently nobody knows just what to do about it. Related problems include disturbed sleep patterns; fatigue from long-duration flights; possible long-term and short-term effects of limited physical movement on digestion, dehydration, and nutrition; the various toxic agents voluntarily taken or involuntarily encountered in the flight environment; and other sub-acute environmental pollutants such as cockpit noise and vibration and X-ray emission from CRTs. Understanding the relationships of these variables with our various biological rhythms calls for systematic multi-factor, multi-criterion investigation.

Category: Learning from accidents and incidents
Issues: Investigation, analysis, modelling, and simulation of aircraft
accidents and incidents normally stop with the determination of
'probable cause', most frequently 'pilot error'. What caused the
pilot to err is seldom discovered and even less often stated in
accident reports, despite presentation of relevant evidence in public
hearings. Although physical evidence of what happened in an
accident is carefully searched for, collected, re-assembled and
analysed, and the physical events are then modelled and re-created
through simulation, investigation of physiological and behavioural
events stops short of modelling and re-creation through simulation.
Even urgently needed procedures and computer programmes for
assisting local authorities in the recovery and identification of the
dead, and the rescue, handling, and treatment of survivors are lacking.

Category: Pilot vision and cockpit visibility
Issues: While all of the problem areas mentioned above deserve additional
attention, visual abilities and visibility restrictions have been
virtually ignored by the aviation community despite their early
recognised importance and their frequent continuing contributions
to landing accidents, mid-air collisions, and countless non-fatal
incidents involving visual perceptual factors.

References

1.   Finnegan, J. P. (1977) 'Transfer of a Computer-Assisted Instrument
Procedures Trainer to Flight'. *Proceedings of the 21st Annual Meeting of the
Human Factors Society*, Human Factors Society, Santa Monica, California.
2.   Lintern, G., and Roscoe, S. N. (1980) 'Visual Cue Augmentation in Contact
Flight Simulation', in Roscoe, S. N. *Aviation Psychology*, Iowa State
University Press, Ames, Iowa.
3.   Randle, R. J., Roscoe, S. N. and Petitt, J. C. (1980) *Effects of Magnification
and Visual Accommodation on Aimpoint Estimation in Simulated Landings
with Real and Virtual Image Displays*, National Aeronautics and Space
Administration, Technical Paper NASA-TP-1635, Washington, DC.
4.   Roscoe, S. N. (1980) *Aviation Psychology*. Iowa State University Press,
Ames, Iowa.
5.   Simon, C. W. (1971) *Considerations for the Proper Design and Interpretation
of Human Factors Engineering Experiments*, Hughes Aircraft Company,
Technical Report P73-325, Culver City, California.
6.   Simon, C. W. (1973) *Economical Multifactor Designs for Human Factors
Engineering Experiments*, Hughes Aircraft Company, Technical Report
P73-326A (AD A035-108), Culver City, California.
7.   Simon, C. W. (1977) *Design, Analysis, and Interpretation of Screening
Designs for Human Factors Engineering Research*. Canyon Research Group,
Technical Report CWS-03-77A (AD 056-985), Westlake Village, California.

8.   Simon, C. W. (1979) *Applications of Advanced Experimental Methodologies to AWAVS Training Research*, Naval Training Equipment Center, Technical Report NAVTRAEQUIPCEN 77-C-0065-1 (AD 064-332), Orlando, Florida.

9.   Simon, C. W. (1981) *Applications of Advanced Experimental Methods to Visual Technology Research Simulator Studies: Supplemental Techniques*, Naval Training Equipment Center, Technical Report NAVTRAEQUIPCEN 78-C-0060-3 (AD A095-633), Orlando, Florida.

10. Simon, C. W. and Roscoe, S. N. (1981) *Application of an Efficient Approach to Transfer of Training Research*, Canyon Research Group, Report NAVTRAEQUIPCEN 78-C-0060-6, Lakewood Village, California.

11. Westra, D. P., Simon, C. W., Collyer, S. C., and Chambers, W. S. (1981) 'Investigation of Simulator Design Features for Carrier Landing Tasks'. *Proceedings of the IMAGE Generation Display Conference II*, Williams Air Force Base, AZ: USAF Human Resources Laboratory, Flying Training Division.

Chapter 10
Portents and Challenges *R. Hurst*

This work closes with a brief survey of some significant events and developments of relevance to human factors in aviation which must be considered as formative influences in the 1980's. Some discussion will also be opened on an especially intriguing area of investigation in which the role of a further 'neglected human factor' is examined for its possible contribution to aircraft hazard.

It is worth recalling that the first edition of this book was permeated to some extent by the claims and counter-claims of specialist contributors. Classic conflicts of interest between pilots, operators, manufacturers, air traffic controllers and legislators were then in evidence. The permutation of these confrontations could be manipulated at will: the totality, however, faithfully reflected the strains within an industry which, by 1976, had not yet reached a philosophical maturity.

We are hopefully today a little nearer that aim: yet it must be said while many of the earlier problems have been solved, or have been overtaken by those of the developing technology, a variety of basic issues ventilated in that first edition are still preoccupations at this time.

In Chapter 1 Martin Allnutt wrote that. . .by and large, research workers know more about the effects of physical stresses than they do about those which are physiological: and more about those which are physiological than about those rooted in psychology. It may be added, too, that while there is an enormous wealth of knowledge about the technology of aviation there is also distressingly frequent evidence that in vital areas, human relations within the aviation community remain at a devastatingly primitive level. It is in these areas that the conflicts of interest have been and continue to be acted out, occasionally with a bitterness and ferocity of quite startling impact. Such episodes have residual and long-term effects on aviation safety which are not to be ignored, unless the study of human factors is to limit itself to and perhaps spend itself in, the quest for near immaculate performance in the cockpit. Thus, at one end of the scale the interpretation of a 'conflicting interest' made it possible for an air traffic controller who had been overwhelmed by a crisis to be sentenced to seven years rigorous imprisonment following a most disputable allegation of criminal negligence on his part: and this despite the demonstrable inadequacy of his working environment and the equally clear — and later admitted — responsibility of his employers for those shortcomings.*

Inevitably, this event left its dangerously sensitive scar on a profession already burdened by the physical and psychological pressures described in Chapter 7,

*For a detailed study of this case see Weston, R. and Hurst, R., *Zagreb One Four — Cleared to Collide?* Granada Publishing Ltd (1982).

since the possibility that he might meet a similar fate effectively jeopardises the objectivity of controller decisions and hence the safety of air traffic. It will be much more difficult for the researcher to repair, if not to erase, this type of psychological damage and it may prove to be even more important that he should attempt to do so rather than concern himself entirely with the ergonomics of the workplace.

The Troubled Air

At the other end of the scale — and again in this profoundly underestimated sector of operations — came President Reagan's abrupt dismissal of 12 000 striking air traffic controllers subsequent to their walk-out on 3 August 1981. The strike was initiated by the US Professional Air Traffic Controllers Organisation (PATCO) and triggered sympathetic action by Canadian and Portugese controllers.

The justice or otherwise of the controllers' claims for improvements in pay and conditions is not discussed here. The negative factors arising from this episode are, however, pertinent since they must exert their influence on the civil aviation system and press a further potential for hazard on the pilot group.

There is, therefore, cause for unease as to the future in the assertion by the National Transportation Safety Board that. . .there is no evidence (that) the underlying problems that caused the air traffic controllers strike have been resolved and they could surface again in a few years if the FAA does not improve management of the air traffic control system.[1]

It is also of concern that in an industry so dependent for its operational efficiency on personal integrity and, for the researcher, on the integrity of data supplied, that the facts of a critical issue can be buried in the claims of opposed parties. Thus, despite the expulsion of so many highly-skilled controllers the Safety Board also offered the assurance in December that. . .there is no evidence that the air traffic system has been made unsafe since the walk-out began. . .'[2] It is not surprising that this view was immediately rejected by PATCO officials who pointed not only to the introduction of military controllers and even in the Safety Board's own words 'marginally qualified' personnel to fill the gaps. . . but also, to what they considered to be the biased nature of information released to the public.

'Data collected by NTSB investigators from the FAA, the Aviation Safety Institute and the Air Line Pilots Association show the number of operational errors per million operators committed by the system *decreased* by 12—66 per cent during the first two months of the walk-out compared with a year earlier. *PATCO figures showed a 46 per cent increase.*[3]

There is, therefore, confusion and frustration for the researcher as well as bitterness and recrimination between striker and non-striker: there is also the uneasy outlook for the future in the "avowed intent of the FAA to rebuild the staffing level of the air traffic control system to about 12 000 controllers, approximately 25 per cent fewer than the number working for the agency prior to the strike. It is expected that large-scale hirings of some 14 500 new entrants would result in an additional 10,500 controllers on-the-job due to washouts in the training process."[4]

These then, are the shifting sands promising future instability for the world's busiest air traffic control system. One is left to ponder the sagacity and practicability — to say nothing of the ethos — of instituting such a massive turnover of skilled and experienced personnel in response to industrial action, and the effect of such a managerial approach on the quality of those surviving these purges. It may well be that this is yet another area in which the human factors specialist is impotent, thankful that these matters are the province of the practitioner in labour-relations: but he — or she — need not at the same time be blind to or silent on the incongruity of mediaevalism in aviation, nor should they fail to reflect on the potential of this syndrome to impose a serious degree of hazard, not only on the pilot but also on that Cinderella figure, the innocent passenger.

But perhaps the most perceptive comment on the meaning of this dispute was that made by James P. Woolsey, Editor of the journal *Air Transport World**.[5]

'. . .Leadership is not always best expressed in willingness to use power. It is best demonstrated by the ability to resolve crises for the best interests of all those concerned. If the current scenario runs its course, the PATCO group will be the losers. The air transport system, already beset by problems, will again be humbled by what is becoming industry's frailest element, the human equation.

The new technology rolling out of Boeing and elsewhere will not be produced just to make air travel more efficient and pleasant. It will become, even more than it already is, a vehicle to make air transport as free of human dependence as possible. In that game, losers will always outnumber the winners. That applies to air traffic controllers, presidents and the rest of us.'

The Three Decade Debate: Two Pilots or Three?

In the context of formative influences it is important to highlight yet another issue of current discord and hence, latent menace, namely, the crew-complement debate. If it is permissible to speak of a healthy skeleton then this apparition is in excellent shape, and indeed, has now been rattling its bones for almost three decades, since the resolution that there should be three pilots on the flight-deck of a large jet originated at the 1958 conference in Bogota of the International Federation of Air Line Pilots Associations.*

Time and the self-evident revelation of perfectly conducted two-place operations have somewhat diminished this aspiration and in the 80's the pilot groups

*See Captain Arne Leibing, Airline Management — Pilot Relationship: in *Pilot Error*, 1st Edition.

find themselves fighting a rearguard action wherein, as protagonists of the three-man crew — now conceived as comprising two pilots and an engineer — they are accused of job-protectionism: meanwhile manufacturers and operators anxious to introduce two-place cockpits are in their turn reviled for an allegedly cynical disregard for safety in the pursuit of economic — and thereby profitable — operation.

Once again it is stressed that in this chapter there can be no useful evaluation of the factors in dispute. It would in any event be sterile to proceed on the basis of the simplistic propositions outlined above for these emotive terms are of no value whatsoever in any attempt to visualise what vital situations may be determined by the presence or absence of a third crew member.

It is, however, legitimate and necessary to register the phenomenon of the significant change in the pattern of flight-deck manning which is inexorably coming about, to note the reactions of those concerned and again, to consider these observations in the light of their possible relevance to future events. Certainly there are important implications for cockpit, system design and work-load: that is easily foreseen — the unknowns are represented by the entirely new area of investigation which will be opened into interpersonal relationships in the two-place environment.

Features of this phenomenon include firstly, the recommendation by a United States Presidential 'task force'* on aircraft crew complement that '. . .the addition of a permanent third crew member to the McDonnell Douglas DC-9-80 *or to future transport aircraft, regardless of their size or type of operation*, in the light of current technology, is not justified in the interest of safety.[6]

The task force also recommend that new aircraft such as the Boeing 757 and 767 and the Airbus Industries A310 short-to-medium haul transport could be operated safely by a crew of two. . .'In our view', stated their report, 'there is nothing in the size of the aircraft per se that requires a flight crew larger than two persons.' Major issues involved in the consideration of crew complement included the safety record of transport aircraft, the air traffic environment, cockpit systems and technology, human factors and the certification process. . .[7] It was also noted, in contesting the pilot unions claim of less safe operation in crowded skies that '. . .as air carrier jet transport accident rates have declined, the number of two crew member transports has been increasing. In 1980, two crew member transports accounted for 24 per cent of the scheduled airline fleet and performed 42 per cent of the scheduled airline passenger departures. A characterisation by the unions that the air traffic environment is 'hostile' and 'dangerous' was refuted by the task force etc., etc. . .[8]

Currently and doubtless for years ahead, pilot response is and will continue to be ambivalent. The executive board of the US Air Line Pilots Association disagreed with the task force conclusions but voted to support the study because of a prior commitment to the Government that it would do so. Nevertheless, reported Aviation Week and Space Technology on July 13, 1981. . . 'it is doubt-

*Members were John L. McLucas (Comsat World Systems), Fred J. Drinkwater 3rd, of NASA and Lt. General Howard Leaf of the Air Force.

ful if (the conclusions of the study) came as a great surprise. Too much hand-writing has already lettered the wall (and) pilots themselves are divided on the subject. . .'

Perhaps the most ominous demur was entered by Europilote, the European Organisation of Airline Pilots Associations: its members reserved the right to challenge and refute any legislation in their countries presented on the basis of the task force study. . .especially where and when an accident investigation should disclose airworthiness implications deriving from the task force report, directly, in the case of US manufactured aircraft or indirectly, in the case of European manufactured airplanes. This position would be made known to insurance companies and travellers' associations in order to properly assess the product liability aspects involved.[9]

Coupled with announcements early in 1982 that KLM Royal Dutch Airlines was to take delivery of ten Airbus A310 aircraft despite the protests of the KLM flight engineers and the Dutch Airline Pilots' Association and the counter by KLM management that its decision was based on the company's experience with Airbus Industrie, the task force report, the airline's considerable experience with aircraft operated with two-man crews (notably DC-9's which have been operated by KLM for more than 15 years), the conviction that the workload will in all probability be lighter and that it was in any case impossible to give the flight engineer a meaningful task[10]. . .one fact remains unobscured: yet another unpropitious element has been decanted into the mix before the human factors researcher. It may be that this too, is beyond his capacity for intervention: but as before, he must remain cognizant that this ingredient has its significance in the real background to his theoretical work.

Research — and Wider Horizons

The strengths of the civil air transport industry and in particular, the strength of the research effort, are not to be underestimated: it may be seen from the pro-ceedings of the First Symposium on Aviation Psychology conducted by the Aviation Psychology Laboratory of the Ohio State University that there is a special emphasis — perhaps too special — on pilot behaviour: it may be argued that this is a complex enough field to fully occupy battalions of research workers and of course, it is and does. And may it continue to do so.

It is nevertheless not churlish, and certainly not disrespectful to the fomidable professionalism of those who contributed to the First Symposium to suggest that the field should be broadened: that the immense effort concerned with cockpit efficiency as exemplified by pilot performance might be to some extent a diversion of talent from the examination of equally important peripherals such as external support systems and their personnel and the deeper understanding of their relationship to aircraft operations.

This problem was ventilated by Gary R. Church, Manager, Air Traffic Control, Air Transport Association of America, in a presentation at the 1980 ATCA Convention:[11]

'Research and development in human factors for air traffic control has been limited. An FAA Contact Report published in January of 1978 determined three broad areas with only seventeen specific human factors to be considered relevant to future ATC automation issues. Job satisfaction and motivation, man-machine interface and failure mode operations were considered the only general areas of concern. . .'

Buried among the clearly necessary concentration on the ergonomics of system design are nevertheless gems offering the hope of a more catholic approach:

> Technological concepts and state-of-the-art developments may enhance software and hardware redundancy and reliability, but the reduction of simple human error by proper consideration of human factors may provide the greatest system benefit to increased safety. . . The study of the nature and cause of human error is absolutely essential in designing automated systems to minimise human-generated error. Donald A. Norman, Professor of Psychology at the University of California at San Diego has categorized these types of mental errors. These classifications are: description error related to abstract reasoning, activation and triggering errors related to memory and capture errors related to habits of behaviour.
>   Each category explains a mental slip that leads to a human error. By understanding how human errors occur it should be possible to design computer systems to block such errors, by selectively forcing functions which detect specific types of mistakes.

Command — Intimidation or Leadership?

In the simplest hypothesis of the vital value of support systems it is sufficient to point out that a controller or briefing error may impinge fatally upon the pilot. If this is accepted then there is a strong case for increasingly widening the focus of individual research projects in order to take fully into account those other components of the system — however abstract they may appear to be — which may detract from the desirable level of safety. In this category lie such subjectives as personality and ill-temper: most notably in the intimidation of flight deck crew by the aircraft commander.

Examples were offered to the Symposium on Aviation Psychology by H. Clayton Foushee of Ames Research Center, NASA.[12]

> I was the copilot on a flight from JKF to BOS. The captain was flying. Departure turned us over to centre and we were given Flight Level 210 (21 000 ft) which was our flight plan altitude. I noted that we had reached FL210 and were continuing through it, but was reluctant to say anything. As we climbed through to 21 300 feet I mentioned it to the captain, but not forcefully enough, and he did not hear me.
>   I mentioned it again and pointed to the altimeter. We were at 21 600 feet when the climb was stopped and we descended back to 21 000 feet. As we started our descent, center called and told us to maintain FL 21 000. The captain said he had misread his altimeter and though he was 1 000 feet lower than he was.

I believe the main factor here was my reluctance to correct the captain. This captain is very approachable and I had no real reason to hold back. It is just a bad habit that I think a lot of co-pilots have of double-checking everything before we say anything to the captain.

Clayton Foushee also quotes the 1979 crash of a north-eastern commuter carrier wherein the first officer failed to take over control of the aircraft when the captain apparently became incapacitated. The captain was a company vice-president, the first officer a newly hired pilot on probation. The captain, according to reports, was a gruff personality and was observed to be visibly upset on the day of the accident: further this captain apparently had a history of not acknowledging call outs. Now I suspect, states Foushee, that about the last thing that that particular first officer would have been willing to do was take over control of his aircraft. It would appear that the first officer was intimidated and that the accident might not have occurred given a different orientation by the captain.

There is unfortunately no lack of similar illustration in Foushee that the destiny of a flight, for all the careful and wondrous technology involved, may nevertheless hinge on the idiosyncratic behaviour of a single individual: and if, indeed, we should seek for some index of the potential for disaster inherent in the abuse of the command role -- for it is nothing less -- then we need look no further than the study conducted by Dr C. R. Harper of United Air Lines:[13]

. . .Captains feigned subtle incapacitation at a predetermined point during final approach in simulator trials. In that study, roughly one-third of the aircraft "hit the ground" because, for some reason, the first officers did not take control.

This finding, says Foushee, is disturbing despite the fact that 'simulator complacency' may account for some of these occurrences. . .but it is not difficult to read into his observations — and indeed, that author closes with just such an appeal — the need for a critical examination of the traditional command situation. Aircraft operation is acknowledged now to consist of system-management: it is simply not supportable that the efficiency of those systems should be vulnerable, particularly in emergency situations, to aberration protected by an archaic concept of rank.

The imperative is there. There may, after all, be some four hundred trusting souls in the passenger compartments who piously — and quite properly — hope that the captain will always make the right decision.

The idea may be a chimaera: but if it is nothing else, the study of human factors in aviation is surely the endeavour to attain this state of affairs. If that endeavour suggests the need to tamper with taboo by questioning the captain's current role and prerogative then the researcher must take a deep breath, reach out and thereafter protect himself as best he may against the lightning bolts of the pilot group. They will surely arrive.

Yet among the sensible responses which Foushee addresses to this problem is one of quite tantalising attraction and, in terms of challenge to the established order of things, considerable daring:

Of the socio-psychological dynamics of flight crew in emergency situations'. . . . it is probably true that the decision-maker is the least appropriate person to be overburdened in such situations. In stressful circumstances, humans tend to exhibit a narrowing of perceptual attention such that it is perhaps not optimal to have the captain involved in flying the aircraft, co-ordinating the activities of the flight and cabin crew and making the ultimate decisions regarding actions to be taken. . .'.

Foushee speaks of the importance 'of effective delegation of responsibility '. . . and, quoting Ruffell Smith,[14] the immediate benefits (which) were derived by captains who elected to hand over flying of the aircraft to the first officer while making decisions about how to handle problems. In addition to allowing the captain more time to serve as an effective decision maker, such a strategy allows other crew members a greater sense of responsibility.

The importance of personality traits as a factor in aviation safety is thus receiving attention: but there must be vigilance that it is not pursued in a frame which may not long continue to be relevant. As noted, we are now moving into the era of the two-place cockpit and in those circumstances the ploy of task delegation may not be so readily available as an easement of psychological pressure. Similarly it is known that the pattern of behaviour and the relationships between two people are vastly different from the interplay typifying groups of three or more. The potential for harmony or tension in the new situation i.e., of the two-man crew, or, vide Foushee, the crew which more commonly now may include a female pilot — remains to be seen and explored in the enigmatic future. All we can be sure of at this time is that there must be exploration and that it must never lose sight of the fragility of human equilibrium: that variable is documented in other chapters of this book and most vividly in Chapter 7.

All those examples support the relevance and importance of human factors research: no words, however, offer more emphatic confirmation of this than those of the stricken Captain Katigiri, pilot-in-command of the Japan Air Lines DC-8 which crashed in Tokyo Bay on 9 February 1982, on the approach to Haneda Airport. In that accident 24 passengers died: the total complement was 166 passengers and eight crew. At this time the findings of the accident investigators have not yet been published: but it was reported that 'a struggle' had taken place in the cockpit as the co-pilot and engineer strove to restrain the captain 'from applying reverse thrust to one engine. . .'. Flight International quoted Captain Katigiri thus:

". . . immediately I switched off the autopilot and started controlling the aeroplane manually, I felt a feeling of terror and completely lost consciousness".[15]

The report also revealed that '. . .Katigiri had been grounded for a year some time ago, because he suffered from a stress-related physical disorder.' The

Japanese authorities (were said to be) considering bringing a charge of criminal negligence against JAL for failing to monitor Katgiri's health effectively in the light of his medical history.

Communication and Hearing Deficiency

The need for clarity and lack of ambiguity in aviation communication with special reference to pilot and controller dialogue has been a recurrent theme in many post-accident reports: yet it is possible that the incidence of deafness in aviation arising from acoustic trauma may be higher than is 'formally' noted and that the contribution of this impairment to confusion and hazard may be considerably underestimated.

Much attention has been given to what might be termed the 'mechanics' of the spoken interchange whereby diction, volume and mutual understanding of the transmission have all been scrutinized in the effort to eliminate or at least reduce the possibility of error. Much consideration, too, has been given to the problems arising from an assumed acceptance, knowledge and universal use of English as the 'official' language of aviation. It is to be noted that Anglophone pilots in Canada made their own forceful protest at the introduction of French as the premier language of air traffic control in the Province of Quebec. Their apprehensions were, however, set aside in the face of the nationalist pressures: bilingualism thus flourishes and sets a precedent which may one day be acclaimed by like-minded aspirants. Civil aviation, struggling for rationalisation, will not benefit from the resultant strife.

It can be no coincidence that a recent proposal for a 'universal language of aviation'[16] was offered by four Anglophone researchers of the Canadian Society of Aviation Medicine all of whom are members of the Aerospace Linguistic Foundation. In describing UNIGEN — the name chosen for this language is an acronym from Genesis 11:1 — the authors point out that:

'In 1978, 12 million flights arose from nations where English is a foreign language. From these, crash-deaths averaged 200 per million flights. The Aerospace Linguistic Foundation is incorporated to further coooperative evolution of a suitable speech for universal air use as envisaged by ICAO. UNIGEN reflects the pragmatic monitoring of collective air communications and universal linguistic developments. The Foundation underwrites investigations by existing communication faculties of linguistic problems identified from accidents, etc. (e.g. Tenerife shows English phonemes 'th' and 'wh' are not internationally suitable). Optimum expressions may derive from the world languages. Phonetics may also be selected to monitor the human factor, e.g. plosives to spot hyperventilation or arousals for sleep. Future air communications must exploit hearing and sight concurrently to assure the million-to-one reliability required for perception transfer.'

It is the last sentence which touches upon that 'grey area' of hearing. While researchers such as Stanley Roscoe have done noble service in the cause of investigation into and explanation of visual acuity and performance it is difficult to find a comparable dissemination of information related to the field of aural research.

It is, in fact, possible to sift through literally scores of aviation technology research reports before one comes upon the occasional paper dealing with hearing: it requires, indeed, persistence to find such a paper applying its findings to the man in the cockpit of a commercial transport aircraft. Yet research into aviation deafness dates back certainly to the 1920's and has since attracted numbers of dedicated workers. Studies of hearing capacity in military pilots abound, particularly in the United States, Canada and Germany. It is again, more difficult to obtain truly comprehensive data on commercial aircrew, possibly because of the difficulty of collating information from so widely dispersed a population. For the purposes of this chapter, however, it may be accepted that there has long been an acknowledged relationship between the noise level inside the aircraft, the susceptibility of the listener to acoustic damage and the duration of the exposure to excessive noise, i.e. noise above the 'safe' level of 85dB and therefore hazardous to hearing.

The patterns, sound levels and conclusions illustrated in Figures 10.1, 10.2 and 10.3 were presented in a Polish paper read at the United Nations Seminar on Agricultural Aviation, 1980. These parameters were established on the basis of experiments with a variety of single-engine agricultural aircraft and one helicopter. While similar studies covering the more general range of training and commercial aircraft may be sought, these graphs provide a useful and perhaps disturbing indication of the nature and effect of aviation deafness. The study by Jerry V. Tobias entitled 'Auditory Effects of Noise on Air-Crew Personnel'[17] which examined the effect of aircraft noise on a wide spectrum of professional aviators (aerial application pilots, FAA Flight Inspectors, Flight Instructors, private pilots and stewardesses). . .opened by confirming that 'studies of cabin and cockpit noise show that many planes are potential producers of permanent threshold shifts'*. Tobias, however, did not include airline pilots in his study '. . .because these people are required to have semi-annual physical examinations, including hearing tests and only a tiny minority fail because of hearing problems. Although the precision of our laboratory tests might have turned up some degree of noise-attributable threshold shift, special tests of these men would not be particularly informative: for the most part, they fly in the quietest planes and they do so for relatively few hours per week. The same statements apply to flight engineers. . .' Setting this aside for one moment it is instructive to refer to the order of precedence, in terms of capacity for noise-generation listed in that study. Helicopters, Tobias records, and planes with open cockpits are the noisiest. Then, more or less in order, are light single-engine airplanes, light twin-engine planes, piston-driven planes in air transport use, turboprop planes, planes with wing-mounted jet engines and planes with rear-mounted jet engines. . .'

It is arguable that there are assumptions here which can be questioned. Whatever the current expertise in cockpit soundproofing and whether or not ear defenders are worn it is often observed (and wryly reported to intimates by

*Change in the point at which the stimulus of sound elicits a response.

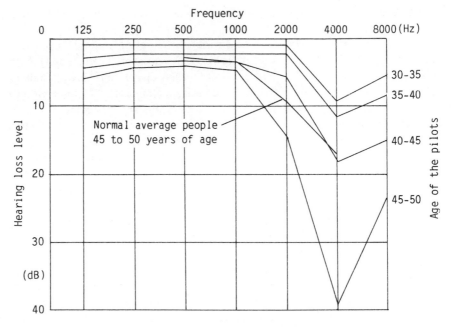

Fig. 10.1.   Hearing loss of agricultural aviation pilots. The mean losses by age function are shown in correlation with those of normal (non-flying) people of 45–50 years of age.

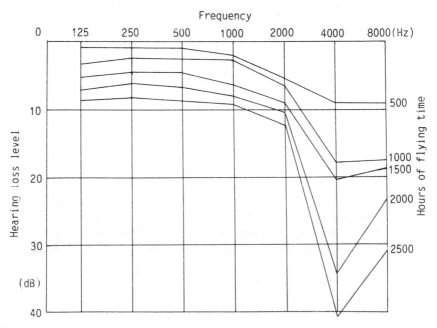

Fig. 10.2.   Mean hearing losses collected as a function of flying hours.

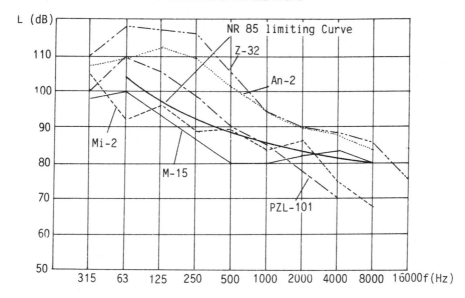

Fig. 10.3.   Sound analysis measured in cockpits of different agricultural aircraft and in one helicopter are shown on the background of a limiting curve representing the guaranteed safety of hearing in continued noise activity (minimum five hours daily). It is apparent from Fig. 10.3 that the quietest of the aircraft tested does not meet this criterion.

junior flight crew) that the first action of many senior captains is to turn up the volume control on radio equipment to a level which the junior officer may regard as unnecessarily high.

In addition, although it is true that the sound proofing of a modern jet transport substantially reduces cockpit noise levels, it is also true that the current generation of airline pilots, like their predecessors, must have undergone more than 300 hours of flight training in those self-same single and twin piston-engine aircraft to which Tobias correctly accords a high noise rating. Given the passage of years before attaining command status, one must also postulate the existence of a corresponding deterioration of hearing initiated among the most susceptible by that early trauma, and this condition may be further aggravated among those pilots with military backgrounds, who may, inter alia, have flown rotary-wing aircraft or suffered percussive shock.

Since careers are at stake, self-preservation becomes a powerful factor: it may therefore be unrealistic to expect too much in the way of voluntary admission of the extent of a hearing deficiency, nor may that deficiency necessarily be fully revealed by audiometric testing. Nor may the assessment of such a test be considered to show sufficient reason for the disqualification of any but the very smallest percentage of examinees. The acid test, however, is the pilots' comprehension of the spoken word under the circumstances of flight-deck pressures, ambient noise and possibly, emergency situations. Personal experience — the author has suffered a classic aviation-induced acoustic trauma — has shown that speech comprehension becomes a casualty if the listener with impaired hearing is given no time in which to interpret the words addressed to him.

The implications here are for the reliability of communication between flight-deck crew and between controller and pilot and appear to reinforce the case for the visual presentation of information in the cockpit. It is possible that there may be a link between this deficiency and specific examples of airborne eccentricity such as departures from controller instructions* or even that forbidding individual taciturnity.

It is instructive to return to Foushee for a succinct comment on the situation generated by non-response:

> '. . .we found a negative relationship. . .between aircraft systems errors and acknowledgements to information which had been provided. In crews in which commands, inquiries and observations were frequently acknowledged, these types of errors were less apparent. Acknowledgements were also related to fewer errors overall. . .
>
> It would appear that acknowledgements serve a very important function of validating that a certain piece of information has, in fact, been transferred. These types of communications also serve as important reinforcements to the input of other crew members. If you think about this relationship it appears very logical. When you make an attempt to communicate with someone and that person does not say anything, are you as likely to initiate further communication with that person? Aren't you more likely to communicate further if they respond, even in the simplest fashion (e.g. yeah, uh-huh, etc.)?'

References

1. Aviation Week and Space Technology, 14 December 1981.
2. Ibid.
3. Ibid.
4. Ibid.
5. Air Transport World, September 1981.
6. Aviation Week and Space Technology, 6 July 1981.
7. Ibid.
8. Ibid.
9. Aviation Week and Space Technology, 30 November 1981.
10. Aviation Week and Space Technology, 15 March 1982.
11. Journal of Air Traffic Control, October/December 1981.
12. Foushee, H. Clayton (1981) 'The Role of Communications, Socio-Psychological, and Personality Factors in the Maintenance of Crew Co-ordination' in proceedings of First Symposium on Aviation Psychology, Aviation Psychology Laboratory, The Ohio State University, Columbus, Ohio, April 21—22.
13. Ibid.

*Particularly where the transmission is not repeated back but merely acknowledged by the single word 'Roger'.

14. Ruffell Smith, H.P. (1979) 'A Simulator Study of the Interaction of Pilot Workload with Errors, Vigilance, and Decisions' NASA Technical Memorandum 78482.
15. Flight International, 27 February 1982.
16. Franks, W.R., Allen, P., Soutendam, J. and Taylor, I., (1980) 'UNIGEN — Universal Language of Aviation' in Aviation, Space, and Environmental Medicine, Vol. 51, 339–343, April.
17. Tobias, Jerry V., (1972) 'Auditory Effects of Noise on Aircrew Personnel' FAA Civil Aero Medical Institute, PO Box 25082, Oklahoma City, Oklahoma 73125, FAA Report No: FAA-AM-72-32, November.

Index